MW00769936

PRAISE FOR *ENTREPRENEURIAL MARKETING*

"Kotler and colleagues are at it again. There are no parts of marketing that Phil and his collaborators have not had their imprint. This book takes us from the previously established omnichannel literature on how we go to marketing through a multiplicity of interrelated channels to an inner perspective on the need in 2023 to redesign the organization on how we work in an omnihouse model. They outline how the interconnectedness of every part of the organization is essential with all the changes in the world and how we operate today. They define the new structure for today's firm to survive and thrive. Bravo!!!"

—David J. Reibstein
Professor of Marketing
The Wharton School, University of Pennsylvania

"Marketing people often get caught up merely in tactical matters. This book provides a holistic perspective so that business people, especially marketers, can understand things more strategically in providing solutions for customers and other stakeholders while maintaining satisfactory profit margins and being concerned about the company's market value."

—Hermann Simon
Founder and Honorary Chairman
Simon-Kucher & Partners

"I love the fundamental idea of having an entrepreneurial mindset and tools to augment the existing professional competence rather than replace it. This book shows how an entrepreneurial mindset, with its creativity, agility, and 'can-do' attitude, needs to augment the professional competence of the modern firm faced with dynamic marketing places."

—David Aaker
Professor Emeritus
University of California, Berkeley's Haas School of Business

"*Marketing Entrepreneurship* is an expertly-conceived book that puts front and center the role of marketing in the success of new enterprises. It is a "must-read" for entrepreneurs, new and seasoned alike."

—Stanley F. Stasch
Professor Emeritus
Loyola University Chicago

"The horizons of marketing science are continuously expanding. Entrepreneurial marketing is also developing, more strongly intertwined with many aspects, and showing a progressively crucial role in business performance. I am happy that this book can simplify those complexities and take us to the new frontier of entrepreneurial marketing."

—Marc Oliver Opresnik
Chief Research Officer Kotler Impact and
Distinguished Professor of Marketing and Management
Technical University of Lübeck

ENTREPRENEURIAL

MARKETING

PHILIP KOTLER
HERMAWAN KARTAJAYA
HOOI DEN HUAN
JACKY MUSSRY

ENTREPRENEURIAL
MARKETING

BEYOND PROFESSIONALISM
TO CREATIVITY, LEADERSHIP,
AND SUSTAINABILITY

WILEY

For general information on our other products and services or for technical support, please contact our Customer Care Department within the United States at (800) 762-2974, outside the United States at (317) 572-3993 or fax (317) 572-4002.

Wiley also publishes its books in a variety of electronic formats. Some content that appears in print may not be available in electronic formats. For more information about Wiley products, visit our web site at www.wiley.com.

Library of Congress Cataloging-in-Publication Data:

Names: Kotler, Philip, author. | Kartajaya, Hermawan, 1947- author. | Hooi, Den Huan, author. | Mussry, Jacky, author.
Title: Entrepreneurial marketing : beyond professionalism to creativity, leadership, and sustainability / Philip Kotler, Hermawan Kartajaya, Hooi Den Huan, Jacky Mussry.
Description: First edition. | Hoboken, NJ : Wiley, [2023] | Includes index.
Identifiers: LCCN 2022054469 (print) | LCCN 2022054470 (ebook) | ISBN 9781119835202 (hardback) | ISBN 9781119835448 (adobe pdf) | ISBN 9781119835431 (epub)
Subjects: LCSH: Marketing—Management. | Organizational change. | Decision making. | Strategic planning. | Creative ability in business.
Classification: LCC HF5415.13 .K635 2023 (print) | LCC HF5415.13 (ebook) | DDC 658.8—dc23/eng/20221110
LC record available at https://lccn.loc.gov/2022054469
LC ebook record available at https://lccn.loc.gov/2022054470

Cover Design: Paul McCarthy
Author Photos: Courtesy of the Authors

SKY10041676_013023

"To my nine granddaughters and grandsons: Jordan, Jamie, Ellie, Abbie, Olivia, Sam, Saffire, Shaina, and Dante."
—Philip Kotler

"To Joko Widodo, the president of the Republic of Indonesia (2014–2024), who leads the G20 Indonesia Presidency (2022) and ASEAN Chairmanship (2023), which will bring Indonesian wisdom to world humanity. I am very proud of you."
—Hermawan Kartajaya

"To my wonderful parents, wife, daughters, and sisters."
—Hooi Den Huan

"To my family who always believed in me, teachers, and those who passed away too soon due to COVID-19."
—Jacky Mussry

Contents

Foreword

This book is a timely gift to the next generation of marketers. *Entrepreneurial Marketing* could be the playbook for what Henry David Thoreau described as "a conscientious corporation . . . a corporation with a conscience for humanity."

The book lays out pragmatic and proven frameworks for 21st-century marketers to create a collaborative and sustainable civilization. Its intellectual rigor is impeccable.

I recommend you keep *Entrepreneurial Marketing* within arm's reach (as a sequel to Kotler's renowned *Marketing Management,* now in its 16th edition!). *Entrepreneurial Marketing* is a must-read for CEOs, CFOs, CIOs, and other senior staff people. It does an excellent job with accounting and financial analytical tools. It does an insightful job in looking at future developments in marketing and how to remain flexible and alert for the inherent managerial tensions inside any firm.

—Russ Klein, former ad agency executive, Leo Burnett; Foote, Cone & Belding; former CMO of Inspire Brands (Arby's, 7-Eleven, Dr Pepper/7UP, Church's Chicken); former global president Burger King

Former CEO American Marketing Association

Prologue

Marketing in the Post-Normal Era

So much has changed in the last years, from technological advances that revolutionize the way we communicate to globe-shaking events like COVID-19. Although much uncertainty surrounds these shifts, one factor remains clear. Business will never be the same.

And that includes marketing. In the past, a traditional or procedural approach to marketing might have produced reliable results, time and again. In this book, we'll refer to this setup as *professional marketing*. It is often associated with concepts such as segmentation, targeting, positioning, and product and brand management. The slow-moving, one-step-at-a-time methodology may have been a great fit for a less connected era.

That's no longer the case. Today's fast-paced, shifting world calls for a marketing strategy that can fit in everywhere—and be agile enough to move when needed. An entrepreneurial approach may be the ticket for organizations to be interconnected, flexible, and results-driven.

Although the concept of entrepreneurial marketing isn't necessarily new, a more expanded version is essential. Its original definition referred to a combination of marketing and entrepreneurship elements. However, due to recent developments around the world, this approach must encompass a broader scope, a holistic perspective, if you will. One that integrates all the other departments of a company. One that doesn't remain in a silo, as marketing (and other functions) has often done in the past. It also converges an entrepreneurial mindset and a professional mindset.

This new genre of entrepreneurial marketing takes the center stage as we consider how our world has been disrupted by the pandemic. It remains important as we evaluate the technologies currently available that can connect us. When we look ahead to the coming years, we see approaching finish lines for initiatives like the Sustainability Development Goals. The United Nations adopted these in 2015 as a framework to end poverty and protect the planet. Their time line aims to achieve these goals by 2030.

In some ways, the foundation has been laid for this new version of entrepreneurial marketing. Think of online technology, for instance. Customers can easily search for what they want, get to know companies, and make purchases. Small and large companies alike can get involved in this interactive communication. The arrangement creates paths for stronger engagement, increased customer retention, and higher levels of loyalty.

Entrepreneurial marketing takes these capabilities to the next level. It seeks ways to not only connect with customers but also to speak directly to them. It is more hands on. (Want to know if a solution is working? Rather than running a report, just ask the customers!)

In addition, digital advances have made it easier than ever to integrate various functions of an organization. Entrepreneurial marketing interacts with other areas, including finances, technology departments, and operations. It supports leadership (and takes on a leadership role itself) and strategizes initiatives. It advocates for innovation and responds quickly to change. Effectively, it adds value for the organization and its shareholders.

If you're starting to think the new genre of entrepreneurial marketing sounds quite a bit like an entrepreneur, you are correct. This methodology encourages risk-taking and is results-oriented.[1] It craves productivity and is always on the lookout for opportunities to improve.[2] There are so many great potentials in the new genre of entrepreneurial marketing that you can take advantage of.

---

[1]Retrieved August 20, 2022, from https://www.marketing-schools.org/types-of-marketing/entrepreneurial-marketing/
[2]Based on several definitions as explained in Robert D. Hisrich and Veland Ramadani, "Entrepreneurial Marketing: Entrepreneurship and Marketing Interface," *Entrepreneurial Marketing* (Elgar, 2018).

Acknowledgments

The authors are grateful for the invaluable support and encouragement from the entire management team of MarkPlus, Inc., especially the leadership team: Michael Hermawan, Taufik, Vivie Jericho, Iwan Setiawan, Ence, Estania Rimadini, and Yosanova Savitry.

A special thank-you and highest appreciation to Richard Narramore, who has been very patient and committed to overseeing and directing the preparation of this book from the beginning until its publication. Without Richard, this book would not exist.

The authors would like to thank the editorial team at Wiley for their amazing attention and collaboration at every stage of the writing process for this book: Angela Morrison, Deborah Schindlar, Susan Geraghty, and Rene Caroline. Our thanks also go to Kevin Anderson at Kevin Anderson & Associates and his editorial team, who helped ensure that each chapter would be much more concise and easy to read: Emily Hillebrand, Amanda Ayers Barnett, and Rachel Hartman.

We would also like to thank and give thumbs up to the MarkPlus Institute team, who have worked tirelessly for almost two years to help conduct research, brainstorm with authors, and prepare many valuable materials: Ardhi Ridwansyah, Giovanni Panudju, and Thasya Fadilla.

We also wish to acknowledge, with deep appreciation, the support from the World Marketing Summit and the following member organizations of the Asia Marketing Federation and the Asia Council for Small Business (ACSB):

Member Organizations of the Asia Marketing Federation:

- China Council for the Promotion of International Trade – Commercial Sub-Council
- Hong Kong Institute of Marketing
- Indonesia Marketing Association
- Institute of Marketing Malaysia
- Japan Marketing Association
- Macau Marketing Institute
- Marketing Association of Cambodia
- Marketing Association of Thailand
- Marketing Institute of Singapore
- Marketing Society of Bangladesh
- Marketing Society of Korea
- Mongolian Marketing Association
- Myanmar Marketing Society Institute
- Nepal Marketing Association
- Philippine Marketing Association
- Sri Lanka Institute of Marketing
- Taiwan Institute of Marketing Science
- Vietnam Marketing Association

Member Organizations of the Asia Council for Small Business

- ACSB Bangladesh
- ACSB China
- ACSB Indonesia
- ACSB Philippines
- ACSB Sri Lanka
- ICSB Laos
- ICSB Macau

- ICSB Taiwan
- ICSB Thailand
- ICSB Vietnam
- ICSMEE Malaysia
- ICSMEHK
- Korea ICSB
- SEAANZ

CHAPTER 1

The Omnihouse Model

A Holistic Perspective of Entrepreneurial Marketing

The rapidly changing business environment, especially after the world was hit by the COVID-19 pandemic, demands a new, more holistic marketing approach—a concept that can be a strong foundation for organizations when facing various challenges in the present and especially in the future. In this chapter, we look at the various elements that are part of the new genre of entrepreneurial marketing.

To make it easier to understand this new genre of entrepreneurial marketing concept, we'll use a framework called the *omnihouse model* (see Figure 1.1). This model demonstrates our vision of how entrepreneurial marketing should be carried out. It also shows how the approach integrates with an entire organization. We will use it as a guide throughout this book.

Omni—which comes from the Latin *omnis*—means "to combine." In the model's name, it is used with the word *house*, which represents a place, facility, or business. Thus, *omnihouse* refers to an organization that combines multiple elements. Each of these components plays an individual role and also collaborates with the other parts of the business.

The omnihouse model is a framework that can be used to implement strategies and achieve specific goals. We'll discuss it briefly here. We'll also refer in depth to its different components in the following chapters.

The core of this model is housed in two clusters. The first cluster is the *entrepreneurship* group, comprising four elements: *creativity*, *innovation*, *entrepreneurship*, and *leadership* (CI-EL). The second cluster is *professionalism group*, which also comprises four components: *productivity*, *improvement*, *professionalism*, and *management* (PI-PM).

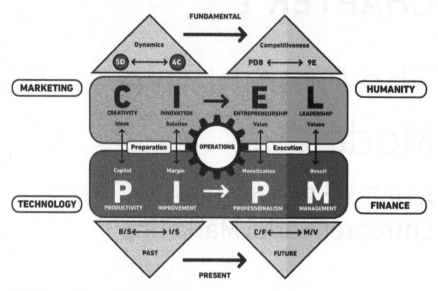

FIGURE 1.1 The omnihouse model

Notice these clusters are surrounded by other functions and interact with them. They are affected by *dynamics* (see the top left of Figure 1.1), which constitutes five drivers: *technology, political/legal* (including regulations), *economy, social/cultural,* and *market*. These drivers, which collectively are called *change,* affect the other 4Cs elements: *competitor, customer,* and *company.*

This dynamics component serves as the foundation to develop marketing strategies and tactics, as outlined in the competitiveness triangle at the top right of the model. Within the triangle, PBD stands for *positioning, differentiation,* and *brand.* This is the anchor for the other main elements of marketing: segmentation, targeting, marketing mix, selling, service, and processes.

The dynamics element is also the basis for developing ideas, which leads to creativity. These ideas can be converted into innovation in the form of tangible solutions for customers. These creative ideas must use various company's capital productively. The solutions provided to customers need to result in improvements, as reflected in the company's better profit margins. Thus, the convergence of creativity/innovation and productivity/improvement elements affects the balance sheet (listed as B/S) and income statement (listed as I/S).

Elements of creativity and improvement can generate competitiveness only if we involve people with solid mindsets of entrepreneurship and leadership to manage them. Value creation is the responsibility of entrepreneurs, and leaders maintain values. However, we also need to support entrepreneurship and leadership with solid professionalism and management. This condition, in turn, can propel the company forward.

What we see in the balance sheet and income statement is a result of the past. What we are doing now, especially through the strong convergence of entrepreneurship/professionalism and leadership/management elements, will determine a company's cash flow (listed as C/F) and market value (listed as M/V). Thus, we gain a picture of how the organization will perform in the future.

As laid out in the omnihouse model, it is essential to integrate marketing with finance and also integrate technology and humanity. The term *humanity* refers to main stakeholders, namely, people, customers, and society. Collectively, these functions support the actions that lead to financial and nonfinancial results.

Note that in the heart of the model we have operations. This function takes marketing objectives and places them into action and, at the same time, ensures financial goals can be achieved. Operations that also bridge that use of technology will ultimately be impactful for humanity. The operations capabilities interact with the other capabilities to keep a company moving forward and competitive within its industry. The operations capabilities also enable the organization to adapt quickly to any changes in the business environment.

Overcoming Marketing Blind Spots

The term *marketing myopia* refers to a condition in which a company is too focused on producing goods or services. It overlooks the customer's actual needs and desires. Theodore Levitt introduced the concept in 1960, and it became widespread during the following decades.

In response to this issue, many companies adopted a customer-centric approach. This places the customer as the starting point in product and service development. It prioritizes the client experience across multiple touchpoints.[1]

The question is, did it work? Perhaps for some. However, this new focus actually led to another set of issues, which we'll call *marketing blind spots*. Let's define it and look at how it can be problematic. We'll then see how entrepreneurial marketing can solve these challenges.

We can define a marketing blind spot as a condition in which a company has carried out various marketing management processes properly but did not realize there are still many unconnected elements. No one has looked

---

[1]According to Accenture, this experiential concept has undergone an evolution that has pushed beyond the customer experience philosophy and organized the whole business on delivering exceptional experiences, and is called *business of experience (BX)*. Please refer to Baiju Shah, "An Experience Renaissance to Reignite Growth." Retrieved January 2021 from https://www.forbes.com/sites/paultalbot/2020/12/07/accenture-interactive-advocates-the-business-of-experience/?sh=78c54bb22ca4

around at other dynamics that could play a role in how marketing is carried out. In turn, these blind spots hamper the company and ultimately cause it to lose its ability to compete.

Some of the common marketing blind spots are discussed in the next sections.

Ignoring the Macroenvironment

What happens in the macroenvironment can affect the microenvironment. In marketing science, there are aspects of strategy and aspects of tactics. The formulation of a marketing strategy must refer to the corporate strategy. Meanwhile, corporate strategy is shaped by, among other things, the existing macroeconomic conditions. However, marketing in practice often does not pay sufficient attention to the macroeconomic aspects. For instance, it may be challenging for marketing executives to link phenomena in the macroenvironment with the tactical policies in the company.

We define marketing as *market-ing* (not *marketing*), which means how we deal with the very dynamic and ever-changing market. If marketing within a company develops at a slower pace than the actual very fast market pace in which a company competes, an advantage is lost. It is ironic: we call it marketing, but it is ineffective in dealing with the market. Figure 1.2 illustrates this condition well.

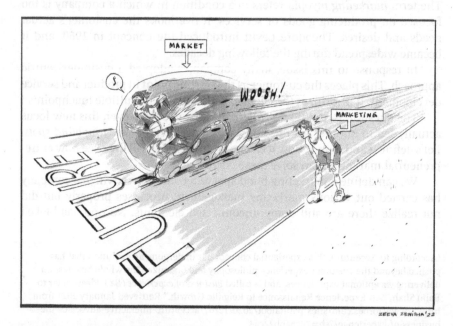

FIGURE 1.2   Marketing versus market.

Source: ZEEVA ZENITHA '22

Misalignment of Marketing and Finance

This classic blind spot often causes a disconnect. Marketers may focus solely on nonfinancial performance, such as increasing brand awareness, forming specific perceptions, and communicating value propositions. These metrics may not hold significance for financial professionals, as they struggle to see the actual value that marketing is trying to achieve.

Financial executives may ask how much the return from an allocated marketing budget is and when it occurs. This question can be difficult for marketing people to answer. It is especially tough if the marketer's mindset doesn't refer to the concept of return, which most financial people always refer to.

A Disharmonious Marketing and Sales Relationship

When marketing and sales aren't fully aligned, it often looks like a "Tom and Jerry" cartoon show. Sometimes they might get along very well. At other points, they could be at odds with one another.

Weak Integration of Online and Offline Marketing

Many brick-and-mortar (offline) companies also have online platforms. Moreover, online companies are adopting offline practices by opening physical stores to strengthen their existence. However, some online companies that do their business purely online can still compete well. If that is the case, what about offline companies that only stay offline? If an offline company decides to remain offline forever, then perhaps soon, they would be off, too. Therefore, we must pay attention, for example, not only to showrooming but also to webrooming.

Overlooking Human Capital

This blind spot may start at the beginning of the recruitment process in a company. It doesn't serve to recruit people whose only purpose is to do limited work as ordered without any initiative. Strong companies need people who have a strong passion and love their work. These candidates should be creative and innovative and, at the same time, individuals who are productive and can make significant improvements.

We are at the end of the era of people who have an "employee mentality"— someone who only wants to work nine-to-five and only on weekdays, follows the job description rigidly, and doesn't want to work extra miles. Therefore, the HR team can no longer look for simple ordinary employees but rather replace them with talented and passionate people who show a calling for their duties and have similar characteristics to the company's character, values, and brand.

Lack of Humanity in Marketing

In the past, we occasionally heard that marketing was being misused by some irresponsible marketers solely for the company's benefit and not for customers' well-being, let alone for broader social interests. In such a situation, the company considers marketing only as a tool for making profits. The company "persuades" customers to buy their products without paying sufficient attention to the employees' well-being, the environment, and other relevant considerations.

Therefore, some of today's companies are trying to incorporate social elements into their business models in an effort to be more human. They may make corporate social responsibility (CSR) efforts merely to be acceptable in the public's eyes and flash CSR as a tool to cover up misuses. Adopting fake CSR is not sustainable, and marketing practices should return to their noble values.

Entrepreneurial marketing solves for these blind spots. By integrating functions, it is able to better track macroeconomic developments and implement strategies that align with the company's overall goals. It helps departments stay connected and even communicate in a similar way. It resolves issues related to talent management and human capital, because it seeks players who are ready to work in a collaborative environment. Finally, it helps a company communicate its social role as a contributor to a community, society, and the planet.

In the pages that follow, we'll look closely at the shift from professional marketing to this new era of entrepreneurial marketing. We'll discuss the changing marketing landscape and how it affects competition, customers, and the company itself. We'll lay out how entrepreneurial capabilities and marketing strategies can be implemented in today's environment, and how an organization ideally should be organized to face the future.

In each chapter, we'll refer to the omnihouse model. It will serve as a guide on our journey toward a more enlightened take on entrepreneurial marketing. By the end, you'll have a better grasp of the potential that your own organization contains. Better yet, you'll know how to address pain points and be fully prepared to take a leading role in a changing world.

CHAPTER 2

From Professional to Entrepreneurial Marketing

The Core Elements of the Omnihouse Model

In 2010, Instagram launched a photo-sharing platform that focused on offering photo-based social media networks. Two months later, it could boast of 1 million downloads.

At its core, Instagram is a fast-moving platform that takes advantage of the latest trends by adding new features, including short-lived content (stories) and short videos (reels). In a crowded social media platform market, the company has taken a leading position with a current focus on four elements: creator, video, shopping, and messaging. In 2022, Instagram's value stood at US$100 million, making the platform Facebook's highest-performing investment with a return on investment more than 100 times.

What can be gleaned from the story of Instagram? Perhaps a good starting point lies in the chance to see that in very dynamic conditions, it's not enough to rely on an overly procedural approach to obtain the desired results. The business environment changes rapidly and companies that want to perform highly will be ready to pivot—often and swiftly. Instagram followed this strategy and on execution developed into a behemoth figure that dominates its industry.

A facile mindset tends to contradict the professional approach that so frequently prevails in the marketing segment. In the past, the marketing department might have set up a plan, outlined the steps to follow, and moved forward. This approach may have seemed appropriate at one time, especially before the internet and technologies took off and created an interconnected, fluid space.

In today's world, the professional method of marketing faces several key risks. First and perhaps foremost, it may not be ready to move with the changes in demand. It might not have the capability to keep up with an agile and changing market. When the tides turn, a marketing department that continues to march down the same path will likely fall short of its goals.

This contradiction in marketing—namely, the "professional" approach versus the entrepreneurial mindset that Instagram exemplified—is precisely what we'll look at in this chapter. Let's explore what's behind each of these marketing methods. In doing so, we'll see that there is value in each. At the same time, companies need to know which method (or combination of the two) is appropriate for their situation and how they can best be used to propel growth and expansion in the years to come.

Understanding Professional Marketing

When we use the term *professional* to describe marketing, it's often to refer to tendencies toward procedures and bureaucracy. In an established organization with clear-cut responsibilities, we typically expect each team member to carry out a specific role within a particular function. In this scenario, executing cross-functional activities can take several routes to gain approval.[1] As such, it can be natural for departments, including marketing, to work in a mindset of "following the procedures." There may be little crossover, and there might be few—or no—attempts to carry out multiple tasks simultaneously.

This approach comes with several notable benefits and drawbacks. Let's start by sifting through the positives that stem from the professional approach of marketing. Then we'll look at a few of the key downsides.

Advantages and Disadvantages of Professional Marketing

In the history of marketing, there is a long line of successful companies that have followed a professional mindset. The following describes some of the main perks that professional marketing brings to the table:

Understanding business models. The professional team sees the value proposition of the product or brand. It can identify where the company's

---

[1]Nina Toren, "Bureaucracy and Professionalism: A Reconsideration of Weber's Thesis," *The Academy of Management Review* 1, no. 3 (1976): 36–46. https://doi.org/10.2307/257271

revenue stream is coming from, master the calculation of various costs incurred, and ensure smooth cash inflow. For example, Netflix developed an effective business model to accumulate 220 million paid subscribers in 2021 and generate US$7.7 billion in revenue in 2022.[2]

Ability to manage resources. The professional marketing approach determines which resources and capabilities are required. The objective is to ensure that there can be an exchange of value with customers.

Capacity to coordinate activities. The professional team understands the interrelationships and interdependencies between the different functions of the company. It organizes procedures so that activities, when carried out, are well coordinated and synchronized with the set direction.

Ability to manage collaboration. The professional team formalizes all forms of cooperating with clear terms and conditions. Tasks follow an established protocol and avoid overlapping or conflicting with other activities.

Knowing how to communicate. The professional team can effectively and efficiently carry out internal and external marketing. They are able to generate strong awareness and appeal as an essential starting point for penetrating the market.

Ability to answer questions. The professional team comprehends the product at a detailed level, including its features, benefits, the buying process, and how it is delivered. Marketers also know how to explain the use of their products so that they can be used optimally by customers.

Ability to provide customer support. The professional team provides support services, including handling customer complaints, repeat purchases, cross- or upsell services, consulting, managing customer loyalty and advocacy, and maintaining a sustainable relationship.

In addition to these skill sets, there are additional advantages that surface when professional marketers have the right attitude. Following are some of these best practices:

Avoiding bias. All thinking and decision-making are free from personal biases such as political views, gender, and social and cultural background. All analysis is fact-based. There isn't prejudice or a personal interest portrayed.

Respecting others. Successful professional marketers appreciate coworkers' opinions, including those of superiors, peers, and subordinates, according to existing boundaries. They treat customers humanely and are aware that these individuals support the company's livelihood. They comply with company regulations, including established company values.

---

[2]https://www.statista.com/statistics/273883/netflixs-quarterly-revenue/; https://www.hollywoodreporter.com/business/digital/netflix-q4-2021-earnings-1235078237/

Demonstrating accountability. The professional team is consistently responsible for all the thoughts, words, and actions they carry out according to the scope of the assignment given. They take ownership for the decisions made, along with their repercussions, both on individual and team levels.

Showing integrity. Professional marketers fulfill their responsibilities correctly and adequately, upholding honesty internally among colleagues and externally with customers and business partners.

Focusing on the task. Professional marketers demonstrate discipline in completing tasks according to a predetermined schedule. They use working hours for productive purposes and do not mix personal matters with business.

Although there are certainly significant advantages that result from a professional mindset, it's important for our balanced discussion to observe several common drawbacks:

Slow to change. There can be a tendency to keep leaders and leadership styles in place, even as times change. If executives unfit for their roles remain in place, it can hinder the company's overall progress. It may also dampen company culture and the spirit of employees.[3]

Grand planning. Spending ample time laying out procedures and processes often leads to slow implementation. When the world around us changes quickly, it can be difficult to keep up.

Becoming stagnant. Organizations that focus on procedures may not spot upcoming opportunities and risk not being ready to pivot when needed.

A nine-to-five attitude. Professional marketers may perceive that their work in the company must take place during set hours. It can be challenging to ask employees to remain for extra hours outside of this time frame.

Inability to adjust priorities. When following procedures and maintaining the bureaucratic status quo, it is often challenging for marketing teams to think and act outside of the box. Even if an opportunity is identified, they might be hesitant to change their priorities and move in a different direction. This hesitancy can put a company at risk of falling behind competitors who are shifting strategies and meeting market demand.[4]

Being reactive. Marketing teams might respond to changes they see over time and follow others instead of leading the way into new markets and segments.

---

[3]https://www.forbes.com/sites/forbestechcouncil/2021/06/15/13-industry-experts-share-reasons-companies-fail-at-digital-transformation/?sh=5aca2d2f7a3f; https://www.forbes.com/sites/forbesdallascouncil/2019/08/23/how-modern-organizations-can-adapt-to-change/?sh=64ea3cf5687e

[4]https://www.weforum.org/agenda/2014/12/8-ways-negative-people-affect-your-workplace/

The Entrepreneurial Approach

Now let's open our minds and consider a different mindset to marketing, one that perhaps aligns with Instagram's approach. Because the term *entrepreneur* has long been associated with start-ups and disruptors, along with high successes (and potential for failure), it's worth starting out this section with a review of the definition. After looking at what it encompasses, we'll apply the term to marketing.

For decades, visionaries have leveraged opportunities, regardless of how small those opportunities might be. When moving forward, someone with an entrepreneurial spirit is fully aware of the risks they will face. At the same time, they have the courage and optimism to give their plans a trial run.

Those who apply an entrepreneurial approach know how to identify the gaps, dare to make decisions, face the consequences of their actions, and collaborate with multiple parties. From this explanation, there are at least three very prominent capabilities related to entrepreneurship, namely, the attitude and ability to see opportunities (opportunity seeker), a mindset that dares to take risks (risk-taker), and the ability to cooperate with other parties (network collaborator). Let's look more closely at each one.

Opportunity Seeker

The opportunity seeker has the ability to adapt and view the positive side of a given situation. They don't dwell on a pessimistic point of view, which can divert a leader's focus from seeking opportunities.[5]

Risk-Taker

Uncertainty surrounds new initiatives. The risk-taker evaluates the circumstance at hand, the options available, and the potential for failure. A decision is then made based on those calculated risks.

Network Collaborator

The network collaborator recognizes they are unable to operate entirely on their own. As such, they build an extensive network and collaborate with other experts who can contribute to areas in which the entrepreneur cannot.

---

[5]https://hbr.org/2021/09/every-leader-has-flaws-dont-let-yours-derail-your-strategy; https://hbr.org/2021/08/leaders-dont-be-afraid-to-talk-about-your-fears-and-anxieties

The Entrepreneurship Model for Marketing

Drawing from our description of entrepreneurship, we can turn the discussion to observing how it applies to marketing. Marketing starts with foresight in seeing opportunities and then undergoes a creative and innovative process to come up with a solution that can be offered to customers. We must position our branded solution clearly to the relevant customer segment. This includes framing the solution by showing its point of differentiation and reasons to believe in it, supported by several competitive advantages.

Marketers must be able to convert solutions into value, which can take on different forms. For the company, it will typically mean higher profits. Investors will be looking for a higher market value of the company, along with an increase in dividends. For customers, the value will be in our products that can solve their problems.

The attitude of daring to take risks, namely, choosing a path that we or others have never tried, shows that marketers aim to be different, and not mainstream. One caveat: although differentiation is essential, we have to ensure that the market will appreciate such an option. It must be consistently realized in marketing campaigns and supported by sales efforts both offline and online.

The sales team needs to understand the characteristics of the targeted segment and how to position an offering (including the brand) relative to competitors. The team will want to grasp the product differentiation and support services offered. They will also need to be careful to ensure efforts are made to maintain the brand's character.

Through solid collaboration, we have a better chance of overcoming challenges. For example, Target and Starbucks connected to deliver a complete shopping experience.[6] Target began to sell Starbucks products, and Starbucks established shops within the Target stores, enabling customers to grab a coffee on their way in or out. As a result, Target received greater brand recognition from loyal Starbucks customers, and vice versa.

From this discussion, we can observe that entrepreneurship in marketing has three main factors: positioning, differentiation, and brand. These components are linked together and will drive decisions. The model shown in Figure 2.1 can help us see these traits and how they are interrelated.

Individuals with entrepreneurial skills may have a specific focus. Opportunity seekers will relate to positioning, which is more broadly part of customer management. Risk-takers will be involved with differentiation and more broadly with product management. Meanwhile, network collaborators will focus on brand development, which is part of brand management.

---

[6]https://globalnews.ca/news/771537/target-starbucks-partnership-brews-up-perfect-blend/

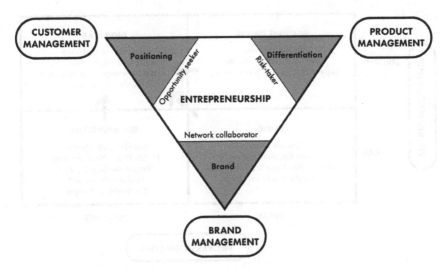

FIGURE 2.1   Entrepreneurship model for marketing

Comparing Professional and Entrepreneurial Marketing

Now that we've studied some of the main characteristics of these two approaches, which is best? The answer isn't simple. There may be times when entrepreneurial efforts should be prioritized, and other moments when professionalism is key. Let's delve into how these approaches tend to stand out, and how they can be blended for optimal results.

Start-ups often have a high entrepreneurial spirit at the beginning of their establishment. At a certain point, however, they can find it difficult to grow. One of the reasons behind this is that it can be challenging for start-ups to build their professional capabilities. Start-ups are often very slow to embed this professional capability. The idea of Pretty Young Professionals—a start-up founded by colleagues at McKinsey who shared the same vision to help women entrepreneurs find resources to run their businesses—attracted several potential investors. However, the friendships could not help them take a solid, professional role in running that company. After 11 months of operations, the company shut down due to an internal dispute.[7]

We often find some companies can exist only for a short time because they do not have these two capabilities. This condition is frequently encountered

---

[7]https://foundr.com/articles/leadership/personal-growth/4-startup-case-studies-failure

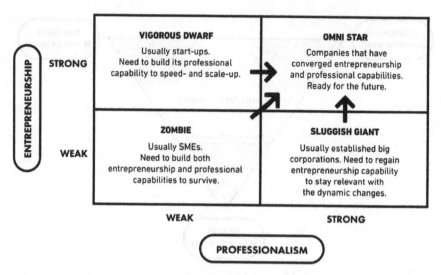

FIGURE 2.2 The shifts: More professional, more entrepreneurial

in small- to medium-sized enterprises (SMEs). It is one of the factors why the percentage of failed SMEs is high.

Figure 2.2 can help us decipher how companies of different sizes can be affected by their level of marketing capabilities.

There can be great potential when we blend entrepreneurial elements into a professional environment. For instance, Google encouraged its employees to spend 20% of their working hours doing things they think can best benefit Google. This strategy resulted in employees coming up with some successful ideas, including Gmail, Google Maps, and AdSense.[8]

The application of entrepreneurship in a professional setup is often called *corporate entrepreneurship* or *intrapreneurship*. The arrangement enables the correct procedures to be followed. At the same time, there is some room for flexibility. The accounting consulting firm PwC has been giving some freedom to their employees, allowing them to focus on their talents. They found that flexibility in work can help the company retain and attract valuable talents.[9]

[8]https://www.forbes.com/sites/georgedeeb/2016/02/18/big-companies-must-embrace-intrapreneurship-to-survive/?sh=6b51f30348ab; https://www.fm-magazine.com/issues/2021/sep/boost-your-career-with-intrapreneurship.html; https://www.cnbc.com/2021/12/16/google-20-percent-rule-shows-exactly-how-much-time-you-should-spend-learning-new-skills.html; https://www.inc.com/bill-murphy-jr/google-says-it-still-uses-20-percent-rule-you-should-totally-copy-it.html

[9]https://www.linkedin.com/business/talent/blog/talent-engagement/how-pwc-successfully-built-culture-of-work-flexibility; https://www.pwc.com/vn/en/careers/experienced-jobs/pwc-professional.html

According to the *Harvard Business Review*, almost every company today has made leaps of faith and major innovations instead of continuous improvement.[10] If we rely solely on professionalism, we will be locked in only to productivity figures and incremental improvements, as we tend to measure success only by financial achievements. This play-safe attitude cannot support increasing the company's market value in the long term because without an innovative breakthrough, the company's future will be bleak. This market value is also important for investors as they place their funds in a company.

However, the entrepreneurial spirit is closely related to seeing the various opportunities outside and learning how to take advantage of them. In addition, creativity and innovation are often attached to the entrepreneurial spirit. A healthy amount of bureaucracy is essential to provide governance in everyday duty. Leaders face constant challenges in putting bureaucracy in the right place. Referring to a survey by *Harvard Business Review*, 7,000 respondents experienced a growing bureaucracy during the year before 2017. However, leaders should minimize multilayer approval to make room for innovations.[11]

Hence, we need to try to bring together the two extremes on the professional and the entrepreneurial continuum. Professionals who usually tend to play it safe with a play-by-the-book approach must have the nerve to take calculated risks like entrepreneurs. In essence, a professional will need to apply the entrepreneurial spirit in various value-creation processes in a company. An intrapreneurial culture enables employees to practice and sharpen their entrepreneurial skills, resulting in more efficient brand management.[12]

Therefore, a company must provide a conducive environment that can support creativity. A company should also be able to carefully see technically feasible creative ideas, choose the best idea, and convert them into an innovative solution that will create value for customers and, in turn, for the company. Curtis Carlson, for example, created the "Champion" program, which encourages his team to submit innovative thinking based on a need, approach, benefits relative to costs, and competition value proposition. This arrangement has had successful results, including the development of technologies such as HDTV and Siri.[13]

No one can rely solely on a professional approach anymore in this highly dynamic business environment. We need strategic flexibility within the company, and one way to make this possible is to have the board of directors and management adopt an entrepreneurial approach. Management plays a role in maintaining various routine processes needed so that the company's day-to-day operations can run smoothly, but if there is a change or even

---

[10]https://hbr.org/amp/2013/10/the-hidden-dangers-of-playing-it-safe
[11]https://www.linkedin.com/pulse/bureaucracy-hindering-your-organisations-agility-adapting-sean-huang/?trk=public_profile_article_view
[12]https://www.investopedia.com/terms/i/intrapreneurship.asp
[13]https://hbr.org/2020/11/innovation-for-impact?registration=success

transformation, management must accommodate and adapt to these changes quickly and make them part of the new routine process. In this way, the company can exist sustainably in the long term.

As imperative as it is to incorporate both professional and entrepreneur elements into marketing campaigns, it's important to note that it's not enough to survive. To fully thrive in this changing world, companies need to be able to integrate these marketing approaches into other departments as well. When all areas are connected, the possibilities will broaden even more. We'll look at this next phase in Chapter 3.

Key Takeaways

- Professional marketing focuses on procedures and a step-by-step approach.
- Some benefits of professional marketing include understanding business models, managing resources, coordinating activities, managing collaboration, communicating well, answering questions, and providing customer support. Its best practices consist of avoiding bias, respecting others, showing accountability, showing integrity, and focusing on the task.
- Drawbacks related to professional marketing involve being slow to change, grand planning, becoming stagnant, a nine-to-five attitude, an inability to adjust resources, and being reactive instead of proactive.
- Entrepreneurial marketing encompasses knowing how to identify gaps, make decisions, face consequences, and collaborate with multiple practices.
- Companies will do well to find a balance of professional and entrepreneurial marketing that best serves their needs.

CHAPTER 3

Rethinking Competition

Collaborating for Sustainability

I f you travel in your electric Renault Zoe across major roads in Europe, you might be able to readily recharge at stations in France, the Netherlands, and Germany. These countries are leading the way in terms of the number of charging stations available in the continent. Other nations have lower numbers but are looking for ways to respond to the growing demand for electric vehicles. Overall, the European Union has more than 300,000 charging stations, with plans to substantially increase that number in the coming years.[1]

In places with the right charging infrastructure, it may be easy to drive up to a station and plug in. If we pull back the layers, however, we'll see that great efforts have been made to get the battery rechargers in their place. This is especially true in Europe, where plans to build efficient battery-renewing stations started long before the charging units popped up.

Interestingly—and of significance for our discussion—the power behind these recharging places didn't come from a single player. This is because the resources required to construct an ultra-fast, high-power charging infrastructure are enormous. The project was simply too much for a single company to take on.

Therefore, several years ago, auto manufacturers from various parts of the world got together. They decided to collaborate to install a charging infrastructure in Europe. The BMW Group, Daimler AG, Ford, and the Volkswagen

---

[1]https://www.euronews.com/next/2022/06/20/demand-for-evs-is-soaring-is-europes-charging-station-network-up-to-speed#:~:text=The%20EU%20has%20more%20than,in%20a%20report%20last%20year

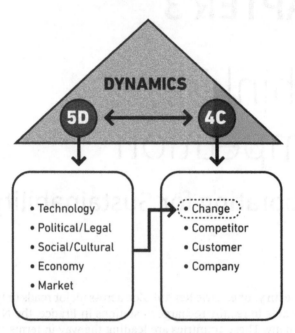

FIGURE 3.1 The "dynamics" section of the omnihouse model

Group, together with Audi and Porsche, pooled their resources.[2] They laid out plans to build charging units, which would support their up-and-coming electric vehicles (EV). The project's goals included making electric-powered cars more acceptable to the public eye and shifting them to become mainstream. This, in turn, could drive up EV sales for all manufacturers involved.

The collaboration exemplifies a key characteristic for companies—and specifically marketers—moving forward. Take note of the players involved. *Aren't they competitors?* you might ask. The answer, of course, is a resounding *yes! Are they working together to create a resource that will serve their individual purposes?* Again, the response is an overwhelming *yes!*

Welcome to the playing field of today and tomorrow. Times have changed and are continuing to evolve. To stay alive, corporations need to look to their competitors and work together, to a certain extent.

There are limitations to this strategy, of course. To fully understand the balance between cooperating and staying competitive, let's explore the dynamics that are affecting these collaborative trends (see Figure 3.1). To do so, we'll turn to our omnihouse model and dive into the "dynamics" section. We'll look at the 5Ds, which stands for the drivers of this collaborative trend.

[2]https://www.press.bmwgroup.com/global/article/detail/T0275763EN/bmw-group-daimler-ag-ford-motor-company-and-the-volkswagen-group-with-audi-and-porsche-form-joint-venture?language=en

What's Shifting Our Marketing World

Let's consider the five drivers that are affecting how companies compete. These factors are related to technology, the political and legal environment, the economy, social and cultural factors, and market conditions. We'll consider each of these briefly.

Technology

The development of electric cars is one example of the significant change technology has brought on in recent years. There's more in the works in the auto industry, too. Take self-driving vehicles, for instance. Many of these advances are bringing companies together in new ways. Organizations rely on a multitude of suppliers and networks to provide the components for these complex cars. Some of the changes in auto technology have also led to greener opportunities, which is important for an industry long associated with a negative environmental impact.

Technology is hitting more than the auto industry, of course. Emerging trends in AI, big data, natural language processing, mixed reality, and robotic and machine learning are making waves in organizations of all sorts. The Internet of Things, blockchain, 3D printing, and video and music streaming are morphing the way businesses operate. These technologies are changing the way consumers live and work as well.

Political and Legal Issues

Politicians from various parts of the world have come together to create written and unwritten policies. These have served as guidelines for communities, organizations, and individuals to follow.[3] Some regulations address ecological issues such as climate change, deforestation, ocean preservation, and biodiversity. Policies often affect trade and the way companies can function in specific regions.

The Economy

Clearly COVID-19 and its related shutdowns slowed global economic growth. As we look to the coming years, the recovery rates remain uncertain. Some countries may recoup their losses at a faster rate than others. David Malpass,

---

[3]https://ctb.ku.edu/en/table-of-contents/implement/changing-policies/overview/main

president of World Bank, stated that the unequal rate of recovery in countries across the globe might slow down collaboration initiatives for shared goals, such as climate change.[4]

Social and Cultural Issues

The changing workforce and population demographics influence how businesses function and whom they hire. Many countries are experiencing an aging population. According to the United Nations, the global population of people aged 60 years or over was 962 million in 2017, more than twice compared to 1980 when there were 382 million older persons worldwide. We expect the number of older persons to double by 2050, with a projection to reach nearly 2.1 billion.

Other issues include rampant inequalities and disparities. In many countries, the rich are getting richer, while the poor are getting poorer. Access to health care and education varies, depending on where individuals live and their social status.[5]

Market Conditions

Many hope that open markets and trade will lead to stronger economies in various countries. Some of the benefits from these trends include new opportunities for workers, consumers, and companies worldwide. Better economic performance is expected to help alleviate poverty and promote stability and security for the wider community.[6]

The character of the market, which has a low barrier to entry, causes it to become a more level playing field. The market is also no longer limited geographically. Still, the local context is becoming increasingly important to consider.

Change Is in the Air

These forces are stirring up change, which we can see in our omnihouse model. In Figure 3.2, you'll find the 4Cs depicted in what we call the 4C diamond

---

[4]https://www.bbc.com/news/business-59946302
[5]An aphorism expressed by Percy Bysshe Shelley. https://en.wikipedia.org/wiki/The_
rich_get_richer_and_the_poor_get_poorer#:~:text=%22The%20rich%20get%20richer%20
and,due%20to%20Percy%20Bysshe%20Shelley.&text=The%20aphorism%20is%20commonly%20
evoked,market%20capitalism%20producing%20excessive%20inequality
[6]https://www.oecd.org/trade/understanding-the-global-trading-system/why-open-markets-matter/

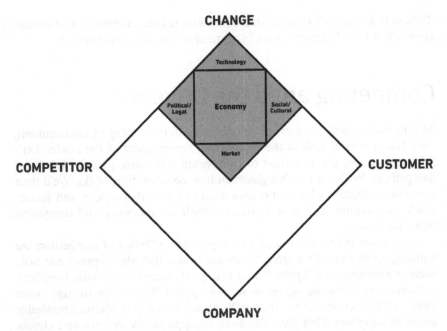

FIGURE 3.2   The 4C diamond model

model. Change, in turn, affects the way companies operate, compete, and interact with customers.

Fujifilm—a giant in the photography film industry—got knocked down when they couldn't shift to the digital age and keep up with others in the space. This could have led to the company's demise. Instead, team members figured out a way to be agile and shift gears. As a result, Fujifilm pivoted its technological applications to serve the health care and cosmetic fields.[7]

In addition to adapting at full force, some players are becoming more aggressive. Take the case of the Industrial and Commercial Bank of China (ICBC), established in 1984. ICBC worked hard to grow and increase in size. In 2007, it beat Citibank, which at the time held the leading position in the banking industry, in terms of total assets. During the following years, ICBC has remained the largest bank in the world.[8]

Much of the success of Fujifilm and ICBC can be attributed to a growth mindset. This goes beyond a focus of offering unique products and services.

[7]https://www.channelnewsasia.com/cna-insider/how-fujifilm-survived-digital-age-unexpected-makeover-1026656

[8]https://www.doughroller.net/banking/largest-banks-in-the-world/; https://www.chinadaily.com.cn/china/2007-07/24/content_5442270.htm

Richard D'Aveni, a US thinker, stated that a traditional competitive advantage approach was no longer relevant in aggressive market competitions.[9]

Competing amid the Drivers

To fully understand the topic of collaborating in this emerging environment, we'll take a careful look at the "competitor" component of the model. Let's think about why it's important to collaborate both with direct and indirect competitors. We'll start with a glance at how collaboration works. We'll then move on to discuss what companies need to know about today and tomorrow's competition, and how to balance both collaborating and competing going forward.

As we saw in the auto industry example, the unlikeliest of competitors are teaming up to a certain degree. There are others that also support our case, such as Samsung and Apple. These two giants found a mutually beneficial collaboration. Samsung agreed to supply Apple with an edge-to-edge Super Retina OLED screen for the iPhone X. Apple, for its part, shares knowledge about its suppliers. This gives Samsung an opportunity to learn and elevate the quality of its products.[10]

Let's go over the three main reasons organizations are collaborating today:

- They cannot face the significant drivers individually. By uniting, they share knowledge, grow more robust, and solve problems quickly.
- A single company may not have the financial backing to overcome a challenge. When facing large issues, firms can pool their resources to share the costs involved.
- Together companies can achieve a win-win situation, as opposed to a zero-sum game. If they establish a standard or platform in their industry, they'll all strengthen their position in the market.

Although collaboration has its strengths, let's keep in mind that companies are still working to achieve their own goals. As we consider entrepreneurial marketing, it's essential to keep several factors in mind when competing today. Here's a brief overview of competency, capabilities, intangible resources, strategy, execution, and domain.

---

[9]https://daveni.tuck.dartmouth.edu/research-and-ideas/hypercompetition
[10]Adam Brandenburger and Barry Nalebuff, "The Rules of Co-opetition," *Harvard Business Review* (January–February 2021).

Building a distinctive competency is urgent. Having a competitive advantage is no longer enough; companies must form a distinctive competency.[11] This might encompass their culture or operating system.

Appropriate capability development is required. Companies need everything from basic capabilities, such as managerial skills, to complex abilities, such as innovation, strong leadership, and customer management. Capabilities that are honed continuously and developed consistently will, in turn, shape competencies.[12]

Intangible resources are increasingly important. Tangible resources, in general, are easier to imitate than intangible resources and can be obtained from the open market. Intangible resources are usually more difficult because they undergo a relatively long formation process. Hence, investment in intangible resources—including human capital and talent—has become a must to establish competitiveness.

Robust strategy must align with policies. A company should develop its strategy based on relevant macro-environmental conditions, competitive situations, and relevant competitors and customers. Developing policies is the next step. Organizations will want policies to fall under the same umbrella; they should complement each other and support the strategy.

Execution should focus on productivity. The company should carry out all business operations efficiently and use assets effectively. When it comes to productivity, we can't compromise. Management can use several financial ratios to measure productivity levels. There are also nonfinancial measures that reflect on performance. Some of these include customer loyalty, product quality improvement, and employee productivity.[13]

Clearly define competition domain. Companies must ensure that they are always compatible and have the necessary competitive advantages wherever they participate in the competition domain. The competition domain can also adjust in line with changes in the business environment and business development can redefine it from time to time.

---

[11]The topic of distinctive competencies was also discussed in depth by Hitt and Ireland in the mid-1980s. Michael A. Hitt and R. Duane Ireland, "Corporate Distinctive Competence, Strategy, Industry and Performance," *Strategic Management Journal* 6, no. 3 (273–293).

[12]The topic related to this competency has been studied in depth by two renowned figures in management science, namely, Prahalad and Hamel, who introduced the term *core competencies*. See C. K. Prahalad and Gary Hamel, "The Core Competence of the Corporation," *Harvard Business Review* (1990). https://hbr.org/1990/05/the-core-competence-of-the-corporation; https://en.wikipedia.org/wiki/Core_competency

[13]https://hbr.org/2003/11/coming-up-short-on-nonfinancial-performance-measurement

The Future of Competition

In line with the increasingly dynamic macro environment, competition will become more challenging because the future is increasingly full of uncertainties. Several issues will define the competition now and in the future. Companies should pay attention to these trends.

More Digitalized

The competition will be based primarily on digital technology and data. This technology will provide a solid capability for the company to obtain fast, accurate, and relevant information related to the business environment, especially those related to competitors and customers. Data will provide substantial predictive and prescriptive insights to make precise strategic and tactical adjustments.

More Unforgiving Players

The sharing economy is becoming mainstream in business. With a wide-open market, new lean and eager companies will jump in. These start-ups will look much different than established, traditional companies. This new breed will have solid digital capabilities that offer various products with good quality, lower costs, faster delivery, and better support services. This digital capability will also enable them to cross borders into new segments and industries.[14]

Level Playing Field

Social media gives everyone an equal chance at the spotlight. It offers a new way to consume a paid promotion, complete with raw, less-edited visuals that provide a sense of realness. Based on this trend, many influencers whose face, body, and identity do not conform to traditional modeling have emerged as a new model.[15]

The more equal opportunities are, the more difficult it will be for a company to form a significant competitive advantage. This phenomenon aligns with emerging policies as well. Many of these focus on a fair game and fair play approach.

---

[14]This refers to Peter Weill and Stephanie L. Woerner, *What's Your Digital Business Model?* (Cambridge, MA: Harvard Business Review Press, 2018).
[15]https://www.bbc.com/news/technology-56592913; https://medium.com/@TheWEIV/how-social-media-has-impacted-the-modeling-industry-a25721549b65; https://www.youtube.com/watch?v=6OKDa9h4lDo

Harder to Differentiate

It is increasingly difficult for companies to maintain strong differentiation. Decision-makers in a company should rely on the customer-centric approach—emphasizing personalization and customization—in building its value proposition. The company's products and services will be quickly commoditized and lead to a price war if it lacks creativity and innovation capability.

Faster Pace

The fast-changing trend will shorten the life cycle of various products and even the company's value proposition. Time to market and the company's entry strategy are crucial in determining the company's competitive advantage. First movers will not benefit if they fail to set a new standard accepted by the market and soon will become mainstream. Flexibility is an essential key to surviving in a very tough competitive environment.

Stronger Interdependency

Almost all elements in the value chain will be more integrated, and the interdependence will be stronger. To a certain extent, even factors in the broader ecosystem—for example, payment platforms, e-commerce, marketplaces, omni-channels, and others—will also be strongly related one to another. Therefore, synchronization between elements is crucial to guarantee an effective and efficient value-creation process.

For example, in the aviation industry, an airline will depend on the airport manager and vice versa. In addition, there are other interdependent elements in the industry, such as ground handling, catering, and fuel suppliers, which all demand robust synchronization. The regulations of technical aspects and the availability of technicians hampered the growth of the low-cost carrier market in several Asian countries.[16]

Balancing Competition and Collaboration

There are several advantages and disadvantages in competing and collaborating (see Table 3.1). Regardless, a challenge for companies is to make the

---

[16]Wiboon Kittilaksanawong and Elise Perrin, "All Nippon Airways: Are Dual Business Model Sustainable?" *Harvard Business Review* (January 29, 2016).

TABLE 3.1	Advantages and Disadvantages of Competition and Collaboration	
	Advantages	**Disadvantages**
Competition	• Forces company to become better in business[17] • More value or service[18] • More options for customers[19] • Access to new customers[20] • Learn from competitor mistakes[21]	• Decreases market share[22] • Shrinks customer base[23] • High cost to compete[24]
Collaboration	• Created to form resources[25] • Saves costs and avoids duplication[26] • Sharing resources to create a competitive advantage[27] • Accelerates the achievement of economies of scale and scope[28] • Provides chance of mutually reducing company costs[29]	• Increases the likelihood of conflict[30] • Free-riding activities and limited rationality[31] • Requires serious and sustained effort[32] • Loss of autonomy[33] • Future selling complications[34]

[17]https://bizfluent.com/info-8455003-advantages-disadvantages-economic-competition.html
[18]https://www.autoritedelaconcurrence.fr/en/the-benefits-of-competition
[19]https://www.marketing91.com/5-advantages-of-market-competition/
[20]https://opentextbc.ca/strategicmanagement/chapter/advantages-and-disadvantages-of-competing-in-international-markets/
[21]https://www.entrepreneur.com/article/311359
[22]https://bizfluent.com/info-8455003-advantages-disadvantages-economic-competition.html
[23]Ibid.
[24]https://www.thebalancesmb.com/what-is-competition-oriented-pricing-2295452
[25]https://www.mdpi.com/2071–1050/10/8/2688/pdf
[26]https://hbr.org/2021/01/the-rules-of-co-opetition
[27]Ibid.
[28]https://www.mdpi.com/2071–1050/10/8/2688/pdf
[29]https://www.forbes.com/sites/briannegarrett/2019/09/19/why-collaborating-with-your-competition-can-be-a-great-idea/?sh=451bd432df86
[30]https://www.mdpi.com/2071–1050/10/8/2688/pdf
[31]Ibid.
[32]https://hbr.org/2021/01/when-should-you-collaborate-with-the-competition
[33]https://www.americanexpress.com/en-us/business/trends-and-insights/articles/what-are-the-advantages-and-disadvantages-of-a-partnership/
[34]Ibid.

most of the advantages. At the same time, they'll look for ways to mitigate the impact or eliminate the causes of disadvantages.

Collaboration also opens the opportunity to increase the company's flexibility in dealing with changes that occur rapidly in the business environment it faces. This flexibility is an essential capability in dealing with conditions full of uncertainties that require modification or even the adoption of new business models. For example, in 2020, JD.com was the only e-commerce brand in China with consistent product delivery during COVID-19, beating Alibaba. JD.com, which is one of the biggest e-commerce platforms, collaborated with their merchants to predict and send supplies to ensure product availability. With this flexibility, JD.com became one of the earliest in delivering virtual night-time party experiences by joining alcohol brands and music groups.[35]

With the same resources, the company can reach a higher level of sales more quickly and easily achieve a better level of economies of scale. Even further, if the company can develop various other products and carry out cross-selling or upselling with the same resources—and core competency—it will also achieve better economies of scope.

For example, the invention and development of additive manufacturing is one way for a company to achieve better economies of scale and scope. Additive manufacturing, popularly known as 3D printing, is a process of creating objects from data input, initially made for a company that needed to make small manufacturing parts that would be expensive to purchase from the available supply chain. This technology helps the company manage low-scale productions because it can print some parts with the exact quantity they need. Hence, additive manufacturing helps the company achieve economies of scale because the company can control the cost of prototyping.[36]

One distinctive trait of a successful company with digital capabilities is collaboration. Digital transformation blurs bureaucracy and compartmental work functions.[37] Collaboration can also shorten the process from the idea stage to commercialization, where it can answer business challenges related to the speed in making a product available in the market according to the rapidly changing customer demands. Another story of collaboration in commercial activities is Marhen J., a vegan Korean fashion brand with a large fanbase in Southeast Asia. When entering Thailand, Marhen J. created a showcase in Samsung stores to show customers how they'd deliver fashion and technology experience to people's daily lives. The campaign resulted from both Korean brands supporting each other and positioning themselves in customers' daily lives.[38]

---

[35]https://www.valuer.ai/blog/examples-of-successful-companies-who-embraced-new-business-models
[36]https://www.3deo.co/strategy/additive-manufacturing-delivers-economies-of-scale-and-scope/
[37]https://sloanreview.mit.edu/article/why-your-company-needs-more-collaboration/
[38]https://www.bangkokpost.com/thailand/pr/2078987/marhen-j-brand-collaborates-with-samsung-in-in-store-launch-showcase

As an African proverb says, "If you want to go fast, go alone. If you want to go far, go together." We can see that "go alone" means we choose an approach to compete, and "go together" means we choose a collaborative approach. Going alone can quickly decide things within our management ecosystem, but we need to collaborate to be sustainable in the long term. The company's challenge is how to combine the dichotomy. Not fast *or* sustainable, but fast *and* sustainable. This illustration explains why a collaborative approach while competing is becoming an increasingly relevant approach.

Cooperation between competing organizations—or coopetition—to achieve common objectives has become a prerequisite for global competitiveness and innovativeness.[39] The ideal coopetition is to seek to obtain the advantages of each partnership and become more competitive. According to this approach, the parties involved can integrate and synergize the increasingly needed strengths to face a challenging business environment, especially in crisis times.[40]

Greater Challenges, Stronger Collaboration

As mentioned previously, a challenging condition that is increasingly difficult for companies to deal with individually, if their resources, capabilities, and competencies—or sources of advantages—are indeed minimal, encourages companies to collaborate. By looking at the two aspects—namely various challenges and sources of advantages—we find three conditions.:

First Condition: Challenges < Sources of Advantages

An overinvestment enables companies to have powerful sources of advantages that can cause them to face productivity problems if they cannot leverage these advantages. Therefore, entrepreneurial efforts are needed to find new business challenges or opportunities that can take advantage of all the company's resources, capabilities, and even competencies. Companies should leverage an out-of-the-box entrepreneurial mindset to build a network and find partners who are willing to capitalize on existing opportunities. In essence, companies must exploit these excessive advantages by focusing on various external conditions to identify multiple opportunities.

---

[39]Refers to the classic concept from the 1990s echoed by Raymond Norda.
[40]Dorothe Kossyva, Katerina Sarri, and Nikolaos Georgopoulos, "Co-opetition: A Business Strategy for SMEs in Times of Economic Crisis," *South-Eastern Europe Journal of Economics* no. 1 (January 2014): 89–106.

Second Condition: Challenges = Sources of Advantages

In this condition, companies need an entrepreneurial approach to consider the various opportunities and risks associated with adequately allocating their sources of advantages. The company focuses more on internal issues related to these advantages because its sustainability is still not compromised. The company should use all its resources to face the existing challenges.

IKEA—one of the leading Swedish companies headquartered in The Netherlands—is very cautious. It pays attention to a few basics when expanding its geographic scope. First, IKEA seeks to understand culture-based preferences across different geographic locations and then ensure that they meet those preferences. Second, the company is very concerned about the price factor as a strategy to compete so that the various products it offers are affordable in each local market. Third, IKEA always endeavors to run the company's operations as efficiently as possible and uses local resources.[41] With these, the company aligns its advantages with challenges in each geographical location. IKEA never bites off more than it can chew.

Third Condition: Challenges > Sources of Advantages

This condition occurs when advantages become limited and companies do not have sufficient time to strengthen, even though the challenges arise quickly. This third condition can threaten the sustainability of the company. That is why entrepreneurial efforts and creativity are needed to build networks with various parties—including competitors—in a business ecosystem. Within this condition, collaboration is necessary to overcome the shortage of sources of advantages and face these formidable challenges.

Contrary to the first condition, in this third condition, we need to build a network to find compatible partners to complement each other's lack of advantages. Companies must focus their attention on external aspects and explore relevant sources of advantages (see Figure 3.3).

From these three conditions, it is clear that collaboration is vital, significantly when the company's sustainability is compromised. Collaboration is in line with the shared-economy principle, which is now commonplace in the era of high connectivity with solid interdependence. Companies can collaborate by becoming part of a platform ecosystem or even becoming a platform provider, and then invite other companies to join.

---

[41]https://myassignmenthelp.com/free-samples/challenges-ikea-faced-in-the-global-market

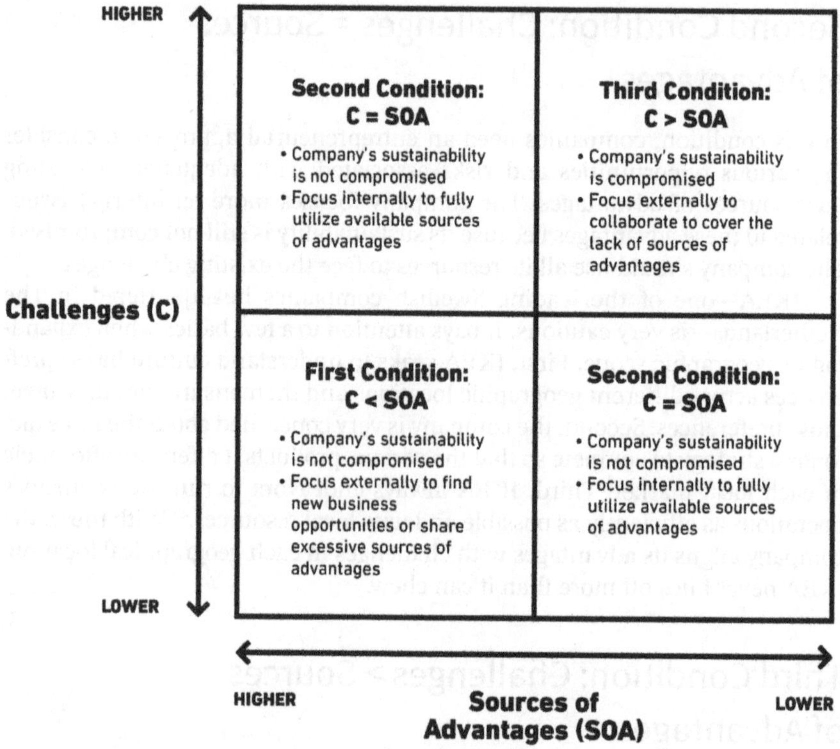

FIGURE 3.3 Challenges versus sources of advantages

A company can also collaborate with elements in a conventional value chain that is more static and linear. This might occur between a company and vendors and channels. With collaborations like this, companies can have a much better product management capability and reach their customers more massively, enabling them to implement better customer management. Companies can achieve product and market suitability more efficiently and effectively because of seamless working relationships, integrated systems, and an open flow of information to other elements in the value chain.

Key Takeaways

- To understand the balance between cooperating and staying competitive, marketers can turn to the five drivers (5Ds): technology, the political and legal environment, the economy, social and cultural factors, and market conditions.

- Organizations collaborate to face the five drivers, to pool their resources, and to strengthen their position in the market.
- When competing, companies need to build a distinctive competency, develop capabilities, invest in intangible resources, align strategies with policies, focus on productivity, and define the competition domain.
- Going forward, competing will be more digitalized, involve more unforgiving players, have a level playing field, be harder to differentiate, move at a faster pace, and have stronger interdependency.
- As they collaborate and compete, companies will look for ways to maximize their advantages and mitigate their disadvantages.

CHAPTER 4

Navigating Customers

Progressive Approach for Stronger Market Position

I n 2012, two people who were struggling to pay their rent had an "a-ha" moment. They were living in San Francisco at the time. They could put mattresses on their floor, provide breakfast services, and charge guests to stay at their place.

Fast forward to 2020. These same individuals, now with a business built on the idea of providing lodging services, underwent the largest IPO of 2020. Their company reached a valuation of over US$100 billion that year, exceeding the three publicly traded hotel chains' value, namely Marriott, Hilton, and Intercontinental.[1]

This is the story of Airbnb, which took the concept of shared lodging and short-term rentals to the next level. In addition to pioneering a new business model in the hospitality industry, in which owners can rent their dwellings to guests via a website and app, Airbnb understands how to solve customers' confusion over travel.

Guests can find what they need in a safe, user-friendly environment. It starts with an inspirational travel experience. Users get to choose their unique spaces, ranging from a simple room to the exotic. Treehouses, caves, boats, condominiums, villas, and tents—they're all available via Airbnb.[2]

It doesn't stop there; Airbnb also offers Airbnb Plus, which provides the highest quality homes managed by hosts who get great reviews and pay great attention to detail.[3] Travelers can even rent a city, village, or country.[4]

---

[1]Retrieved March 2021 from https://en.wikipedia.org/wiki/Airbnb
[2]Retrieved March 2021 from https://econsultancy.com/airbnb-how-its-customer-experience-is-revolutionising-the-travel-industry/
[3]Retrieved March 2021 from https://www.airbnb.com/luxury; https://www.airbnb.com/plus
[4]Retrieved March 2021 from https://www.wired.co.uk/article/liechtenstein-airbnb

Airbnb pushes all hosts to facilitate an experience by creating a "You belong here" initiative. It measures the extent of the hosts' feelings of belonging and rewards them if they can show it. Conversely, if they fail to provide an experience expected by the guests (based on their reviews), the Airbnb algorithm will make the host's property hard to find.[5]

To support this, the three cofounders consistently visit and live at the homes of key hosts worldwide, which significantly affects loyalty formation. Airbnb also navigates these hosts through various activities in groups. Hosts can share knowledge, integrate into a host application that embeds hospitality standards and guidelines, and participate in stand-alone meetups to exchange information.[6]

During the pandemic, Airbnb launched Flexible Search. This service enables users to choose a flexible date, making it easier to search for a weekend getaway, week-long vacation, or month-long vacation without setting specific dates. Flexible Search restores the users' traveling mindsets without worrying about future travel restrictions or cancellation fees.[7]

The Airbnb case illustrates how today's advances, coupled with consumer expectations, have enabled us to provide new navigation systems for customers. In this chapter, we'll continue discussing the "dynamics" section of the omnihouse model. We'll look at the customer element, which is positioned in the 4C diamond model (see Figure 4.1). Together with elements of change and competitors, the customer is one of the main determinants of a business landscape. Change, competitors, and customers are the sources of various business risks that the company must consider.

As we have seen, today's customers have extreme bargaining power. Thus, companies generally adopt a customer-centric approach. However, customers are also increasingly stuttering with the piles of information they can get, including false information, hoaxes, and other misleading information. There is so much available that they can get caught in confusion. Companies need to supply customers with robust navigation systems so they can find the solutions they need.

In line with the advancement of information and communication technology, which triggers digital democratization, the world is increasingly connected. On the one hand, this provides new strength for every individual. On the other hand, it floods everyone with an extreme amount of information. There is so much to digest, and it is hard to ensure accuracy.

---

[5]Retrieved March 2021 from https://www.mycustomer.com/customer-experience/loyalty/four-customer-experience-lessons-from-the-airbnb-way

[6]Retrieved March 2021 from https://hbr.org/2014/11/what-airbnb-gets-about-culture-that-uber-doesnt

[7]Retrieved March 2021 from https://techcrunch.com/2021/02/24/airbnb-plans-for-a-new-kind-of-travel-post-covid-with-flexible-search/

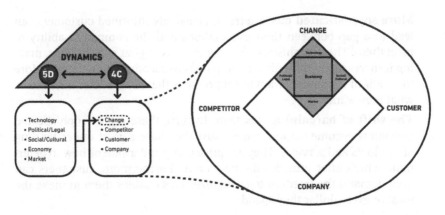

FIGURE 4.1   Customer element in the "dynamics" section and 4C diamond model

These circumstances open opportunities for companies to provide navigation that enables customers to better understand what they want. This maximizes their experience and enables them to enjoy the solutions. Clear, transparent, and honest navigation is essential in the post-truth era marked by rampant hoaxes throughout the world.

The Connected Customers

In line with today's digital world, customers—who have been and will be served by companies worldwide—are also more connected. This leads to a number of factors:

Customers are more informed. With almost unlimited access to a large amount of data and information, everyone will do their research before deciding on trivial or monumental decisions.[8] In general, more than 80% of consumers do online research before making a purchase to validate their choice, such as ensuring originality and reviewing user experiences. Consumers appreciate detailed information about the product or service.[9]

---

[8]Retrieved March 2021 from https://www.thinkwithgoogle.com/marketing-strategies/search/informeddecisionmaking/
[9]https://www.inriver.com/resources/inside-the-mind-of-an-online-shopper/#resource-gated-content; https://www.ge.com/news/press-releases/ge-capital-retail-banks-second-annual-shopper-study-outlines-digital-path-major; https://insights.sirclo.com/

More sophisticated customers. Increasingly informed customers can lead to a gap between their expectations and the company's ability to meet them. These sophisticated shoppers have higher expectations, making it increasingly difficult for companies to accommodate them.[10] More than 90% of consumers want to get products that are predetermined to be what they want.[11]

The shift of bargaining position. In turn, these highly sophisticated customers become empowered because they have a great understanding of products and services. They are price savvy and aware of how to determine which offer provides the best value. Furthermore, customers can even demand the freedom to customize. This enables them to make the most of every dollar they spend.

With the increasingly strong position of customers since the early 2010s, there have been several recent issues facing businesses. Let's look at these here.

More challenging to satisfy the customers. For some product categories, customers seek product function over brand. Other times, they choose the brand with which they feel most strongly connected. However, there is a tendency for customers to ditch the brand immediately when neglected.[12]

More challenging to have loyal customers. Consumers are dynamic, quick to understand, and at the same time change rapidly in line with their latest insights, which in turn has sparked a wave of disloyalty to brands in various parts of the world. As a result, only about 8% of consumers globally are committed to the brands they buy.[13] Marketers put a lot of effort and money into delighting customers, but sometimes they don't care because most make buying decisions automatically. Therefore companies need to develop a "cumulative advantage."[14]

More difficult to get positive advocacy. In the pre-connectivity era, we often used the level of retention and repurchase to indicate customer

----

[10]Retrieved March 2021 from https://www2.deloitte.com/content/dam/Deloitte/uk/Documents/consumer-business/consumer-review-8-the-growing-power-of-consumers.pdf

[11]https://www.inriver.com/resources/inside-the-mind-of-an-online-shopper/#resource-gated-content; https://www.ipsos.com/en-nl/exceeding-customer-expectations-around-data-privacy-will-be-key-marketers-success-new-studies-find

[12]https://www.businesswire.com/news/home/20211021005687/en/TruRating-Announce-the-Release-of-New-Report-Investigating-Consumer-Loyalty-in-2021-Following-Survey-of-180000-US-Consumers

[13]Retrieved March 2021 from https://nielseniq.com/global/en/insights/analysis/2019/battle-of-the-brands-consumer-disloyalty-is-sweeping-the-globe/

[14]Retrieved March 2021 from https://hbr.org/2017/01/customer-loyalty-is-overrated

loyalty. Now, we include the willingness to support our brand in a connected world as part of loyalty. However, advocacy often puts customers at greater risk than merely making repeat purchases of a product or service, because customers who recommend a brand to others face "social risks." For example, if others follow someone else's recommendation but the results are disappointing, the recommendation provider may receive social punishment. This risk causes customers to be cautious in expressing their advocacy.[15]

Customer Management Toward 2030

Facing this new breed of customers requires a serious overhaul of a company's customer management to survive and remain competitive. To do so, in the future, many more businesses will become internet businesses and work across all types of channels and devices. They will use a large number of tools in their tech stack and must have the ability to see their customers up-to-date and in real time. Customer data will be a valuable asset, and companies have no choice but to make digital transformation efforts, which will lead to the adoption of the customer data platform (CDP). In the next stage, CDP will determine a company's ability to provide the best customer experience.[16] Let's look at what this means for digitalized marketing and the future business model.

The Need for Digitalized Marketing Capabilities

Digital marketing can bring many benefits, including more substantial brand equity, increased sales, improved customer service quality, efficiency in spending on media, and significant savings in research spending.[17] These capabilities to support marketing are fundamental, but to ensure a company's flexibility in facing a very dynamic market, a company must implant updated and real-time data in their DNA. Leveraging big data means that we will encounter volumes of data from multiple sources at an incredible speed.

Digital technology will also support various automation processes. Jobs that will be automated in the near future include customer service,

---

[15]Philip Kotler, Hermawan Kartajaya, and Den Huan Hooi, *Marketing for Competitiveness: Asia to the World; In the Age of Digital Consumers* (Singapore: World Scientific, 2017).
[16]https://segment.com/2030-today/
[17]Retrieved March 2021 from https://jcirera.files.wordpress.com/2012/02/bcg.pdf

data entry, proofreading, courier services, market research analytics, and manufacturing.[18] The human talent needed by 2030 will include problem sensitivity, deductive reasoning, information ordering, fluency of ideas, oral comprehension, written expression, and speech clarity.[19]

Companies need individuals who can communicate with customers through various digital platforms, understand digital technology, and use it. Employees must move fast and flexibly, have an entrepreneurial mindset, and make decisions based on facts that refer to the data.[20]

Data-driven marketing works for businesses on any scale. For example, small health care services using digital marketing have shown a faster growth rate in recent years. Paid media advertising used to target the locals accurately is one of the driving factors for this growth.[21]

Toward 2030, the marketing culture will be increasingly rooted in creativity and technology. Almost everything will take place in the form of a frictionless experience to help people in their lives.[22] One-to-one segmentation will be even more mainstream because of the support of big data, AI, and analytics that enable full customization and personalization. Brands will have to be highly adaptive, and companies will have to reposition themselves in response to a very dynamic market.[23] The role of AI in brand strategy is vital, and marketers who cannot apply AI to form customer engagement at various customer journey stages will be out of the competition.[24]

The Need to Review the Business Model

Only focusing on the digitalizing aspect of marketing will not guarantee survival. Companies need to revisit their business models and create a digital business model. The book *What's Your Digital Business Model?* discusses that there are two poles in one continuum from the business design aspect.

---

[18]https://firsthand.co/blogs/career-readiness/jobs-that-will-likely-be-automated-in-the-near-future
[19]Retrieved March 2021 from https://www2.deloitte.com/content/dam/Deloitte/ch/Documents/innovation/ch-en-innovation-automation-competencies.pdf
[20]Adapted from https://www.fintalent.com/future-enabled-digital-banking-skill-sets/
[21]Retrieved March 2021 from https://www.mckinsey.com/business-functions/marketing-and-sales/our-insights/the-big-reset-data-driven-marketing-in-the-next-normal
[22]Retrieved March 2021 from https://www.thinkwithgoogle.com/future-of-marketing/creativity/marketing-in-2030/
[23]Retrieved March 2021 from https://www.ignytebrands.com/adaptive-brand-positioning/
[24]Xóchitl Austria, "13 Marketing Trends for 2030." Retrieved November 2022 from https://www.studocu.com/es-ar/document/instituto-educativo-siglo-xxi/comercializacion-en-marketing/13-tendencias-de-marketing-para-2030/19069461

These are the value chain and the ecosystem. We can divide the knowledge of end customers into two, namely, partial or complete.[25]

In general, the more a company's business design leads to the ecosystem—both as a modular producer and as an ecosystem driver—the more likely it is for the company to obtain higher revenue growth and net profit margins. Furthermore, if a company's understanding of customers is complete and broad, it will be better equipped to achieve higher performance. The ecosystem enables a company to expand its business network and portfolio and sell more new products and services. An ecosystem could increase total revenue by approximately 30% by 2025.[26]

We see that big is no longer enough in this even more social era. The key to winning the competition is to be faster, more fluid, and more flexible. Constantly fiddling with the value chain is no longer suitable for establishing high competitiveness.[27]

The *New York Times*, a global media company that focuses on creating, collecting, and distributing high-quality news and information, was the fastest to enter the online subscription business model in 2011. It applied a freemium business model to attract subscribers to the news product and delivered many advertising opportunities. In recent years, when freemium became universal, the *New York Times* acquired the gaming company, Wordle, to expand their game business. The newspaper giant is ready to engage younger, more digitally in-touch customers to expand the company's reach. Besides gaming, the *New York Times* also has a podcast, along with its long-standing international journalism. As of February 2022, the *New York Times* had successfully collected 10 million paid subscriptions.[28]

In a dynamic ecosystem, we can see that the boundaries of value-creation activities are expanding, becoming more integrated and strengthening business partners' interdependence. The various elements in a digital platform or ecosystem will have an interdependence that is not linear like the classical value chain approach.[29] Therefore, we must expand value chain analysis to cover various trends and factors that influence them.[30]

[25]Peter Weill and Stephanie Woerner, *What's Your Digital Business Model? Six Questions to Help You Build the Next-Generation Enterprise* (Cambridge, MA: Harvard Business Review Press, 2018).

[26]https://www.mckinsey.com/~/media/McKinsey/Business %20Functions/McKinsey %20Digital/Our %20Insights/How %20do %20companies %20create %20value %20from %20digital %20ecosystems/How-do-companies-create-value-from-digital-ecosystems-vF.pdf

[27]https://hbr.org/2012/02/why-porters-model-no-longer-wo

[28]https://theconversation.com/wordle-how-a-simple-game-of-letters-became-part-of-the-new-york-times-business-plan-176299; https://www.forbes.com/sites/mikevorhaus/2020/11/05/digital-subscriptions-boost-new-york-times-revenue-and-profits/?sh=1c459ea96adc

[29]https://cissokomamady.com/2019/04/02/debunking-the-myth-of-competitive-strategy-forces-disrupting-porter-five-forces/

[30]Retrieved March 2021 from https://www.cgma.org/Resources/Reports/DownloadableDocuments/The-extended-value-chain.pdf

Navigating Customers

Customers are overwhelmed by product information available in the market, making their decisions less accurate. A company must proactively act as a trusted navigator for these customers by following these processes:

Provide a platform. Companies can provide a physical and digital platform for customers to use as a tool to identify their problems, find solutions, and learn how to get them. It's important to make sure customers can immediately understand the benefits of the platform. Ensure all the platform features are complete, relevant, and user-friendly, especially for Generations Y and Z.

For example, mobile apps for banking services are beneficial and remove all customer pain points. One famous quote says, "people do not need banks, but they need banking." For example, a mobile app review on the *Forbes* page states that the complete banking services in a mobile interface are sufficient to address customers' needs, such as account statements, expense tracking, and debit card lock security, without face-to-face, on-the-spot verification.[31]

Engage partners. Companies must involve relevant partners on the platform to support the resources, activities, capabilities, and even competencies needed to serve customers' multiple needs. These partners' involvement must be seamless and provide a hassle-free experience for customers. They must ensure that the architecture platform is flexible and compatible with partners but has strict governance control.

Focus on the solution. Through this platform, the company must provide complete solutions to customers that free them from pain at each point of the customer journey. The company must provide an understanding of how to use the platform and produce solutions that can solve the core problems of customers through customization and personalization. It should also offer opportunities for co-creation and collaboration with customers.

Provide supporting services. This support service aims to provide assurance to customers and must be accessible anytime and anywhere. Companies need to be ready to receive calls from customers at any time. They must make sure all support services can strengthen engagement with customers.

Communicate value and values. Check that the company's value proposition focuses on experience and even transformation. Ensure that the

[31]https://www.forbes.com/advisor/banking/capital-one-360-bank-review/

company's values, especially those related to the broader community's interests, are embedded in the business model and communicated clearly to customers to understand and appreciate them. Engage customers in a community to interact with each other, help one another, share ideas, provide input, network, and even have fun.

The Choice: Conservative or Progressive

The terms *market-driven* and *market-driving* have been around for some time. Referring to the explanation by Bernard Jaworski, Ajay Kohli, and Arvind Sahay, market-driven is a business orientation that seeks to understand the behavior of players in a particular market structure and then react to it. Meanwhile, market-driving implies influencing the structure of the market and/or the behavior(s) of market players in a direction that enhances the business's competitive position.[32]

Both business orientations are optional and highly dependent on various factors in a company, including those related to resources (tangible and intangible), capabilities, and core competencies. A more robust market orientation will give a company the potential to achieve better performance. We also know that business challenges are too massive for one company to face alone, so a company's involvement in a digital business ecosystem will provide a better chance for the company to survive in the long term (see Figure 4.2).

By combining the market orientation with the company's model, we can describe and predict that the more it goes to the lower left (in Figure 4.2), the more the company will be market-driven. However, the more it goes toward the top right, the more it will have the market-driving capability. This market-driving capability will be even more powerful, especially if a company can drive the ecosystem, not only participate in it.[33]

On the lower-left section are conservative companies, and companies on the upper-right section are progressive. We name the continuum between these two company characteristics the conservative–progressive firmographic continuum. Most companies will be somewhere in the continuum (or perhaps even outside of it), regardless of whether the company deliberately chooses its position or merely ends up with it by chance.

---

[32]Bernard Jaworski, Ajay K. Kohli, and Arvind Sahay, "Market-Driven Versus Driving Markets," *Journal of the Academy of Marketing Science* no. 28 (2000): 45–54.
[33]Companies like this are called *ecosystem drivers*. Please refer again to Weill and Woerner (2018).

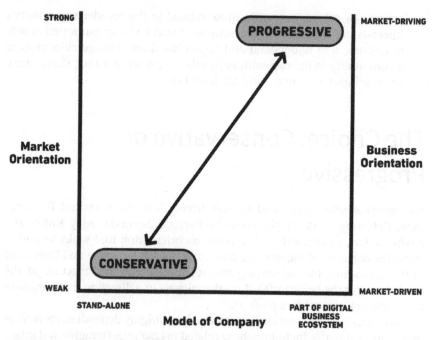

FIGURE 4.2 Conservative–progressive firmographic continuum

Progressive companies have a strong market orientation, are part of a digital business ecosystem (and may have the power to control this ecosystem), and have a market-driving business orientation. For example, TikTok is available in every ecosystem. It drove short video content to such popularity that it has pushed other platforms to follow suit. Three billion users downloaded TikTok in under four years.[34] TikTok video is now available in a three-minute duration to support some video categories, such as cooking videos.[35]

By contrast, conservative companies have weak market orientation. They are stand-alone or are not part of a digital business ecosystem. They are market-driven in terms of their business orientation.

Companies with both conservative and progressive characteristics can exist, but progressive companies will have a better chance of building strong competitiveness in the long run. A conservative company is suitable for a static business landscape. By contrast, a progressive company is ideal for a very dynamic business environment, as we are now witnessing—and will continue to toward the year 2030. Progressive companies rely on their dynamic capability, enabling them to become market-driving companies.

[34]https://backlinko.com/tiktok-users
[35]https://www.theverge.com/2021/7/1/22558856/tiktok-videos-three-minutes-length

Conservative companies can survive in a business environment that tends to be static. To a certain extent, they are able to continue in a dynamic business environment but find it difficult to form a strong market position. Meanwhile, progressive companies can always follow—and can even help shape—this very dynamic business environment.

Conservative companies have a stand-alone model that relies on conventional value chains. Progressive companies rely on networks with highly coordinated and interdependent partners within the digital business ecosystem, enabling them to strengthen their bargaining position relative to their customers. For instance, the cloud kitchen business model, adopted by ride-hailing company Grab, enables many brands to cook in one central kitchen. These arrangements are often designed for online food orders. This concept allows Grab riders to pick up food faster than picking up orders in a restaurant. Started in 2018, this business model enabled the brand to stay operating during the pandemic.[36]

Conservative companies still tend to apply conventional marketing approaches in contrast to progressive companies who commonly use a digital marketing approach to navigate their customers fundamentally, holistically, and proactively. For example, the DBS Digibank app launched LiveBetter to be a one-stop digital platform that aims to help transition to a greener life simply by adopting green retail financial solutions across home renovation, car loans, and investment. This initiative enabled DBS to be one of the most profitable banks in the world. In 2021, DBS reported higher-than-expected profit, marking ten consecutive years of this achievement. DBS's transformation to adopt a digital banking system to serve their customers has made them one of the best Singaporean digital banks.[37]

Both types of companies can navigate their customers. Still, conservative companies can guide their customers only in a limited way to things that are not fundamental, which tend to be technical, through various platforms, such as how to get information, how to purchase, the payment methods, how to use products, and so on. Meanwhile, progressive companies navigate customers more fundamentally, for example, by setting new game rules, making many incumbent players irrelevant in a competition, and changing the mindset and behavior of customers and competitors.

Progressive companies can present disruptive shock waves. Progressive companies are also able to significantly affect the macro environment. For example, they may force the authorities to revise regulations, create social/cultural changes, or even affect the market structures.

---

[36]https://www.kompas.com/properti/read/2021/04/10/135228821/membaca-peta-persaingan-cloud-kitchen-di-jakarta-ini-7-pemainnya?page=all

[37]https://knowledge.insead.edu/blog/insead-blog/how-dbs-became-the-worlds-best-bank-17671; https://www.reuters.com/world/asia-pacific/singapore-lender-dbs-q2-profit-jumps-37-beats-market-estimates-2021-08-04/

Based on these explanations, we can start to understand why conservative companies tend to have a temporary competitive advantage. By contrast, progressive companies can establish a sustainable competitive advantage. Those reasons also show that the more progressive a company is, the higher the competitiveness that company can achieve (see Table 4.1).

TABLE 4.1 Summary of Conservative and Progressive Company Characteristics

	Firmographic	
	Conservative	**Progressive**
Business landscape	Suitable for the static business landscape	Ideal for the dynamic business landscape
Strategic capability	Market-driven	Market-driving, dynamic capability
Company model/ platform	Stand-alone with conventional sequential value chain	A network of highly coordinated and interdependent partners within the digital business ecosystem
Bargaining power	Customers have a stronger bargaining position	The company has a stronger bargaining position
Organization	Rigid, strong inertia	Adaptive and flexible
Marketing approach	Conventional marketing	Digital marketing
Level of navigation	Basic, narrow scope, and reactive	Fundamental, holistic, and proactive
Center of gravity	Customer-centric	Solution-centric
Market	Niche, segmented, specific target market, focus on economies of scale	Broad, transcendent, one-to-one, concentrate on both economies of scale and scope
Tech and touch	Low-tech, low-touch	High-tech, high-touch
Brand and positioning	Only name with no precise positioning	Living brand: ubiquitous, relevant, and seamless
Differentiation	Based on functional and emotional benefits through the use of products and services	Based on customer experience or transformation through strong engagement

TABLE 4.1 *(Continued)*

	Firmographic	
	Conservative	**Progressive**
Selling point	Just product features and benefits	Customized or personalized customer experience/ transformation in each touchpoint
Product and services	Standard product with a ray of variants	Allow comprehensive options of customization, co-creation, and collaboration
Price	Fixed price	Dynamic pricing
Loyalty	By design, based on a lock-in mechanism through high-cost loyalty programs because customers are liable to switch	By default, based on a "natural" lock-in mechanism because the company is essential in the customer's life, so customers are reluctant to switch
Key performance indicators	Financial and nonfinancial, subjective and objective	Comprehensive financial and nonfinancial (subjective and objective) and digital traction
Competitive advantage	Temporary competitive advantage	Sustainable competitive advantage

Several points need attention. First, a progressive company does not merely refer to its customers' perspective, as conservative companies do. It also comprehensively looks at various aspects of the 4C diamond model where the customer is only one of the elements. Companies cannot just focus on making products and services that are attractive only in their customers' eyes to guarantee business continuity. However, they must also comprehensively pay attention to the business environment dynamics, including what happens in the macro environment and the competitors.

Second, the new progressive approach, particularly how companies deal with their customers (and their communities), requires inspiring educational efforts to be immediately accepted and adopted as part of people's daily lives. Educating the market to achieve critical mass is a crucial matter that progressive companies must carefully consider.

Third, a progressive company's business model will differ from a conservative company's that relies heavily on forming competence based on its capabilities in using various tangible assets. By contrast, progressive companies build their competitiveness by leveraging intangible assets of companies that are very difficult to imitate, not available for sale in the market or rare, and have high value. Meanwhile, a company can obtain other assets that it does not own from multiple partners who are members of the business ecosystem, eventually forming an ecosystem advantage.

Fourth, 2030 is a strategic point in time and is a stepping stone toward 2045. According to Ray Kurzweil's predictions, there will be exponential increases in technologies such as computers, genetics, nanotechnology, robotics, and artificial intelligence, referring to the law of accelerating returns. Singularity is the point where human and machine intelligence will eventually merge.[38]

Thus, every company must determine its future from now on. A firm cannot miss the momentum toward 2030 if they want to survive in the era after that. For this reason, companies must plan where their foothold will be in the conservative–progressive firmographic continuum.

Key Takeaways

- The customer, which is part of the 4C (customer, change, company, competitor) diamond model, takes center stage in the business landscape of today and tomorrow.

- Customers are more connected, which makes them more informed and sophisticated, and they have greater bargaining power. It's challenging to satisfy them, keep them, and have them advocate positively for a company.

- Going forward, companies will need to adapt digital marketing capabilities and review their business models.

- To navigate customers, firms can provide a platform, engage partners, focus on the solution, provide supporting services, and communicate value and values.

- Companies need to evaluate their conservative and progressive status and consider how they want to operate to prepare for the future.

---

[38]Ray Kurzweil, *Singularity Is Near* (New York: Penguin, 2005).

CHAPTER 5

Unifying Capabilities

Converging Mindsets Within an Organization

D o you want to listen to music or a podcast on your phone? What about your laptop, or tablet, or other devices?

For an all-in-one solution, turn to Spotify. Founded by Daniel Ek and Martin Lorentzon in 2006, this Sweden-based company has made audio accessible from anywhere. Consumers can opt for a free or paid subscription.[1] Currently, Spotify has nearly 350 million users; of those, about 155 million are premium users.[2]

How did this company take music, considered by many to be a basic necessity for thousands of years, and meet today's standards of connectivity? Certainly, the industry has come a long way, shifting from live music to record, from phonographs to tape cassettes and then compact discs, followed by iPods. All these innovations served a purpose. Yet Spotify leveraged technology to make it possible for anyone to access any song from anywhere.

Let's go behind the scenes of this aggressive, globally expanding firm. Clearly it fulfilled a desire among music enthusiasts, as shown how it has grown significantly during the last few years. From 2018 to 2021, the company increased in size from about 3,600 employees to more than 6,500.[3]

To keep up with this pace, it has recruited employees from various geographic areas with different cultural backgrounds.[4] This is no small task. Its biggest challenge is to keep attracting the right people (occasionally bringing

---

[1] Retrieved March 2021 from https://www.spotify.com/id/about-us/contact/
[2] Retrieved March 2021 from https://en.wikipedia.org/wiki/Spotify
[3] https://www.macrotrends.net/stocks/charts/SPOT/spotify-technology/number-of-employees#:~:text=Interactive%20chart%20of%20Spotify%20Technology,a%2017.12%25%20decline%20from%202019
[4] Retrieved March 2021 from https://corporate-rebels.com/spotify-2

on hundreds of workers) while maintaining innovation, agility, and its unique culture, according to Katrina Berg, chief human resources officer at Spotify.[5]

To overcome this obstacle, and remain a leader, the company formed cross-functional teams called squads, autonomous groups of between 6 and 12 people. They remain accountable to the firm and strive to keep the workforce both innovative and agile while staying committed to the company's core purpose.[6]

Squads are responsible for new products, including what will be built and who will make it happen.[7] Collectively, several squads form one tribe, and each tribe is also autonomous.[8] One of the duties of the tribe leader is to provide a suitable work environment for all squads.[9] Simultaneously, tribe members with the same skills are grouped into a chapter. Anyone in a chapter can also join a guild, which is formed of individuals with a common interest.

To harmonize such a unique form within the organization, Spotify relies on technology to conduct virtual town hall meetings. Any team member of Spotify worldwide can get involved in these meetings.[10] Technology also allows Spotify employees to work remotely from anywhere.[11] Clear guidelines support how Spotify tracks employee development to maintain a strong growth mindset.[12]

This organizational arrangement intends to avoid the silo phenomenon.[13] It enables Spotify to strike that delicate balance between implementing structure and promoting creativity. It also aims to keep employees engaged, satisfied, well managed, and actively involved in innovation and growth.

Companies that want to follow suit will do well to harmonize mindsets, functions, and resources. In this chapter, we'll discuss strategies to carry out these objectives. We'll look to the omnihouse model to guide our discussion (see Figure 5.1).

We'll start by exploring how to converge different elements in the "entrepreneurship" cluster, followed by connecting those in the "professionalism"

[5]Retrieved March 2021 from https://corporate-rebels.com/spotify-1/
[6]Retrieved March 2021 from https://hbr.org/2017/02/how-spotify-balances-employee-autonomy-and-accountability
[7]Ibid.
[8]Retrieved March 2021 from https://divante.com/blog/tribes-model-helps-build-agile-organization-divante/
[9]Retrieved March 2021 from https://achardypm.medium.com/agile-team-organisation-squads-chapters-tribes-and-guilds-80932ace0fdc
[10]Retrieved March 2021 from https://corporate-rebels.com/spotify-1/
[11]Retrieved March 2021 from https://www.reuters.com/article/us-spotify-employees-idUSKBN2AC1O7
[12]Retrieved March 2021 from https://corporate-rebels.com/spotify-1/
[13]Retrieved March 2021 from https://www.linkedin.com/pulse/thinking-using-spotifys-agile-tribe-model-your-company-schiffer/

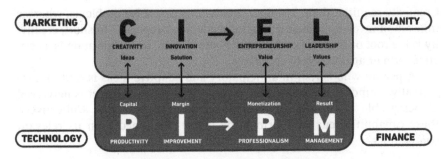

FIGURE 5.1 Dichotomous elements in the omnihouse model

cluster. We'll study the relationship between creativity and innovation, and entrepreneurship and leadership (CI-EL). We'll also look at the connections between productivity and improvement, and professionalism and management (PI-PM). In Chapter 6, we'll delve into the integrations between marketing and finance, and technology and humanity.

Creativity and Innovation Mindset

Innovation and creativity are fundamental to all disciplines and educational activities, not just art. Innovation is related to novelties (ideas, methods, or products) that have value. It is the fruit of ideas, of producing, making something happen, or implementing something new. Innovation involves working hard to ensure that we can eventually realize good ideas. Creativity is an active process that needs to be involved in innovation. The creative process is at the heart of innovation.[14]

Creativity and innovation are two independent constructs that complement each other.[15] Creativity alone does not always lead to innovation.[16]

----

[14]From Cambridge Assessment International Education, "Developing the Cambridge Learner Attributes," which is used in more than 160 countries. https://www.cambridgeinternational .org/support-and-training-for-schools/teaching-cambridge-at-your-school/cambridge-learner-attributes/

[15]Tatiana de Cassia Nakano and Solange Muglia Wechsler, "Creativity and Innovation: Skills for the 21st Century," *Estudos de Psicologia* 35, no. 3 (2018): 237–246. https://doi.org/10.1590/1982–02752018000300002

[16]O. C. Ribeiro and M. C. Moraes, *Criatividade em uma perspectiva transdisciplinar: Tompendo crenças, mitos e concepçõe* (Líber Livro, 2014) as quoted in Tatiana de Cassia Nakano and Solange Muglia Wechsler, "Creativity and Innovation: Skills for the 21st Century," *Estudos de Psicologia* 35, no. 3 (2018). https://www.scielo.br/j/estpsi/a/vrTxJGjGnYFLqQGcTzFgfcp/?lang=en&format=html

Creativity requires ideas, insights, or solutions that solve problems, whereas innovation involves implementing these ideas to progress.[17] In short, creativity is the root or source that determines innovation, and innovation is a concrete form or application of creativity.

A person who is rich in anticipatory and adaptive ideas is said to have a creative mindset. An individual with an innovative mindset is perceived as being able to provide solutions to customers' problems. Collectively, these capabilities enable a firm to be better positioned than its relevant competitors.

Entrepreneurship and Leadership Mindset

In general, we can say that an individual with an entrepreneurial mindset identifies and understands various problems, sees opportunities for those problems, takes calculated risks, and collaborates with multiple parties to find solutions to address those problems. These steps ultimately can create value for both customers and the company. Meanwhile, leadership is demonstrated when an individual builds and exerts influence on others based on their intellectual, emotional, and spiritual abilities.

We can see a number of examples of successful entrepreneurs in the world who demonstrate transformational leadership, which not only solves problems in their companies but also plays a role in solving the world's most pressing problems. Instead of looking at what other people have done in the past to solve a problem, they are more interested in the universal truth behind it. Based on this, they come up with creative solutions.

From the older generation of entrepreneurs like Bill Gates or Ted Turner to the younger generation of entrepreneurs like Larry Page, Sergey Brin, or Adam D'Angelo, they all challenge what humans can think and do. Their entrepreneurial and leadership skills have great potential to impact their organization and the world.

---

[17]L. Zeng, P.R.W. Proctor, and G. Salvendy, "Can Traditional Divergent Thinking Tests Be Trusted in Measuring and Predicting Real-World Creativity?" *Creativity Research Journal* 23, no. 1 (2011): 24–37 as quoted in "Creativity and Innovation: Skills for the 21st Century," *Estudos de Psicologia* 35, no. 3 (2018). https://www.scielo.br/j/estpsi/a/vrTxJGjGnYFLqQGcTzFgfcp/?lang=en&format=html

Productivity and Improvement Mindset

Productivity, in simple terms, is often associated with the comparison of input and output. We can achieve a higher productivity level using less input with greater output. This approach is especially evident in the manufacturing process, where we measure how many output units are produced from a specific input unit.

Although more complex, we can also use it in other management domains. We might measure how many sales are achieved (the output) compared to the headcount or entire company's employees (input). The greater the level of sales achieved with a smaller headcount, in general, the more productive a company is. Oftentimes productivity is directly proportional to a business's profitability.

We also frequently use the combination of efficiency and effectiveness to measure productivity. If the level of efficiency or effectiveness (or even both) decreases, the level of productivity will also decrease. Simply put, effectiveness is about doing the right things, and efficiency is doing things right. Thus, if we do something right in the right way, we start from the right point in achieving optimal productivity. Therefore, effectiveness and efficiency are two different things, but we cannot separate them if we discuss productivity.

Thus, to increase efficiency, we strive to produce more output with the same input. To be more effective, we focus on resources. We prioritize those that will provide the best results in line with the company's goals.

To achieve optimal productivity, the company must be both effective and efficient. A person with a productivity mindset can do various effective tasks, including using company resources and carrying out different value-creation processes efficiently. Meanwhile, someone is said to have an improvement mindset if they focus on better results today over yesterday. They look to continue with even more optimal performance tomorrow.

Professionalism and Management Mindset

Professionalism is often associated with a certain standard (both written and unwritten).[18] It can refer to attributes related to knowledge and competencies, along with characteristics such as integrity, honesty, and mutual respect. Professionalism frequently results from a lengthy formation process.[19]

----

[18]Retrieved March 2021 from https://www.mindtools.com/pages/article/professionalism.htm
[19]Retrieved March 2021 from http://graduate.auburn.edu/wp-content/uploads/2016/08/What-is-PROFESSIONALISM.pdf

Accountability—as part of professionalism—is demonstrated by following through on promises. It encompasses structure, well-laid plans, and an avoidance of procrastination. When commitments are not kept, employee performance can dwindle. According to a study conducted by the LSE Department of Management, a world-class center for research and education in business and management based in London, broken promises deplete employees' mental energy, resulting in unintentional harm to others.[20]

Professionalism is vital for one's career in a company. Still, more than that, it will collectively form a strong reputation and trust from various parties in a business ecosystem. Professionalism will also have an impact on better overall company performance. Therefore, commitment to professionalism is a must, and professionalism must also refer to the values or corporate culture.[21]

A study conducted in Australia underscores the importance of this professionalism to organizations. The paper emphasizes the impact of an individual's pursuit of professionalism on an organization's reputation. Not only that, but professionalism also affects the organization's strategic advantage.[22]

Professionalism is a critical element in an organization because it clarifies what is generally accepted (and not) in a particular community. The foundation of this professionalism mindset leads to a harmonization that transcends throughout functions as a universal protocol. This protocol helps avoid unproductive conflicts and disputes in various interactions between individuals in the same organization and between people from two or more different organizations.

It is hard to separate professionalism from management in business organizations. Management cannot function as intended if no one with professionalism is behind it. According to a survey of 2,580 people in seven Australian hospitals, unprofessional behavior had a moderate or significant negative influence on patient care, the frequency of errors, or the quality of service. Nurses, nonclinical workers, and management and administrative staff were more likely than medical staff to report this influence.[23]

In general, management covers several things that often begin with specific objectives and plans to achieve them. Therefore, planning is crucial in the management process. Strategies (and tactics) will reflect how to achieve

[20]Retrieved February 2022 from https://blogs.lse.ac.uk/management/2018/04/03/breaking-promises-is-bad-for-business/

[21]Brandman University, "Professionalism in the Workplace: A Guide for Effective Etiquette." Retrieved March 2021 from https://www.experd.com/id/whitepapers/2021/03/1583/professionalism-in-the-workplace.html

[22]Jillian de Araugoa and Richard Beal, "Professionalism as Reputation Capital: The Moral Imperative in the Global Financial Crisis," *Social and Behavioral Sciences* 99 (2013): 351–362.

[23]Johanna Westbrook et al., "The Prevalence and Impact of Unprofessional Behaviour Among Hospital Workers: A Survey in Seven Australian Hospitals," *Medical Journal of Australia* 214, no. 1 (2021): 31–37. doi: 10.5694/mja2.50849

the company's objectives. The strategy will have substantial repercussions on what resources should be available, what capabilities are needed, and what competencies the company should focus on to gain a competitive advantage.

The organization is a collection of people working together to achieve a predetermined goal. Companies realize that effective project management is critical to achieving better results. According to Bain & Company, by 2027 the majority of work will be project-based. As a result, the need for project managers is expanding faster than the demand for qualified people in other professions. This increased emphasis on project managers reflects a greater awareness of the influence of good project management on a company's bottom line.[24]

Management is also related to implementing predetermined plans or strategies to achieve the company's goals. Implementation or execution is often challenging because a dynamic environment can create unexpected new constraints that require adjustments to those well-written plans and strategies. That's why people often say it is easier said than done.

The Project Management Institute (PMI) sponsored an Economist Intelligence Unit report titled "Why Good Strategies Fail: Lessons for the C-suite," looking at how C-level executives participate in strategy execution. A survey of 587 senior executives worldwide was used to compile the study. Of the respondents, 61% admitted that their companies frequently struggle to bridge the gap between strategy formulation and day-to-day execution. Furthermore, respondents claim that just 56% of strategic initiatives at their companies have been successfully implemented in the previous three years.[25]

In this implementation process, communication of direction and coordination plays a critical role in guaranteeing the effective and efficient use of all organizational resources and capabilities. Management in a company, for example, requires good coordination between each function, such as finance, marketing, human capital, operations, IT, and others. This coordination is crucial to ensure that a company's value-creation process runs continuously without significant interruptions, even though they have to deal with the unpredictable dynamics of the business environment.

The final management element involves efforts to maintain standards. These are well understood and agreed on by all relevant people in an organization. It is impossible to carry out an objective evaluation without accurate and appropriate measurements.

Cargill Inc.—a Minneapolis-based food producer and distributor—was having trouble motivating and engaging its 155,000 employees worldwide.

---

[24]Retrieved February 2022 from https://www.teamwork.com/project-management-guide/why-is-project-management-important/

[25]https://www.pmi.org/-/media/pmi/documents/public/pdf/learning/thought-leadership/why-good-strategies-fail-report.pdf/

When it debuted its "Everyday Performance Management" method in 2012, which aimed to include daily encouragement and control into on-the-job talks, it became a trendsetter. Cargill claims to have noticed measurable improvements after management began providing constructive, forward-looking evaluation rather than retrospective.[26]

Thus, a person is said to have a professional mindset if they can always build relevant competencies, have strong discipline, and uphold applicable ethics. Someone is said to apply a good management mindset if they always act appropriately and carefully in planning, organizing, implementing, and controlling processes in the company.

As we have seen, an integration of these elements, both in the entrepreneurship cluster and the professionalism cluster, can lead to optimal performance. Establishing connections and valuing the contributions of each mindset reduces the risk of conflict. It also increases cooperation, enables innovative ideas that benefit the company to be produced, and creates a synergy that propels the company forward.

Key Takeaways

- A creative mindset is able to generate ideas; an innovative spirit turns possibilities into tangible solutions that solve problems.
- Entrepreneurship enables companies to leverage the commercial value of innovations; leadership guides and influences the strategy, direction, and morale.
- A productivity-focused individual seeks to increase effectiveness and efficiency; an improvement-minded team member looks for ways to achieve better results than before.
- Professional individuals help make sure ethics are upheld; managers oversee processes and the implementation of protocols.
- Creating harmony among the employees' mindsets can build competitive advantages for companies, including an increase in value.

[26]Retrieved February 2022 from https://www.fastcompany.com/3054547/six-companies-that-are-redefining-performance-management

CHAPTER 6

Integrating Functions

Converging Departments Within an Organization

A company is organized in a way that is conducive to carrying out its required activities. We often encounter several functions within the company, known as divisions or departments. Each can carry out its activities independently or interdependently with other divisions.

Sometimes, a division does not want to communicate openly. This can hamper information dissemination between divisions.[1] Without communication and information exchange, it will not be easy to coordinate to achieve organizational goals.[2]

Silo mentality, as described previously, is counterproductive because it may originate from unhealthy competition from people who sit at the top levels in various divisions in a company. It can also happen between people at multiple levels who essentially have a hidden agenda for their interests.[3] One of the characteristics of the silo is the unwillingness of everyone involved in an organization to share information that is very valuable or even necessary to other divisions or departments in a company.[4]

In the omnihouse model, we can observe four distinct functions: marketing, technology, humanity, and finance. (Don't worry, we will discuss about

---

[1] Retrieved March 2021 from https://www.investopedia.com/terms/s/silo-mentality
.asp#:~:text=In%20business%2C%20organizational%20silos%20refer,shared%20because%20
of%20system%20limitations
[2] Retrieved March 2021 from https://www.adb.org/sites/default/files/publication/27562/
bridging-organizational-silos.pdf
[3] Retrieved March 2021 from https://www.forbes.com/sites/brentgleeson/2013/10/02/the-silo-
mentality-how-to-break-down-the-barriers/?sh=2921022d8c7e
[4] Retrieved March 2021 from https://www.investopedia.com/terms/s/silo-mentality
.asp#:~:text=In%20business%2C%20organizational%20silos%20refer,shared%20because%20
of%20system%20limitations

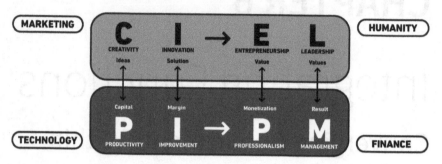

FIGURE 6.1 Dichotomous functions in the omnihouse model

operations later on.) Notice that marketing and finance are in separate corners. The same is true with technology and humanity. These are placed accordingly to stress the fact that in companies, these functions are often siloed or separate. Contradictory characters are also seen between the CI-EL and PI-PM elements. These are the various dichotomies that we can find in the omnihouse model (see Figure 6.1).

In this chapter, we'll observe ways to break down the silo challenges. We'll start by exploring ways to connect marketing and finance. We'll also consider the convergence of other resources, especially those related to technology and humans.

Connecting Marketing and Finance

As discussed in Chapter 1, one of the classic marketing blind spots is the incompatibility of finance and marketing functions—one of the most visible dichotomies (see Figure 6.2). Marketers are often only fixated on nonfinancial measurements. Financial executives usually ask what marketers want to achieve when using their budget. It could be that marketing people will give answers such as increasing brand awareness, creating certain perceptions, and communicating value propositions.

Such answers will sometimes make financial people frown because they may not understand the value of all that the marketing team wants to achieve, especially the terminology used, which is not a normative financial lingo. Finance people then sometimes jump to the further question: what will be the return from the money they would give to marketing people?

Many of the financial domain's primary measurements refer to the idea of return, for example, return on sales, return on assets, and return on investment. Meanwhile, marketing people often use metrics that are nonfinancial, such as loyalty index, satisfaction index, top of mind, and market share.

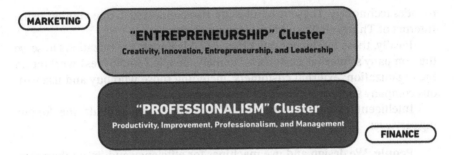

FIGURE 6.2   Marketing and finance dichotomy in the omnihouse model

Some marketing people may also not care about the company's financial statements. The only aspect that is often associated with financial measurement in marketing practice is sales, which is only the top line in the income statement. We can achieve (or even exceed) sales target by at-any-cost efforts, but this will make the bottom line negative. The bottom line is the primary concern of most shareholders because it will determine the dividends that shareholders will receive.

However, sometimes financial people place too much emphasis on cost containment alone without seeing that the money spent will accumulate non-financial results, which can be converted into financial results under certain conditions. As such, it should not only be seen as an expenditure but rather as an investment.

Finance professionals must understand how various departments work to gain a more contextual understanding, which can help other departments when making decisions about budget expenditures.[5] As previously discussed, the inter-departmental collaboration will strengthen a one-firm mentality to deliver the best products and services to customers and positively affect company revenue.[6]

Coupling Technology and Humanity

The definition of machines in this digital era is not limited to machines that work only on the mechanical aspect. Machines with technology such as AI can perform human work with much higher precision and consistency due to

---

[5]Retrieved March 2021 from http://www.managingamericans.com/Accounting/Success/Breaking-Down-Departmental-Silos-Finance-394.htm
[6]Retrieved March 2021 from https://hbr.org/2019/05/cross-silo-leadership

robotics technology. These machines are also connected to one another using Internet of Things (IoT) and blockchain technology.

Ideally, these intelligent machines should support organizations to serve the company's internal customers, namely, people (employees) working in the organization; external customers, including those who buy and use various company support services; and even society.

Intelligent machines with digital technology can provide the following services:

People. We design and use machines for efficiency and, more than that, to make employee work easier, more ergonomic, and free from possible injuries while increasing productivity. Technology will enable workers to carry out their duties more humanely. Technology enables someone to work from anywhere because they can always be connected and access various data and information remotely.

Customers. Technology enables companies to offer personalization, customization, and humane or compassionate navigation. If people in a company are humanized and assisted by technology, they can ultimately provide more humane services for customers. The era of customer exploitation has long ended, and with technology, it is time to fully humanize customers by offering solutions that can improve their quality of life.

Society at large. Even if you don't buy products marketed by a company, it doesn't mean that the company can ignore the wider community's interests. Switching to renewable electricity technology in all its factories, as Mercedes-Benz did, ensures that they are also responsible for the environment's quality. Recycling technology enables companies to reduce waste drastically. Likewise, using biodegradable materials in various products is an indicator of the company's concern for the environment.

The latest technological breakthroughs are routinely incorporated into wildlife protection projects, from monitoring endangered species to detecting poachers. Drones, data, and digital mapping can be used to track endangered wildlife. Increased poaching activity in Africa has decimated the elephant population in Garamba National Park. Garamba's herd once numbered 22,000 elephants, but by 2017 it had shrunk to only 1,200. During the following three years, Garamba cut elephant poaching by 97%. To do so, it adopted location intelligence, which enabled specialized surveillance teams to track and monitor each animal 24 hours a day using a mix of GIS and IoT.[7]

---

[7]https://www.ericsson.com/en/blog/2021/5/technology-for-good-how-tech-is-helping-us-restore-planet-earth

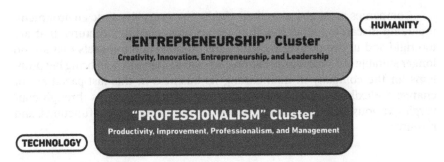

FIGURE 6.3   Technology and humanity dichotomy in the omnihouse model

We can fulfill our obligations to those stakeholders by using very sophisticated digital technology intelligent machines. Ideally, technology and humans should provide humanity for people, customers, and society at large.[8] The essence of using technology together with humans—hence, converging the dichotomy of technology and humanity—will become a growing priority among companies in the years ahead (see Figure 6.3).

The Importance of Unification

It can be tough to break down the silo status quo. Let's consider two obstacles that often need to be overcome to unify the company. Then we'll look at why integrating is key and how to measure your success along the way.

Obstacle 1: Organizational Rigidity

Rigidity is the opposite of the flexibility required to adapt to various internal and external pressures the company faces. This flexibility enables the company to allocate its multiple resources from one division to another, including moving its employees to other assignments in different divisions. Employees will find it challenging to become adaptive and productive people in the future if they are unwilling or unable to converge the various mindsets of CI-EL and PI-PM.[9]

---

[8]Retrieved March 2021 from https://www.businessmodelsinc.com/machines/
[9]Retrieved March 2021 from https://smallbusiness.chron.com/strategic-flexibility-rigidity-barriers-development-management-65298.html

Companies must abandon their rigidity in a very dynamic environment, including discarding strategies that are no longer valid, structures that are too rigid and unresponsive, and company cultures and mindsets that are no longer suitable with current situations. In essence, rigidity will bring big problems for the company in maintaining its business in this fast-paced era of change.[10] Flexibility is the answer; one way to achieve this is through converging various dichotomies of mindsets, various management functions, and resources.

Obstacle 2: Organizational Inertia

Usually an organization that has reached the maturity stage will continue its journey into the future by simply continuing its trajectory for a long time. The organization cannot instantly change its trajectory due to strong inertia. It is not surprising that a long-existing company using various conventional value-creation processes will face difficulties if it suddenly has to change by adopting a more progressive approach.

Consider the Deepwater Horizon explosion, which claimed the lives of 11 people, injured 126 others, and resulted in a three-month-long oil leak. According to a federal study, the disaster was caused by "poor risk management, last-minute plan changes, inability to notice and respond to vital signs, inadequate good control response, and insufficient emergency bridge response training."[11] In a nutshell, the inability to adapt to external challenges and diverse situations can lead an organization into disaster.

Start-ups and the many leading tech companies have a different story. Since inception, they have adopted a progressive approach that suits the highly dynamic business environment. Of course, for the time being they don't need to recalibrate their trajectory. However, if there is another significant wave of disruption, then these companies will have to revisit and adapt their approaches. Sometimes there are some start-ups that have had problems from the beginning so they can't grow, let alone develop (see Figure 6.4).

Large, long-standing companies can indeed avoid inertia. You probably think of a forward-thinking corporation when you hear the name DuPont. However, not many know that E. I. du Pont, a Frenchman with experience creating gunpowder, founded DuPont in Delaware in 1802. Du Pont established his first powder mill on Brandywine Creek in 1804, using willow tree bark for charcoal to generate black powder. Since then, the company has produced dyes, sweater fibers, and film for Hollywood movies, among other things.

[10]Retrieved March 2021 from https://www.linkedin.com/pulse/process-rigidity-leads-organizational-entropy-milton-mattox
[11]Retrieved February 2022 from https://blog.lowersrisk.com/culprits-complacency/

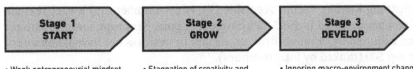

FIGURE 6.4   Summary of start-up stages and its potential problems

DuPont and Dow merged in 2015. It relaunched its brand in 2018, with a new logo, an emphasis on innovation, and a wide range of solutions.[12] In 2018, DuPont spent about US$900 million on research and development. It claims that items introduced in the previous five years boosted new sales growth by more than 5% in 2018.[13]

Reasons to Unify

Although there are many benefits to integrating, three main advantages stand out. Let's consider relevancy, survivability, and sustainability. Each of these underscores the importance of getting together.

Relevancy

Unifying the company by converging the dichotomies will ensure relevance in a specific competition setting. This means that a company seems to have an entrance ticket to participate in the competition but no guarantee that it can win. We call this a necessary condition (to participate in a specific contest) but not sufficient (to win the competition). To be relevant, a company needs relevant people. For this reason, companies must ensure that the people involved have a high level of fitness with the company, at least in terms of values, culture, and competency qualifications.

If we compare the list of Fortune 500 companies in 1955 and 2017, it appears that only 60 companies still exist, only about 12%. Many of the companies on the 1955 list are now unrecognizable and forgotten (e.g., Cone Mills,

---

[12]https://www.businessnewsdaily.com/8122-oldest-companies-in-america.html
[13]https://delawarebusinesstimes.com/news/features/dupont-creates-new-digital-center/

Armstrong Rubber, Pacific Vegetable Oil, Hines Lumber, and Riegel Textile). Of companies listed in 1955 88% have either gone bankrupt, merged with (or been acquired by) another firm, or are still in business but have fallen out of the top 500 (ranked by total revenues).[14]

Survivability

Maintaining cohesiveness consistently at a higher level than competitors will put the company in a stronger market position. The company's organizational ecosystem must be compatible with the business ecosystem in which the organization participates to ensure the company's survivability. Organizations must have dynamic capabilities, which are the basis for the formation of agility, which is very important when adapting to a business ecosystem that is constantly changing rapidly.

Many new small companies enter the competition every month, but the failure rate is quite large. As of 2019, the failure rate for start-ups was over 90%. Of start-ups 21.5% fail in the first year, about 30% in the second year, and that number gets even higher in the third year, with 50% failure, ultimately reaching 70% in the tenth year.[15]

Sustainability

By continuing to ensure that various dichotomous elements remain converged, at the same time, the company must carry out a transformation with all parties in a business ecosystem in line with changes in the business landscape due to the volatility of primary drivers in the macro environment. The conversion can require just a slight shaking if all the elements are entirely converged, allowing for speedy communication and coordination. This perpetual transformation capability can ensure a company remains sustainable in the face of various volatility drivers in the macro environment and micro environment. According to Deloitte, implementing digital transformation can help companies achieve 22% faster progress toward financial returns, workforce diversity, and environmental goals.[16]

---

[14]https://www.aei.org/carpe-diem/fortune-500-firms-1955-v-2017-only-12-remain-thanks-to-the-creative-destruction-that-fuels-economic-prosperity/
[15]https://www.nationalbusinesscapital.com/blog/2019-small-business-failure-rate-startup-statistics-industry/
[16]https://www2.deloitte.com/us/en/insights/topics/digital-transformation/digital-transformation-survey.html

Phases Toward Sustainability

After understanding the various dichotomies in a company—and the converging—we can simplify it into a model (see Figure 6.5).

Here is the explanation of this model.

Phase 0: Potential/Loser Company

Every company, newly founded or established, has various potentials. If it faces an obstacle it cannot overcome, such as being too rigid or having too much inertia, it will lose out among other players.

Phase 1: Relevant Company

If the potential company's rigidity and inertia are not too strong, the company can have a better possibility to converge various dichotomies within the company.

Management also has a broader perspective by referring to a competition setting consisting of relevant competitors and customers. Thus, the company can move up the ranks to become the relevant company in a competition, although it may not survive. However, if the company becomes inconsistent in carrying out the convergence process, it may move down again to become only a potential company or even immediately become a loser.

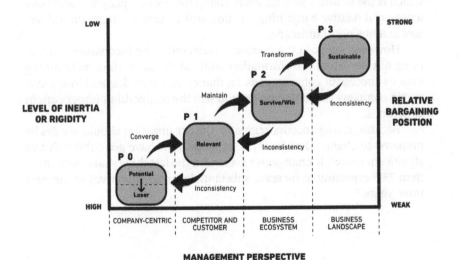

FIGURE 6.5   Company phases toward sustainability

Phase 2: Surviving/Winning Company

If the potential company has an even smaller level of rigidity and inertia, it is more likely to maintain the convergence of the various dichotomies it has carried out.

Management also has an even broader perspective by referring to the business ecosystem, which consists of various partners connected conventionally or digitally while also paying attention to relevant competitors and customers.

In this way, the company can move up to a higher level to become a surviving company. In certain conditions, if its performance is much better than its competitors, it can become a winning company. Simultaneously, the company also has a relatively stronger bargaining position with many elements in the business ecosystem.

However, if the company becomes inconsistent in maintaining the various convergences of dichotomies, it may cause it to drop back into a merely relevant company again.

Phase 3: Sustainable Company

If the surviving/winning company has little or no rigidity and inertia, it will likely carry out a sustainable transformation while maintaining the various convergences they have successfully carried out previously.

Management also has a whole perspective by referring to the overall business landscape, including the main drivers in the macro environment, business ecosystem, relevant competitors, and customers. Thus, the company can reach the highest level to become a sustainable company, which is the ultimate goal for every company. The company will also have a powerful relative bargaining position against various elements and factors in a business landscape.

However, suppose the company turns out to be inconsistent in carrying out perpetual transformation while at the same time maintaining various successful convergences. In that case, it may descend into a surviving company that still enables it to win the competition under certain conditions.

Because change occurs regularly, the organization should always be prepared to change. For example, organizations have gone through five significant firmwide changes on average in the last three years, with more than 75% expecting to increase substantial change initiatives in the next three years.[17]

---

[17]https://www.gartner.com/en/human-resources/insights/organizational-change-management

Every company must understand its current standing in these phases. The organization can study the dynamic elements that exist internally, especially those related to organizational rigidity and inertia. It can also look at external factors, especially including the main drivers in the macro environment. Then the company will be able to determine ways to survive and become sustainable.

Key Takeaways

- Creating strong relationships between the marketing and finance departments can lead to significant financial advantages.
- Balancing technology and humanity, in which employees are supported by automation and are able to focus on high-level tasks, leads to a stronger workforce.
- Organizational rigidity and inertia are the main obstacles on a company's path toward unification.
- Coming together as a company is essential for relevancy, survival, and sustainability.
- Breaking down siloes doesn't occur overnight; companies can move in phases toward sustainability to ensure longevity in the marketplace.

CHAPTER 7

Converging Creativity and Productivity

From Idea Generation to Capital Optimization

In 2008, Diego A. Cárdenas Landeros founded Bamboocycles in Mexico City. The Bamboocycle is an environmentally friendly bicycle product designed and fabricated using 85% bamboo material. Bamboo is a resistant, sugar cane–shaped root tropical plant.

Cárdenas is an engineer who graduated from the Universidad Nacional Autonoma de Mexico. At the end of 2007, he started this bamboo bicycle project, at the beginning only as part of a school project.

Cárdenas came up with a cutting-edge solution. Bamboo absorbs vibrations and is resistant to the fatigue usually experienced by metal materials in general. Carbon fiber is an ultralight material, but it can crack if you hit it hard enough. Bamboo, however, isn't as easy to break.

On the sustainability side, bamboo produces 30% more oxygen than other trees. When it grows, it is ready to be harvested within three years. Other types of wood take much longer to mature. Staying close to home, Cárdenas found bamboo production could be carried out in southeastern Mexico.

Cárdenas's first model hit the streets in 2010 and attracted a great deal of attention. Soon he organized a weekend workshop to show others how to build a bamboo bicycle. Then he designed a three-hour Mexico City bamboo bicycle tour.

Through all his efforts, Cárdenas aimed to raise awareness about sustainable transportation and break stereotypes related to car use. According to a report by the Mexican National Institute of Statistics and Geography, in 2020, more than 6 million vehicles were registered in Mexico City. That number was nearly triple from the number in 1980. So many vehicles on the road caused the traffic to be unbearable in many parts of the city, especially during the week. The bamboo bicycle initiative demonstrated another option that reduced auto congestion, increased exercise, and came at a lower price tag than a vehicle purchase.

This case shows us that the objective of creativity is not about pursuing the amount of production, nor is it related to the outcome of a business organization's performance non financially and financially. Cárdenas wanted to make a positive environmental change. After understanding the problem, he used his creativity to find a solution and then executed a plan productively.

In this chapter, we'll discuss the convergence of creativity (from the "entrepreneurship" cluster) with productivity, (a "professionalism" cluster element). Creativity is needed for innovation. Bear in mind, however, that being creative only must be avoided. Creativity must present various technically feasible ideas that we can materialize (see Figure 7.1).

Therefore, creativity must start from a clearly defined problem. We have to measure the productivity in correlation to the use of capital provided by the company. However, the productivity calculation is not solely based on the input-output approach, especially when there are several intangible input factors. Productivity must be looked at more widely and include outcomes, as well as impact, like we saw in the Bamboocycles story.

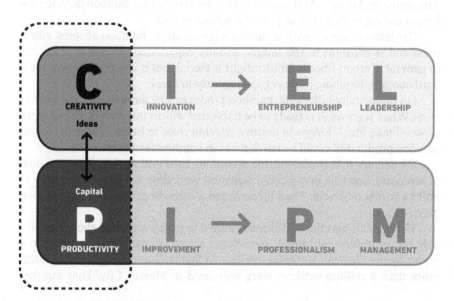

FIGURE 7.1 Creativity and productivity elements in the omnihouse model

The Problem with Creativity

Many easily understand the definition of creativity, yet it is not easy to insert it and run it in an organization. Several factors often cause problems with creativity. Let's look at each one.

Larger Company, Weaker Creativity

When a company is still small, we often find its owner has extraordinary amounts of creativity. Not all of it can be realized due to limited resources and the tendency to have low productivity. However, as a company grows, management is often preoccupied with many operational matters and focuses on intricate and complicated productivity calculations.

If we neglect to hone creativity, it will be increasingly weakened, become very limited, and eventually lost.[1] Companies that are already big are often trapped in a commodification attitude that mainly refers to a commercial or trade orientation. Companies with a commoditization approach usually do not require intense creativity. Commoditization is a catalyst that can lead a company to become a price taker—a company with no market power to influence price and faces so many competitors who sell identical or similar products so that customers are indifferent—which is forced to sell its product at a price according to the market equilibrium, willing to accept a low price, and subsequently get caught in a price war with a thin profit margin. Only creative companies can create differentiation, become price makers, and finally get a significant margin.

Unclear Purpose of Creativity

It is common for a company to be very creative, but the purpose of that creativity is often not clear, resulting in a costly waste of resources. It is not productive if a company follows a creative process that is not in alignment with its vision and mission. Even though, from the start, the company has involved qualified people in being part of the value-creation process, management must be sure beforehand that the character of these people is in line with the company's values and is suitable for carrying out the company's mission.

Creativity without a clear purpose will not produce anything valuable, both commercially and socially. Creativity like this will only be a discourse that wastes the company's capital, which will undoubtedly be contrary to the company's economic goals. We have entered an era in which many businesses are run based on a purpose-driven approach, in line with the increasing global,

---

[1] Creativity will decrease and eventually be very limited if a company stops creating something. Please refer to https://bettermarketing.pub/the-problem-with-creativity-3fdf7c061803

social, and environmental challenges. Given this, companies need a powerful creative capability to work with stakeholders and overcome problems. Therefore, a strong alignment between creativity and the company's business goals is essential.[2] Unfortunately, not all companies can accomplish this alignment effectively.

Intense Creativity, Zero Execution

No matter how strong creative ideas are, if they are not feasible to execute, it is a waste of existing capital or assets, both tangible and intangible. Sometimes many creative ideas can disrupt the long-running routine in a company. This is why management often sees creative ideas as a new burden—even a problem. In other words, management may be resistant to concepts that force them to abandon long-standing habits or routines. They could reject a new challenge because they are already busy managing other problems.[3] No wonder so many great creative ideas usually remain on the drawing board.

Idealism and Reality

Management sometimes develops creative ideas using assumptions based on ideal internal and external environmental conditions. This can be hazardous if the actual conditions are different. Sometimes, a company's management holds onto unrealistic creative ideas.

Both pragmatic and idealistic traits are essential in building a solid team in a company. Therefore, by mixing both ways of thinking and working, a team will be well balanced and ultimately capable of creating the best outputs. An idealistic vision can make people excited and even persuade them to engage. However, we must also acknowledge the reality of the challenges. We should see idealism as a vision that drives and motivates the company and its employees to know that they are working toward something consequential and noble. But with all the difficulties to achieve it, it's still not enough—employees also need to know that their companies' leaders are in touch with reality and are willing to directly step in and engage themselves by working hard on executions. In other words, sticking to one goal is excellent, but it will limit one's creativity in doing business. Therefore, pragmatism will help overcome limitations of creative potential.[4]

---

[2]https://www.anastasiashch.com/business-creativity
[3]https://hbr.org/2002/08/creativity-is-not-enough
[4]https://www.forbes.com/sites/work-in-progress/2010/04/15/are-you-a-pragmatic-or-idealist-leader/?sh=72b90bbf3e67; https://hbr.org/2012/01/the-power-of-idealistic-realis

Underappreciation of Creativity

Creativity is sometimes considered a given. In other words, some have the thought that we can obtain creativity for free. This thinking makes a company reluctant to invest in creativity-related projects, especially if the results are often unreal and difficult to monetize.

Companies are often trapped in spending their money on tangible things such as physical assets—including production equipment and supplies—which are easier to calculate for productivity in terms of input-output and the rate of return on investment. If someone requests that funds be allocated for physical facilities related to creativity, it may raise a few eyebrows among executives.[5]

In Industry 1.0, the top corporation activities were focused on mining, textiles, glass, and agriculture, which rely on tangible assets such as land, factory, and natural resources. However, in Industry 4.0, company performance depends on brand valuation, intellectual property, and knowledge assets for problem-solving. These are intangible assets but will still affect the corporation's profit.[6]

Unclear Orientation of Creativity

Customer problems are an excellent starting point for providing a clear orientation to a creative process. Sometimes, though, it is not easy to define customer problems. Meetings often include discussions of ideas without focusing on the actual issue that consumers are trying to remedy.

Creativity that starts from a well-defined problem—written in a clear problem statement—will significantly assist management's judgment to support the effort with solid reasons, especially if it is in line with company policies reflected in the vision, mission, and strategy. Productive creativity depends on the process of defining a problem (see Figure 7.2).[7]

We also need to pay attention to how pressure will affect creative abilities. Some argue that we cannot force creativity. We often find that in conditions where pressure is too high, creativity cannot emerge. However, if the motivation of a group of thinkers is unusually powerful, no matter how heavy the pressure is, they will not crack under it. They can even come up with various creative ideas that lead to innovation.

---

[5]https://www.linkedin.com/pulse/problem-creativity-its-free-tom-goodwin
[6]https://www.irwinmitchell.com/news-and-insights/newsletters/focus-on-manufacturing/edition-6-industry-40-and-property
[7]https://hbr.org/2012/09/are-you-solving-the-right-problem

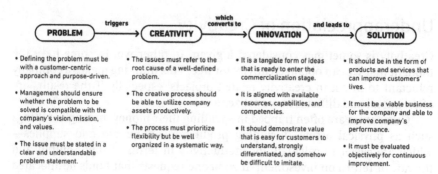

FIGURE 7.2 Several critical considerations from problem to solution

The Problem with Productivity

It would be remiss to end with the issues related to creativity. Certainly, challenges arise on the productivity side as well. We'll briefly look at some of the main challenges that tend to arise in this area, which can hinder the ultimate connection between creativity and productivity.

Status Quo on Productivity

Productivity is often associated with routine activities, leading management to stagnancy in a business-as-usual cadence. This status quo condition is typically oxygen-depleting for creativity. Anything viewed as "rocking the boat," which creativity usually does, doesn't fit in. The culture prefers stability, consistency, and rigid standardization.

Herein lies the challenge, because the status quo mindset as the basis for calculating productivity does not leave much room for creativity. We must not forget that creativity—converted into innovation—may directly or indirectly affect productivity.[8] Management sometimes prefers to avoid problems because of ideas that are not viewed as mainstream. When these ideas are ignored because they are considered "not-invented-here," it will, unfortunately, cause the company to be unable to innovate and will eventually bring the company into a crisis. If companies can't even get out of that crisis, how can they think about customer problems?

---

[8]https://www.mantu.com/blog/business-insights/is-the-status-quo-standing-in-the-way-of-productivity/

Productivity Is Everything

A company's pursuit of productivity can lead to an excessive burden on employees, in which workers feel unappreciated, inadequately rewarded, and burned out.[9] Too much emphasis on time management—meant to make an employee less stressed—sometimes has the opposite result.[10] There has to be room for other activities too, including rest and employee well-being.[11]

Inflexibility in Productivity

It is not easy to calculate productivity if there is no consistency. Companies usually build this consistency through standard operating procedures. The processes are sometimes so complicated that they cause headaches for the people who carry them out. Yet their essence aims to achieve high efficiency and a certain level of productivity.

Deloitte, in one of its publications, said that efficiency undermines creativity. Productivity is built with savings in mind, and reducing waste, so that there is less room to experiment with new things, including creative ideas and different approaches.[12] We often hear the expression that it will be difficult to manage appropriately without measurement. Unfortunately, an applied measurement sometimes focuses more on tangibles such as machinery, equipment, other physical assets, and working capital. The management often overlooks the intangibles because they are difficult to calculate with the "machine" approach.

Input-Output Perspective

The calculation of productivity in some companies solely relies on production factors as inputs, which then undergo processes and eventually become the company's output. Unfortunately, this approach often cannot include multiple intangible and indirect factors. The setup refers to the output but not the outcome. It is not surprising that a company is reluctant to spend money and invest in creative ideas because the comparisons refer to items that are quantifiable and not abstract.

Quantifying ideas that come from creative thoughts often can be challenging. Moreover, no one knows whether they will work until we implement them and then evaluate them. Indeed, we still have to use the input-output approach, but that does not mean it is sufficient. In the end, we are not merely looking at the output, but also the outcome and impact (see Figure 7.3).

[9]https://krisp.ai/blog/why-do-people-hate-productivity-heres-how-to-embrace-it/
[10]https://www.bbc.com/worklife/article/20180904-why-time-management-so-often-fails
[11]https://happilyrose.com/2021/01/10/productivity-culture/
[12]https://www2.deloitte.com/xe/en/insights/topics/innovation/unshackling-creativity-in-business.html

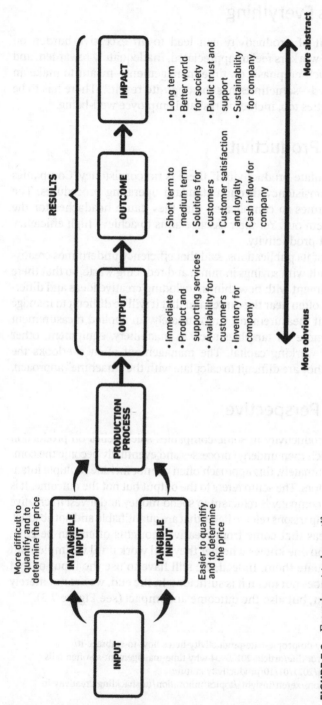

FIGURE 7.3 From input to impact[13]

---

[13]The concept of results consisting of output, outcome, and impact refers to the OECD explanation.

Output is the immediate result of a production process that we often call products (both goods and services). We can measure output immediately after the completion of a given production process. In simple terms, an outcome is the positive effect of the output from a given production process offered and enjoyed by several stakeholders, such as people in the company, customers, the community, and the company itself. We can see an outcome in the short and medium term, whereas the impact is a result that we can see in the long term.[14]

Attracting Customers and Investors

Companies can generate new ideas and use them to attract customers and investors through the creative process. Customers often seem to impatiently anticipate the launch of a new product. They may be willing to preorder for an interesting new product idea, even though the physical form does not yet exist. Investors will be interested if the company has unique business ideas. Let's look at how to balance these segments in terms of the creativity and productivity elements.

Impatient Customers

Customers are the lifeblood of a company. Their expectations can affect how creativity and productivity are handled. Here are some main challenges in dealing with customers in today's environment.

> **More demanding.** Consumers, empowered by social media and digital gadgets, increasingly control when, where, and how they interact with brands. They are now more demanding than ever for more personalized service. Because of this, the customer experiences at all points of the omni-channel must be seamless. Products and services need to be offered at affordable prices with fast and hassle-free delivery. This condition also forces companies to collaborate and co-create with customers—both B2C and B2B—to ensure a stronger level of engagement.

> **More challenging to satisfy.** Connectivity of one person to another on various platforms makes it easier to exchange information and educate more customers. Customers are increasingly demanding higher standards and becoming more stringent in their choices by constantly comparing the options available. They study ratings that other customers have given.

---

[14]https://www.oecd.org/dac/results-development/what-are-results.htm

More difficult to gain loyalty. Even if we can satisfy the customer, it is not a guarantee that the customer will remain with us. A study of more than 34,000 consumers worldwide by Verint® Systems Inc. shows customer loyalty and retention are dropping. More specifically, two-thirds of consumers surveyed indicated that they are inclined to move to a competitor that offers superior customer service or an exceptional experience.[15]

Craving for new products. Changes in functional and emotional needs, tastes, and contemporary trends occur quickly, causing consumers to feel deprived and influencing them to look for new, better products that are available ASAP. Shoppers are constantly looking for new and higher value from products. They may be willing to pay an advance even before a new item is available in the market so they can gain the title of becoming one of the first owners or users.

Highly Cautious Investors

Investors are often a vital source of funding for a company. However, it is not easy to convince them to contribute to a company because it is full of creative people, and therefore, has a very high creative capability. Investors will be interested in a company's potential to provide a rate of return on the money invested. If it is difficult to give a convincing calculation, then they will also be hesitant to make a commitment.

Here are some reasons why investors may be skeptical about creativity:

A huge investment. Generating creativity requires enormous effort and resources. Yet it does not usually produce the desired results right away. Sometimes we see a scarcity of creativity in a company because of the reluctance of parties to contribute the heavy funding needed to support the initiatives.[16]

Difficult to assess the value. Investor hesitancy usually increases when an investment offer is too complicated to understand. Creativity is often abstract. We cannot see the results immediately. We need to find a way for investors to see and understand that creativity has a high value and deserves to be considered when investing.[17]

High rate of failure. According to Harvard Business School professor Clayton Christensen, there are about 30,000 new products introduced to the market every year. Of those, 95% fail. Meanwhile, according to

---

[15]https://businessrealities.eiu.com/in-brief-shifting-customer-demands
[16]Robert J. Sternberg and Todd I. Lubart, "An Investment Theory of Creativity and Its Development," *Human Development* 34, no. 1 (January–February 1991): 1–31.
[17]Ibid.

University of Toronto Professor Inez Blackburn, the failure rate of new products in grocery stores ranges from 70–80%.[18]

Play-it-safe attitude. The management team's view of creativity often shows high distrust. Instead of making "rational" investment efforts, management usually sets aside a small budget for creativity. If it does not provide any results, it will be considered or calculated as an insignificant loss. Investors also play it safe in the same way, because they cannot see the results of creativity in financial terms.[19]

Unsolved hidden problems. In addition to considering the investment amount, investors tend to spot hidden issues that increase risk. If a company's culture is not in line with the spirit of creativity, if it does not involve people who have a calling for creativity, or if the management team is not committed to supporting creativity (in the form of time and resources), it will raise doubts for investors.[20]

Overpromised creative proposal. Investors will be reluctant to invest when they hear a pitch that seems too good to be valid or too complex to be understood. They may be familiar with creative ideas that look good on paper but do not materialize as expected and even end up failing. It's only natural that investors are then more interested in other investment portfolios that make more sense in their view.

The founder of Segway—a two-wheeled personal transporter—predicted the device would be a game-changer to the transportation industry. The founders also envisioned that sales would explode to 10,000 units per week, and that the company would reach US$1 billion in sales faster than any company in history. Unfortunately, this did not happen. In fact, Segway only sold 24,000 units in four years. This issue was rooted in the fact that Segway made the products for general purposes. The outcome was that Segway could not compete with other forms of transportation such as motorcycles, bicycles, and cars. Some people even prefer to walk (which is free!) rather than use a Segway.[21]

By understanding these obstacles and finding solutions to overcome them, we can increase the likelihood of attracting investors. Having their support often leads to the development of creativity in a company. Bottom line, their investments matter.

---

[18]https://www.inc.com/marc-emmer/95-percent-of-new-products-fail-here-are-6-steps-to-make-sure-yours-dont.html

[19]https://www.vttresearch.com/en/news-and-ideas/business-case-creativity-why-invest-organizational-creativity

[20]In line with Chris Savage's opinion (2018). Please refer to https://wistia.com/learn/culture/investing-in-creativity-isnt-just-a-money-problem

[21]https://www.forbes.com/sites/adamhartung/2015/02/12/the-reason-why-google-glass-amazon-firephone-and-segway-all-failed/?sh=69676682c05c

Key Takeaways

- There are challenges achieving creativity in large corporations and in environments with no clear purpose, no execution, overly idealistic perspectives, low levels of appreciation, and an unclear orientation.

- Too much emphasis on productivity can lead to status quo challenges, employee burnout, inflexibility, and an input-output perspective.

- Today's customers are more demanding, harder to satisfy, and eager to have new products.

- Investors find it difficult to invest in creativity because it could be costly, is hard to value, has a high rate of failure, isn't well supported within an organization, or is too difficult to understand.

- Merging the best aspects of creativity and productivity can help companies keep customers and attract investors.

CHAPTER 8

Creativity and the Balance Sheet

Securing Funding for Imaginative Capabilities

I f a company has a powerful creative ability and can produce innovations that lead to profitability, or at least has the potential to generate profits in the future, it will attract investors. The word *investment* means that investors will contribute their money to the company and expect a return. These investors automatically become shareholders in the company. As implied, investors are not loan providers.

If the intention is to provide loans, one will see only the company's ability to pay interest on loans and return the loan principal within a certain period. The party lending the money does not care about various creative ideas or processes in a company. It is interested in knowing that the company can repay the principal loan plus the agreed-on interest rate. In a default situation, the borrower will submit a request to bankrupt the company. The lender will have the right to take existing assets to replace the loan provided.

Given this, we can relate creative capabilities to what happens in the company's balance sheet depending on how one party appreciates creativity and whether creativity is indeed a primary consideration.

Lender Perspective

Lenders or debtholders will be concerned only about the company's revenue because, from that amount, the company will pay the principal and interest of the loan. Sometimes, companies sell some of their shares to generate cash, which can also be used to pay off their debts.

Evergrande—the biggest China property company—expanded its business aggressively and borrowed more than US $300 billion from international lenders. When the pandemic hit, their real estate business slowed down. This situation affected the company's capability to pay back what they owed. In December 2021, Fitch—an agency that rates the financial risk of companies—declared Evergrande in default. Evergrande went beyond the due date to pay their debts of US$1.2 billion to the international lenders and had to sell some of its assets to pay its debts.[1]

Investor Perspective

On the one hand, if a party is willing to invest their money in a company, then that party fully believes in the proposal of the creative ideas submitted by the company, although the company may first have to suffer losses in the first few years. The party who invests the capital is referred to as an investor and they own a portion of the company's shares. In the balance sheet, we will see an increase in equity. Investors will monitor the productivity of their invested capital by looking at the calculation of return on equity and return on assets.

Investors will also monitor the company's market value movement, be it below or above the book value. Suppose the market value increases rapidly. This indicates that the company's various intangible assets or nonfinancial assets—including creativity, which is actually very valuable but is often hidden and not recorded as assets in the balance sheet—are genuinely appreciated by the market. Furthermore, investors may wait for the right time to sell their shares at a higher price (see Figure 8.1).

The Essence of Creativity

After we understand the importance of creativity for a company and relate it to the balance sheet, we need to further identify the essence of a creative process. The starting point has to do with the various dynamic conditions triggered by multiple change drivers. These consist of four elements

---

[1]https://www.bbc.com/news/business-58579833; https://www.investopedia.com/terms/v/venturecapital.asp; https://www.investopedia.com/terms/p/privateequity.asp

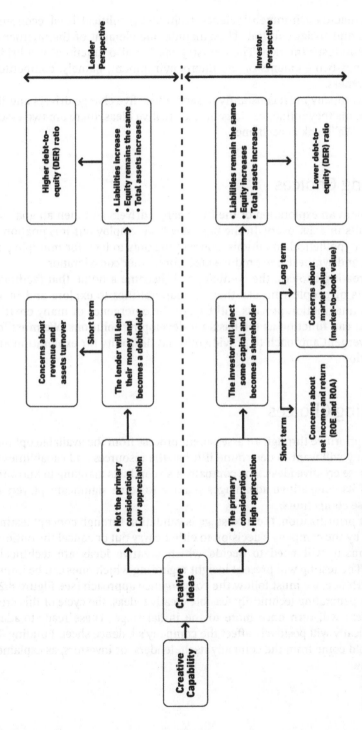

FIGURE 8.1 Lender and investor perspectives

81

from the macro environment: science/technology, political/legal, economy/ business, and social/cultural. They include one element of the microenvironment: industry/market. The industry/market also functions as a bridge to the other two elements of the microenvironment, namely, competitors and customers.

The company must constantly observe these five change drivers and the two elements they influence. To generate creative ideas, there are two essential parts. We'll look at each one.

Creating Choices

It starts with an exploration of the five change drivers and then an analysis. This results in a discovery. In the next stage, we employ our imagination to visualize hypothetical conditions, connect the dots to look for multiple possibilities, and synthesize to produce ideas for further consideration.

In creating choices, the company will become a home that facilitates the efforts of people who use their human abilities to explore and imagine. This imagination process will trigger the emergence of many creative ideas that can function as the basis for developing solutions. We must follow a divergent approach to provide optimal flexibility for exploration and imagination.

Selecting Choices

We then prioritize through an assessment process from the available options. A company will want to determine if it has the resources and capabilities to realize these creative ideas. The company also conducts mapping to know the extent of its competitive advantages relative to some significant players or other close competitors.

After prioritization, the next stage is validation through concept testing, followed by the company's decision to either carry out or cancel the options. The company will need to decide which creative ideas are technically feasible. The testing will present insight regarding which ones can be implemented. Hence, we must follow the convergence approach (see Figure 8.2).

After generating technically feasible creative ideas, the cycle of this creative process will turn once more to the initial stage. These ready-to-adapt ideas typically will positively affect the company's balance sheet. Funding for them could come from the company itself, lenders, or investors, as explained previously.

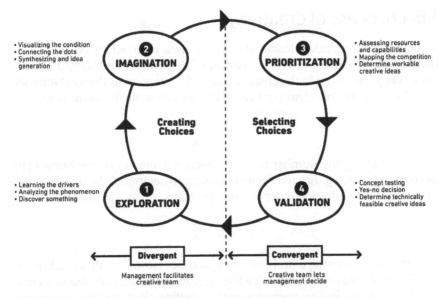

• Visualizing the condition
• Connecting the dots
• Synthesizing and idea generation

②
IMAGINATION

③
PRIORITIZATION

• Assessing resources and capabilities
• Mapping the competition
• Determine workable creative ideas

Creating Choices

Selecting Choices

• Learning the drivers
• Analyzing the phenomenon
• Discover something

①
EXPLORATION

④
VALIDATION

• Concept testing
• Yes-no decision
• Determine technically feasible creative ideas

← Divergent → ← Convergent →

Management facilitates creative team

Creative team lets management decide

FIGURE 8.2 Divergent and convergent approach in the creative process

Measuring the Productivity of Creativity

Though measuring creativity in terms of productivity is not easy, we can agree first on one point. Productivity combines effectiveness and efficiency that we borrow from a financial approach. Conceptually, the creative team, as an asset of a company, should produce technically feasible creative ideas within a specific deadline (T_1). From these technically feasible creative ideas, the company must decide which ideas—in part or whole—they will develop into actual products within a specific time limit (T_2) (see Figure 8.3).

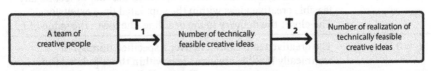

A team of creative people
T_1 →
Number of technically feasible creative ideas
T_2 →
Number of realization of technically feasible creative ideas

FIGURE 8.3 People, creative ideas, and realization of creative ideas

Effectiveness of Creativity

Hypothetically, we can calculate the effectiveness of creativity ($C_{Effectiveness}$) by dividing the total number of technically feasible creative ideas (I) by the number of people involved in the creative team (P). This gives us the total number of technically feasible ideas per headcount. We can write the formula as:

$$C_{Effectiveness} = \frac{I}{P}$$

By replacing the number of people with the amount of the budget (B) devoted to financing the creative process, we can determine the total number of technically feasible ideas per one unit of money spent. This formula is:

$$C_{Effectiveness} = \frac{I}{B}$$

After encountering a problem from potential customers that needs to be solved, a company might set a deadline for several technically feasible creative ideas. If the creative team misses the deadline, then the company might lose its momentum to market timing, and the novelty of those creative ideas begins degrading. After the deadline passes, the company might provide some extra time in certain conditions. It now solely depends on whether the creative team can come up with any, or several, creative ideas before this spare time runs out. Thus, we can add a coefficient (t_1) whose magnitude is between 0 and 1 to the earlier effectiveness of the creativity formula with the conditions shown in Table 8.1.

TABLE 8.1 **The Value of Coefficient t_1**

Coefficient	Conditions
$t_1 = 1$	The creative team can deliver a specified number of technically feasible creative ideas sooner or according to the stipulated deadline.
$0 < t_1 < 1$	The creative team can deliver a specified number of technically feasible creative ideas within the stipulated time extension. The closer the delivery to the deadline, the lower the value of t_1.
$t_1 = 0$	The creative team cannot deliver a specified number of technically feasible creative ideas within the stipulated time extension. Or the creative team can deliver those technically feasible creative ideas—all of them, partly, or even none at all—after the stipulated time extension.

Figure 8.4 can illustrate those conditions as follows:

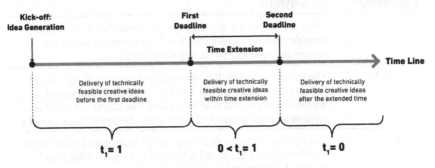

FIGURE 8.4 The value of coefficient t₁ in a timeline

The two formulas to calculate the effectiveness of creativity can be modified as follows:

$$C_{Effectiveness} = \frac{I}{P}t_1$$

or

$$C_{Effectiveness} = \frac{I}{B}t_1$$

Efficiency of Creativity

We can hypothetically calculate the efficiency of creativity ($C_{Efficiency}$) by dividing
the total number of realized creative ideas in the form of concrete products that
can prove to be solutions for customers and are ready for commercialization
(R) by the total number of technically feasible creative ideas (I). The formula is:

$$C_{Efficiency} = \frac{R}{I}$$

Similar to the calculation for effectiveness, when calculating this efficiency,
the company sets a deadline for realizing the various technically feasible creative
ideas. If the creative team exceeds the given deadline and the extended deadline,
then the realization and commercialization efforts will be too late and will be
futile to continue. Therefore, we can add a coefficient (t_2) whose magnitude is
between 0 and 1 in the efficiency formula with the conditions shown in Table 8.2.

TABLE 8.2 The Value of Coefficient t_2

Coefficient	Conditions
$t_2 = 1$	The company can realize the specified number of technically feasible creative ideas and is ready for commercialization sooner or according to the stipulated deadline.
$0 < t_2 < 1$	The company can realize the specified number of technically feasible creative ideas and is ready for commercialization within the stipulated time extension. The closer the readiness for commercialization to the deadline, the lower the value of t_2.
$t_2 = 0$	The company cannot realize specified numbers of technically feasible creative ideas and is ready for commercialization within the stipulated time extension. Or the company can realize those technically feasible creative ideas—all of them, partly, or even none at all—and is ready for commercialization after the stipulated time extension.

Figure 8.5 can illustrate those conditions as follows:

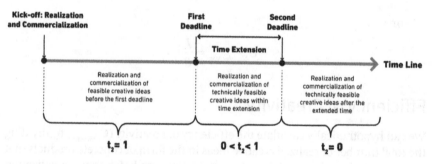

FIGURE 8.5 The value of coefficient t_2 in a timeline

Thus, the two formulas to calculate the efficiency of creativity can be modified as follows:

$$C_{Efficiency} = \frac{R}{I} t_2$$

Productivity of Creativity

By combining the two formulas, namely, effectiveness and efficiency of creativity, we can hypothetically measure the productivity of creativity ($C_{Productivity}$). This can be done non financially based on people as assets (that is, the productivity of creativity per headcount) or financially based on the budget amount allocated to the people (that is, the productivity of creativity per unit money spent). The formula then is:

$$C_{Productivity} = \frac{I}{P} t_1 \times \frac{R}{I} t_2$$

$$C_{Productivity} = \frac{R}{P} t_1 t_2$$

$$If\ T = t_1 t_2\ then\ C_{Productivity} = \frac{R}{P} T$$

or

$$C_{Productivity} = \frac{I}{B} t_1 \times \frac{R}{I} t_2$$

$$C_{Productivity} = \frac{R}{B} t_1 t_2$$

$$If\ T = t_1 t_2\ then\ C_{Productivity} = \frac{R}{B} T$$

Of course, the formula for measuring the productivity of creativity is loaded with simplification. It ignores many other factors (e.g., originality of creative ideas, level of difficulty to imitate, pressure on creative teams) and various changes (e.g., sudden changes in the business environment) that may take place during the creative process. All of these can affect the formulation. However, we can use those formulas for indicative purposes.

Creativity for Productive Capital

In this context, *capital* is referring to the value of assets used by companies to support creativity, which produces commodities available for sale and generates earnings. Therefore, companies need to understand how much capital they should allocate to support creativity for optimal results. For simplicity, we will link the capital allocated to support creativity to the number of technically feasible creative ideas generated. Each increase in the allocation to support creativity will increase the number of technically feasible creative ideas at different rates. At one point, there will be a decrease in technically feasible creative ideas. There are four conditions for seeing the relationship between capital employed or invested in the support of creativity with technically feasible creative ideas. Let's look at each one.

Underinvestment Range

If there is an additional investment, there will be an increase in the number of technically feasible creative ideas with an increasing rate pattern. This condition shows that the capacity of the creative team is still not fully used, and the investment to support them is still very low to moderate. Therefore, companies need to allocate additional capital to support creativity, and the number of technically feasible creative ideas will increase. The creative team's motivation is usually very high in this range, yet the pressure is still low.

The short-video social network Snapchat was invented by Evan Spiegel, Reggie Brown, and Bobby Murphy, Stanford University students, in 2011. It began when Spiegel presented an app to share funny moments with friends for 24 hours during product design class. The moments would then be deleted. During Snapchat's development, the team's motivation was still high to achieve its mission to communicate with the full range of human emotion—not just what appears to be aesthetic or perfect.[2] At that time, they were all students in college, not thinking too commercially, so there was no investment in developing Snapchat, even though Snapchat's potential was very promising.

Near-Optimum Investment Range

This pertains to circumstances in which every additional investment, up to a certain amount, causes an increase in the number of technically feasible creative ideas, but at a decreasing rate. This condition indicates that the creative team has begun reaching its maximum capacity. The company has two options: first, add more people involved in the creative team and increase its investment to enhance creativity; second, invest more but maintain the same number of people until they reach their capacity limit to deliver new technically feasible creative ideas. The creative team's motivation is still high in this range, and the pressure is between moderate to high.

Capital A Berhad is the new holding of the AirAsia Group that was announced on January 28, 2022, in Kuala Lumpur. This holding reflects the new core business strategy from the airlines industry toward the synergistic travel and lifestyle business. During the COVID-19 pandemic, the revenue of AirAsia dropped significantly, and it was immensely challenging to bring back the revenue they had before the pandemic. Therefore, Capital A added more people to diversify business with a financial product, BigPay, education technology, and the grocery business. This transformation got positive feedback from South Korean conglomerate SK Group, which funded US$100 million to develop BigPay in Asia. CEO of Capital A, Tony Fernandes, said that

---

[2]https://www.topuniversities.com/student-info/careers-advice/7-most-successful-student-businesses-started-university

it's not just a new logo but a significant milestone that marks a new era since the group has gone beyond being an airline.[3] Here we see that increasing the scope of business (because of pivoting) requires additional investment and additional people so that the installed capacity is in line with high business demands.

Optimum Investment Point

If the company decides not to increase the number of people in its creative team in near-optimum conditions, the creative team will soon peak its capacity. At this point, the creative team's work pressure has become very high. The work situation grows uncomfortable and less conducive for creativity. The company then reaches the optimum point regarding the investment allocated to support creativity. The company can create a second curve of creativity for productive capital, one of which is to increase the capacity of the creative team by increasing the number of people. At this point, the creative team experiences very high pressure, and their motivations become very vulnerable.

Working in Silicon Valley might at first seem like a dream job for some tech workers. Companies in that space often offer free lunches and competitive salaries to attract top talent. However, top-performing workers are often under loads of pressure to make innovative products and grow the company's revenue.

Being at a "dream company" does not guarantee high working motivation and loyalty to the company. That is why many Americans quit their jobs during the Great Resignation, which coincided partly with the pandemic. Some were looking for new perks, like working remotely, flexible working hours, and more time for more meaningful tasks.[4] We can see that not everyone is suitable for working where the job is very demanding—even if the pay is high.

Overinvestment Range

We will see a decrease in technically feasible creative ideas within this range on every additional amount of capital. The company must immediately stop investing and think about the steps necessary to ensure a rise in the curve (see Figure 8.6). If the company decides not to increase the number of people in its creative team at the optimum point but continues to expand its investment and demands that the creative team still produce more technically feasible creative ideas, the results will be counterproductive. Excessive workload

---

[3] https://newsroom.airasia.com/news/airasia-group-is-now-capital-a
[4] https://www.wired.com/story/great-resignation-tech-workers-great-reconsideration/

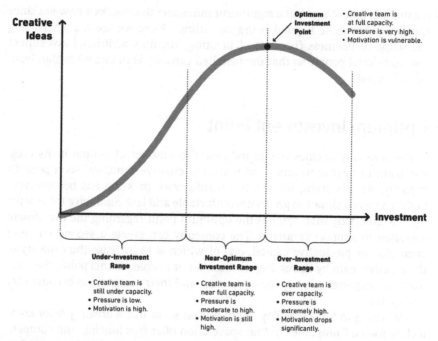

FIGURE 8.6 Ranges of investments in creativity

makes the pressure on the creative team exceptionally high, and in turn, will make them demotivated. Consequently, we can see a decrease in technically feasible creative ideas.

Quincy Apparel is a company that designs, manufactures, and sells working apparel that offers the fit and feel of a high-end brand at a lower price for young professional women. To increase market penetration, they pitched to some investors. However, it turned out to be the other way around because investors only worsened Quincy's conditions. The founders were disappointed with their guidance from those venture capitalists, who pressured them to grow at full tilt—like the technology start-ups the investors were more familiar with. Doing so forced Quincy to build inventory and burn through cash before it had resolved its production problems. This made the pressure on the founder extremely high.[5]

We can see a need for an excellent managerial capability to allocate capital, especially those given for activities related to creativity. Management must also know when to increase, slow down, and stop their investment. In addition, the management team will need to convince investors that the creative capability in the company is indeed valuable. They want to show that it will

---
[5]https://hbr.org/2021/05/why-start-ups-fail

be able to create strong differentiation and is indeed feasible to be realized commercially at a later stage.

In addition, an increase in investment is directly proportional to the rise in the workload of the creative team, which will increase their work pressure. Therefore, management will want to maintain the motivation of creative team members in order to ensure that they can continue to perform at their best. Strategies to avoid brain fatigue and demotivation, which lead to decreased productivity, are key.

Not all companies are suited for implementing the crunch culture, and not all creative teams can be productive in the work culture that is often the case in some highly competitive industries. Work pressure that is too high to meet tight deadlines can make a person demotivated and unable to be creative optimally. Therefore, the role of talent management becomes very decisive. Equally creative people can show different performances in the same work environment because each person or talent has unique characteristics or psychographic profiles. Hence, the compatibility between talent and the workplace becomes increasingly essential for competitiveness.

In the omnihouse model, there are alternating arrows between creativity and productivity, which means that we must always balance these two aspects. Small- and medium-sized companies that are very strong in terms of creativity need to start considering the importance of calculating the productivity of various capitals used, especially those related to supporting creativity. However, already established companies that sometimes feel trapped in complex calculations related to productivity must re-present and strengthen their weakened creative abilities.

Understanding the essence of converging creativity and productivity will enable us maximize results—not only output—and also provide us with better judgment in reviewing the productivity of our capital employed for boosting the creative capability of our company.

Key Takeaways

- Lenders typically look first and foremost at whether a loan can be repaid and place a lower value on creativity.
- Investors chip in their money for various creative ideas that can provide returns and increase market value. There is a time to sell their shares for a gain.
- Creativity can be measured for its effectiveness, efficiency, and productivity levels.
- Companies need to invest the right amount of capital for optimal creativity results.

CHAPTER 9

Converging Innovation and Improvement

Solution-Centric Approach for Higher Profit Margin

W hen we innovate, does it always lead to improvement?

Not necessarily. In fact, it's easy for things to go astray. So much is at play when we innovate that nothing is guaranteed. It takes a lot of orchestrated effort to move the needle in improvement.

Take the case of Bytedance. Established in 2012, the company has produced so many apps that it has earned the nickname "app factory." Among the most well-known are TikTok and Toutiao. Its recent innovations have spurred on tremendous growth, including a 60% revenue increase in 2021.[1] That same year it was valued at more than US$425 billion.[2] Let's look further at how the innovations of TikTok and Toutiao have led to their significant growth.

Created in 2017, TikTok is a short-video sharing platform. It has reached 1 billion users faster than any other social media company. TikTok's most substantial competitive advantage comes from its speed, ability, and AI technology,

---

[1]https://www.scmp.com/tech/big-tech/article/3156192/tiktok-owner-bytedance-post-60-cent-revenue-growth-2021-media-report
[2]https://asia.nikkei.com/Business/36Kr-KrASIA/TikTok-creator-ByteDance-hits-425bn-valuation-on-gray-market

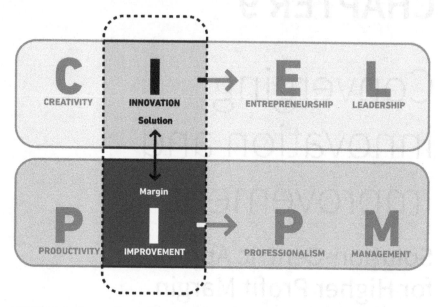

FIGURE 9.1 Innovation and improvement elements in the omnihouse model

which together offer consumers a mix of products and services. For instance, the app features hashtags, audio and video editing, and image filters—all in one place. Previously, these elements weren't available in a single app. Users can easily grab what they need and seamlessly produce content.[3]

Toutiao ("Headlines") is a news app that uses the same business model. It provides news and content from more than just official news agencies. Bloggers and influencers participate, too. This integrated app combines many pieces of information, which is highly appreciated by its users; users spend an average of 74 minutes every day on the app.

In addition to these, Toutiao incorporated a bot to write original news coverage for real-time events such as the 2016 Olympics.[4] It also has a localized feature to help find anyone who has gone astray, known as the "Missing Person Alert," which sends out a push notification to all users within a certain radius.

From Bytedance, we can learn that innovation must focus on customer solutions to provide improvement for the company (see Figure 9.1). Its pro-

[3]https://hbr.org/2020/07/how-spotify-and-tiktok-beat-their-copycats
[4]https://www.ycombinator.com/library/3x-hidden-forces-behind-toutiao-china-s-content-king; https://digital.hbs.edu/platform-digit/submission/toutiao-an-ai-powered-news-platform/
[5]The innovation process based on desirability, feasibility, and viability criteria originated from IDEO and used in the human-centered design. Please refer to IDEO, *The Field Guide to Human-Centered Design* (IDEO, 2015), 14; Kristann Orton, "Desirability, Feasibility, Viability: The Sweet Spot for Innovation," Innovation Sweet Spot (March 28, 2017). https://medium.com/innovation-sweet-spot/desirability-feasibility-viability-the-sweet-spot-for-innovation-d7946de2183c

cesses are based on desirability, feasibility, and viability.[5] Consumers will want something only if it solves a problem for them. To make it feasible, the right resources, capabilities, and core competencies must be optimized.

Viable innovations lead to business growth, both in the short and long term. In the short term, this might include customer acceptance, higher levels of satisfaction among users, and the emergence of a lock-in mechanism or loyalty. Long-term growth is reflected by improved profit margins, which increase profitability. Affecting the community at large can lead to ongoing sustainability.

Certainly, Bytedance seems to have connected the bridge between innovation (i.e., providing solutions to customers) and improvement (i.e., increasing the company's profit margins). For best results, we can't have one without the other. In this chapter, we'll lay out the steps needed to tie these two together and, by doing so, build a competitive advantage. It starts with a 4C analysis.

The 4C Analysis

In Chapter 3, we discussed the five change drivers (technology, political/legal, social/cultural, economy, and market). These trigger creative ideas that, together with the company's internal sources, lead to solution-oriented innovations. Someone with an entrepreneurial marketing mindset can see various phenomena in change. This becomes the basis for looking at opportunities (from the customer aspect) as well as the existing challenges (from the competitor aspect).

The entrepreneurial mindset approach emphasizes what innovative solutions we can provide to customers while simultaneously increasing the company's profit margins. At this stage, we can test the sharpness of implementing an entrepreneurial marketing mindset as indicated by the extent of our foresight in understanding the other three elements in the 4C model (customer, competitor, and the company itself). This exercise ensures the innovations produced are solution-oriented.[6] Here are the analyses we'll want to carry out.

Customer Analysis

We must understand the customer based on data. This might be qualitative, quantitative, primary, or secondary data, depending on the solutions we would like to offer. We're looking for information on preferences, opinions, suggestions, and the problems customers face.

That's exactly what Ariston, an Italian-based tech company, did. Based on consumer preference to have a perfect shower, Ariston built a smart water heater with Wi-Fi connectivity. This invention enables the customer to control

---

[6]The competitor, customer, and company elements refer to the concept of Kenichi Ohmae, *The Mind of the Strategist: The Art of Japanese Business* (McGraw-Hill, 1982).

the temperature remotely from their phone.[7] Consumers can save on energy by turning down the heat. The water heater also uses algorithms to pick up on consumer habits and adjust accordingly.

Competitor Analysis

We also have to comprehend our competitors—direct and substitutes—to ensure the solutions we offer have an advantage and can therefore strongly compete. The goal here is to create the highest perceived value. This is in relation to other existing solutions.

Mercedes-Benz spotted a solution-oriented approach that had not been widely implemented by its competitors. It used this to create a competitive advantage. Its efforts led to Actros, a heavy-duty truck model that is designed and assembled according to the requests of customers. Mercedes-Benz uses virtual reality technology in the development process. Daily, the main plant in Worth, Germany, delivers up to 470 units for each model. Actros is also available for customization to fit B2B business requirements.[8]

Company Analysis

We need to know our company to determine what our resources, capabilities, and competencies can realize and to market these solutions. One of the most crucial things in this analysis is to identify the company's core competencies (see Figure 9.2). We'll want to make sure that the innovations we come up with do not deviate too far from these core competencies.

Uniqlo, a Japanese fashion brand, inspired the world to dress casually. Additionally, they have begun offering breakthrough fashion selections for customers. The company offers HeatTech products to keep the body warm, AIRism products as quick-drying clothes, and UV Cut as sunscreen for the body. These solutions use the company's resources to keep the customer coming back for suitable, comfortable clothing with an innovative functional benefit.[9]

To conduct these analyses, two approaches are available. One is inward-looking and the other is outward-looking.

- **Inward-Looking Approach**

    Innovative solutions are done by first looking at what resources the company possesses. This approach aligns with the concept of the

---

[7]https://www.ariston.com/en-sg/the-comfort-way/news/ariston-launches-singapores-first-ever-wifi-enabled-smart-water-heater-with-app-controls-the-andris2-range/
[8]https://www.autocarpro.in/news-international/f1-legend-niki-lauda-dies-aged-70–43064
[9]https://martinroll.com/resources/articles/strategy/uniqlo-the-strategy-behind-the-global-japanese-fast-fashion-retail-brand/; https://www.fastretailing.com/eng/group/strategy/uniqlobusiness.html

CUSTOMER	**COMPETITOR**	**COMPANY**
Understand customers' problems and provide innovative solutions to customers	Understand the market segments and innovate to create winning product	Understand how much sales will be achieved and at what cost and innovate business process

FIGURE 9.2 Customer, competitor, and company analysis

resource-based view, which evaluates existing resources—both tangible and intangible—and then finds the right market for the resulting innovative solutions.

- **Outward-Looking Approach**

We can also develop innovative solutions through the exploration of opportunities in the market and observation. This approach aligns with the concept of market-based view (or market positioning view). It is based on providing—either organically or collaboratively—the necessary resources and capabilities to deliver innovative solutions that fit a market demand.

Conservative Versus Radical

Whatever approach we take is not a matter of right or wrong. It is a choice and depends on the conditions we face. Regardless, companies can choose to be conservative or radical during these processes.

In a conservative approach, a company tends to play it safe by focusing on what competitors do and how customers develop. The company will then consider what the right solution is to provide. In this approach, the company is more reactive and follows the wave. Changes made by the company are incremental in nature and often market-driven (see Figure 9.3).[10]

If a company takes a radical approach, it uses the analyses of the five drivers of change to identify what significant impacts might occur. The company then considers what solution will provide more disruption and creates new game rules that will affect other players and customers. When an organization carries this out, we often refer to it as a market-driving company (see Figure 9.4).

---

[10]To understand further about the differences between market-driven and market-driving companies please refer to Nirmalya Kumar, Lisa Scheer, and Philip Kotler, "From Market Driven to Market Driving," *European Management Journal* 18, no. 2 (2000): 129–142. https:// ink.library.smu.edu.sg/lkcsb:research/5196; Andrew Stein, "9 Differences Between Market-Driving And Market-Driven Companies." http://steinvox.com/blog/9-differences-between-market-driving-and-market-driven-companies/

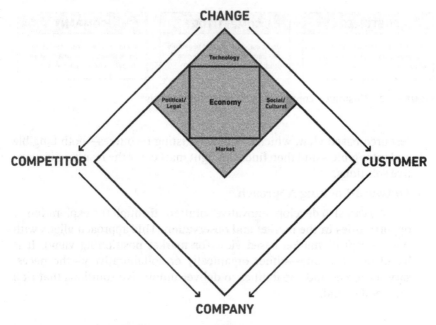

FIGURE 9.3   The 4C model for a market-driven company

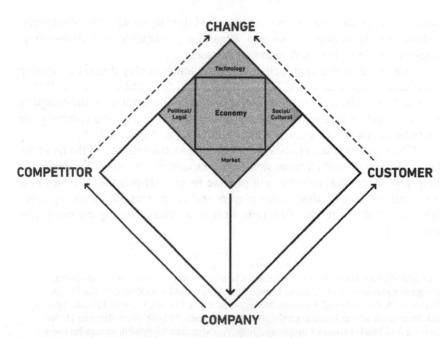

FIGURE 9.4   The 4C model for a market-driving company

Innovative Solutions
for Improved Margins

As people with an entrepreneurial mindset, we cannot be satisfied with only nonfinancial outcomes. If the nonfinancial results that we achieve are pretty good, but the financial results are not satisfactory, then there is something wrong. We must look at the execution or operational aspects of the company.

Innovative solutions must increase the company's profitability margins. This includes the gross margin, operating margin, net profit margin, and EBITDA (earnings before interest, taxes, depreciation, and amortization) margin. Thus, we must look at our profit-and-loss report or the company's income statement for results. Let's consider how we innovate and the financial impact it can have.

Ways to Innovate

A company can innovate its business model, product, or customer experience.[11] By changing its business model, an organization can secure a stronger position in a business ecosystem. For example, Rolls Royce, which manufactures jet engines, created a pay-by-the-hour subscription service for airlines. By paying a flat hourly rate to Rolls Royce, airlines receive installation, check-ups, maintenance, and decommissioning.[12]

In terms of customer experience, innovation can be delivered through omni-channel, service, brand, and so on. 23andme provides an easy way for individuals who wish to know their DNA and genome tests. Their first service, Ancestry + Traits Personal Genetic Service, helps people understand their true selves in terms of their origins. 23andme sends the package to collect saliva from individuals, and then sends the test results via email. Customers share what they learned through online conversations. People love to know themselves better, and DNA tests, as they claim, are indeed a personal experience.[13]

Not all innovations can be carried out by a company due to limited resources, capabilities, and even competencies. Therefore, many innovations

---

[11]https://www.ideatovalue.com/inno/nickskillicorn/2019/07/ten-types-of-innovation-30-new-case-studies-for-2019/

[12]https://www.linkedin.com/pulse/subscription-economy-did-start-power-by-the-hour-gene-likins

[13]https://www.23andme.com/en-int/; https://www.mobihealthnews.com/news/23andme-heads-public-markets-through-spac-merger-vg-acquisition-corp; https://www.virgin.com/about-virgin/virgin-group/news/23andme-and-virgin-groups-vg-acquisition-corp-successfully-close-business

are also made possible through collaboration with various parties. For example, take N26 banking, LEGO's crowdsourcing, and AXS Lab. N26 Bank collaborates with Transferwise to provide better service in money transfer across the bank, and across the globe.[14] LEGO's crowdsourcing is a winning way for a brand to deliver the most popular products by directly interacting with their customers.[15] AXS Lab, in partnership with PwC, collaborates to deliver a map for disabilities.[16]

The Three Strategic Suitabilities

We need to consider three conformity requirements in applying the entrepreneurial marketing mindset approach to ensure the achievement of innovative solutions.

- **Problem–Solution Fit**

    This customer-centric approach is an essential foundation for applying solution-centric principles. We must understand real customer problems from the customer's perspective. We want to fully understand the customer's problem and then provide the right solutions to the right customers. With the compatibility between the problem and the solution, our products can become the answer customers seek.

- **Product–Market Fit**

    Companies offer a wide-ranging variety of products in a very crowded market. Therefore, the products we offer must be the most appropriate for a specific market segment. We can create the highest perceived value through differentiation, best quality, unforgettable customer experience, and even very competitive prices.

- **Get–Give Fit**

    The greater the product the customer gets in terms of functional and emotional benefits, and the less money they spend to buy and own the product, the more highly preferred the product will be. However, these customer preferences must also create value. So, a company should understand what level of sales it can achieve and at what cost to ensure significant value creation (see Figure 9.5).

---

[14]https://www.retailbankerinternational.com/news/n26-transferwise-expand-alliance-to-support-fund-transfers-in-over-30-currencies

[15]https://open-organization.com/en/2010/04/01/open-innovation-crowdsourcing-and-the-rebirth-of-lego

[16]https://www.pwc.com/us/en/library/case-studies/axs.html

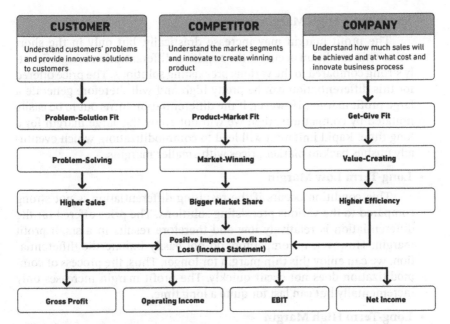

FIGURE 9.5   Impact of strategic suitability on profit and loss

Incremental Versus Drastic Change of Profit Margin

Given that an innovation carried out by a company is already oriented to providing relevant solutions for a customer segment, we must evaluate how strong the differentiation generated by the innovation is, and how hard it is for competitors to imitate. If the differentiation is strong, the company can become a price maker. Conversely, if the differentiation is weak, the company must become a price taker.

In this regard, we can identify four conditions of profit margin that a company can achieve.

- **Short-Term Low Margin**

    This condition occurs if the resulting differentiation is not too significant compared to other solutions that are already available. The price offered for the differentiation is not too high, and therefore it produces only a slight profit margin. In addition, if the differentiation becomes easily imitated by competitors, we will not enjoy the margin for the long term because the imitation will lead to commoditization in a short time. Finally, we have to sell at market prices with increasingly depressed profit margins. So, profit margin may increase incrementally but only in the short term.

- **Short-Term High Margin**

  The profit margin may increase drastically, but only in the short term. This condition occurs if the resulting differentiation is significantly strong compared to the various preexisting solutions. The price offered for this differentiation can be pretty high and will therefore generate a large profit margin. However, if the differentiation turns out to be easily imitated by competitors, then we will not enjoy this large margin for a long time. Rapid imitation will lead to commoditization, which eventually pushes back to market prices with smaller margins.

- **Long-Term Low Margin**

  This condition occurs if the resulting differentiation is not strong compared to the various preexisting solutions. The price offered for the differentiation is relatively low and therefore results in a small profit margin. However, if competitors do not easily imitate the differentiation, we can enjoy this thin margin for longer. Thus, the process of commoditization does not occur quickly. The profit margin increases only incrementally but can last for quite a long time.

- **Long-Term High Margin**

  This condition occurs if the resulting differentiation is significantly strong compared to the various preexisting solutions. The price offered for the differentiation can be pretty high and favorably generates a large profit margin. If competitors do not easily imitate the differentiation, we can enjoy the considerable margin for the long term. The commoditization process does not occur quickly, and profit margins will increase drastically and last for the long run (see Figure 9.6).

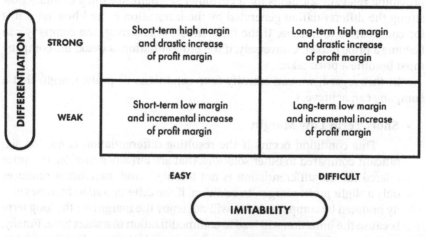

FIGURE 9.6 Incremental versus drastic change of profit margin

Entrepreneurially, we should continue to look for opportunities where we can obtain high margins based on these descriptions. From a marketing perspective, we should create strong differentiation that provides relevant solutions for customers. We'll want the solutions to be difficult for competitors to imitate over the long term.

Reciprocal Relationship of Innovation and Profitability

In the omnihouse model, there is an arrow going back and forth between the elements of innovation and improvement for the depiction of a reciprocal relationship between the two aspects. An innovation produces solutions relevant to customers. At the same time, it is expected to improve the company's profitability margins.

That explains the arrow from innovation to margin improvement. But how about the other way around? Do not let the increase in profitability occur, but put aside investment in innovation capabilities that are in alignment with the company's core competence. On the contrary, the company should allocate more to the budget to maintain or strengthen its innovation capability with a better margin.

Using a study from PwC (The Global Innovation 1000), we can see the company's revenue, R&D expenditures, and R&D intensity (depicted in Figure 9.7 in the form of a bubble), which is the percentage of R&D expenditures to total revenue. We use this data to indicate the commitment level of a company in maintaining its innovation capabilities. We only selected 25 companies from the PwC list, which were also included in the Best Global Brand list released by Interbrand.[17]

From the reprocessed data, there are several exciting points to make. We can divide the 25 companies into three groups. The first group is tech-based companies, the second group is automotive, and the third group is a mixture of companies from different industries, most of which are consumer products.

In the tech-based companies group with revenues below US$200 billion, the R&D intensity is about 10–20% regardless of the total revenue of the companies (see Table 9.1).

---

[17]Data sources are from PwC and Interbrand. This analysis uses Interbrand data for 2018 to be consistent with the year of the study published by PwC.

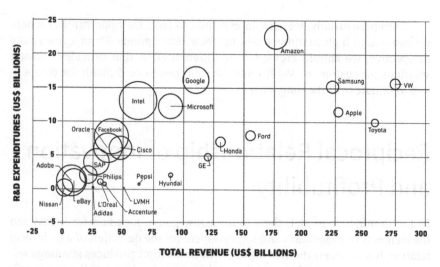

FIGURE 9.7 Revenue, R&D expenditures, and R&D intensity[18]

TABLE 9.1	First Group (Tech-Based Companies) with Revenue Under US$200 Billion[19]		
Company	R&D Expenditures (US$ billions)	Revenue (US$ billions)	R&D Intensity (%)
Intel	13.10	62.76	20.9
Facebook	7.75	40.65	19.1
Adobe	1.22	7.30	16.8
Oracle	6.09	37.73	16.1
Google	16.23	110.86	14.6
SAP	4.02	28.17	14.3
Microsoft	12.29	89.95	13.7
eBay	1.22	9.57	12.8
Amazon	22.62	177.87	12.7
Cisco	6.06	48.01	12.6

[18]Ibid.
[19]Ibid.

In the tech-companies group, only Apple has a relatively low R&D intensity (5.10%) compared to other tech-based companies (see Table 9.2). With an R&D value of almost US$12 billion, it is ranked number 7 out of the 25 selected companies because Apple's revenue exceeded US$200 billion. Samsung, whose revenue is also above US$200 billion—with a broader product range including mobile, TV, and home appliances—has an R&D intensity slightly above Apple, which is 6.8%, but in R&D value, it is ranked fourth with expenditures of more than US$15 billion.

For the automotive group, the R&D intensity ranges from 2% to almost 10% (see Table 9.3). However, we should note that Nissan showed an immense R&D intensity, but was at the bottom of the 25 selected companies in terms of revenue. Even the closest company to Nissan in terms of revenue, namely, Adobe, has more than four times more revenue than Nissan. Excluding Nissan, the R&D intensity of the automotive group averages about 4.5%. The higher the revenue, the higher the R&D expenditures.

TABLE 9.2	First Group (Tech-Companies) with Revenue over US$200 Billion[20]		
Company	R&D Expenditures (US$ billions)	Revenue (US$ billions)	R&D Intensity (%)
Samsung	15.31	224.27	6.8
Apple	11.58	229.23	5.1

TABLE 9.3	Second Group (Automotive)[21]		
Company	R&D Expenditures (US$ billions)	Revenue (US$ billions)	R&D Intensity (%)
Nissan	0.16	1.70	9.6
VW	15.77	277.00	5.7
Honda	7.08	131.81	5.4
Ford	8.00	156.78	5.1
Toyota	10.02	259.85	3.9
Hyundai	2.12	90.22	2.3

[20]Ibid.
[21]Ibid.

TABLE 9.4 Third Group (Various Industries)[22]

Company	R&D Expenditures (US$ billions)	Revenue (US$ billions)	R&D Intensity (%)
Philips	2.12	21.35	9.9
GE	4.80	121.25	4.0
L'Oreal	1.05	31.25	3.4
Accenture	0.70	34.85	2.0
Pepsi	0.74	63.53	1.2
Adidas	0.22	25.48	0.9
LVMH	0.16	51.20	0.3

In the last group, which consists of various companies, the R&D intensity is generally below 5% (see Table 9.4). Only Philips is close to 10%, but we should note that the company's revenue is the smallest in this group.

Of those three groups, there are some interesting takeaways. Generally—apart from the R&D intensity—we can see that the greater a company's revenue, the greater its R&D expenditures. This finding indicates a positive relationship between revenue and budget allocation for innovation. Those companies show their commitment to having a strong innovation capability to maintain competitiveness.

To innovate well, a company will allocate the required resources and direct efforts toward solving customer problems. Through changing how business is done, creating new products that fit a niche, or solving specific issues that are important for customers, revenue and profit margins can increase. A positive relationship between innovation and profitability will support a company's growth and build its competitive edge.

Key Takeaways

- To ensure that the innovations produced are solution-oriented, analyses on customers, competitors, and the company itself can be carried out. Both inward-looking and outward-looking approaches, along with conservative or radical takes, are useful for these assessments.

---

[22]Ibid.

- To innovate, a company can change its business model, product, or customer experience.
- In entrepreneurial marketing, innovative solutions will be evaluated for three conformity requirements: problem–solution fit, product–market fit, and get–give fit.
- Innovations can generate four types of profit margin: short-term low margin, short-term high margin, long-term low margin, and long-term high margin.
- The relationship between innovation and profitability is reciprocal.

CHAPTER 10

Converging Leadership and Management

Maintaining Values and Increasing Market Value

Reed Hastings, the founder of Netflix, set a vision for the company that involves pursuing financial results while also showing concern for environmental issues. To address emissions from its supply chain, Netflix is funding programs that preserve and restore nature's ability to store carbon dioxide. The corporation invests in projects such as worldwide forest protection.[1]

Netflix began as a DVD-by-mail rental service that didn't impose late fees if customers kept a movie for a long time. Customers only had to pay a subscription fee to rent the DVD. The movies they wanted to see were mailed to them, along with a prepaid return envelope.[2]

Over time, Netflix added on-demand streaming services, which proved to be successful. Following Blockbuster's bankruptcy in 2010, Netflix continued to develop rapidly. During the pandemic, Reed capitalized on chances by employing the correct marketing methods and dramatically increasing the number of customers.[3] Netflix brought in 37 million new memberships in 2020 and 18.2 million more subscribers in 2021.

[1]https://about.netflix.com/en/sustainability
[2]https://press.farm/founder-ceo-netflix-reed-hastings-definitive-startup-guide-successful-entrepreneurs/#:~:text=Born%20in%20Boston%2C%20Massachusetts%2C%20Reed,a%20Master's%20in%20artificial%20intelligence
[3]https://www.bbc.com/news/business-60077485

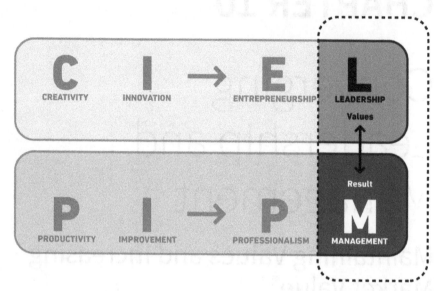

FIGURE 10.1   Leadership and management in the omnihouse model

From the study of Netflix, we learn that leadership is crucial in entrepreneurial marketing. Reed's example shows how he oversaw the firm's beginning and ongoing innovation efforts. The company continued to grow and expand during the pandemic. Its sustainability investments help solidify its commitment to both consumers and the planet's well-being.

Moving from this example to the omnihouse model, we can see that leadership is the rightmost element of the CI-EL elements. We discussed creativity and innovation in previous chapters. We also looked at the shift from professionalism to entrepreneurship. Now we come to the last two elements, namely, leadership, which must be converged with management (see Figure 10.1).

In the following sections, we'll explore the connection between leadership and entrepreneurial marketing. We'll observe the relationship between leadership and management. We'll close by tying in the value components for shareholders and looking at how these can be measured.

Leadership and Entrepreneurial Marketing

Much has been researched and published on the topic of leadership. Literature has discussed in-depth the types of leaders, leadership styles, and characteristics of great leaders. Several theories and models have been developed from the ongoing and broad study of leadership, as well as how leaders and their subordinates interact.[4] Various views about leadership are popular among practitioners and academics, including transformational leadership, situational leadership, and authentic leadership.

One factor often associated with leadership is a vision, or dream, of what an organization will achieve in the future. Leadership is often associated with transforming an organization.[5] This change can encompass monetary and other goals. Daniel Goleman once expressed his opinion that a leader's main task is to achieve results that go beyond the financial aspects.[6]

According to Gallup's 50 years of research, there are five primary roles of great leaders:

- Inspire teams to do exceptional work.
- Set goals and provide resources for teams to excel.
- Influence others to act, pushing through adversity and resistance.
- Build committed and collaborative teams with deep bonds.
- Take an analytical approach to strategy and decision-making.[7]

Discussions are often separated between leadership and entrepreneurship, and leadership with marketing. It can be challenging to find sources that cover the relationship between leadership and entrepreneurial marketing. When the keywords *leadership* and *entrepreneurial marketing* are searched together in scientific journal databases, the results often do not discuss the two together.

Leadership and Entrepreneurship

Ruth Gunther McGrath and Ian MacMillan initially proposed the entrepreneurial leadership concept in 2000. "The world is becoming too volatile and unpredictable to adopt conventional leadership tactics," MacMillan wrote in

[4]Alan Gutterman, *Leadership: A Global Survey of Theory and Research* (August 2017). 10.13140/RG.2.2.35297.40808
[5]To understand further about transformational leadership, please refer to James M. Kouzes and Barry Z. Posner, *The Leadership Challenge: How to Make Extraordinary Things Happen in Organizations*, 6th ed. (Wiley, 2017); Abdullah M. Abu-Tineh, Samer A. Khasawneh, and Aieman A. Al-Omari, "Kouzes and Posner's Transformational Leadership Model in Practice: The Case of Jordanian Schools," *Leadership & Organization Development Journal* 29, no. 8 (2009). https://www.researchgate.net/publication/234094447
[6]Daniel Goleman, "Leadership That Gets Results," *Harvard Business Review* (March–April 2000).
[7]Jim Clifton and Jim Harter, *It's the Manager: Moving From Boss to Coach* (Washington, DC: Gallup Press, 2019).

the book *The Entrepreneurial Mindset.*[8] Examples of how this plays out in business are still being widely discussed.

An individual who applies an entrepreneurial approach in their professional career requires qualified leadership skills. Unfortunately, this leadership ability—from developing a vision, communicating it, setting an example for others, and creating new leaders—is sometimes taken for granted.[9] According to scientific research, the combined influences of nature and nurture play a significant role in leadership development. Data have revealed that environmental impacts have a more substantial effect on people's leadership paths.[10]

Entrepreneurial leadership can have a positive influence on company performance. Strong leadership is defined as the ability to direct the management team in line with company goals and strengthen team morale and confidence, which in turn increases employee engagement and commitment.[11] In this sense, strong entrepreneurial leadership is one of the essential factors for establishing a company's competitive advantage.

Entrepreneurial leadership also plays a vital role in the development of the people in an organization. Data collected from the manufacturing industry in a developing country found that entrepreneurial leadership is positively related to employee creativity.[12] Another study in China found that entrepreneurial leadership can reduce employee turnover.[13] In essence, leadership must be able to build competitive advantage through the development of personnel, including coaching, mentoring, learning-by-doing, and other formal courses.

Leadership and Marketing

Without strong leadership, marketing will only run normatively or by procedure and will not cope with the fast changes triggered by the increasing role of digital technology. We cannot implement marketing based merely on

---

[8]Rita Gunther McGrath and Ian C. MacMillan, *The Entrepreneurial Mindset: Strategies for Continuously Creating Opportunity in an Age of Uncertainty* (Boston, MA: Harvard Business School Press, 2000).

[9]https://www.bdc.ca/en/articles-tools/entrepreneurial-skills/be-effective-leader/7-key-leadership-skills-entrepreneurs

[10]https://www.ccl.org/articles/leading-effectively-articles/are-leaders-born-or-made-perspectives-from-the-executive-suite/

[11]https://www.antoinetteoglethorpe.com/entrepreneurial-leadership-why-is-it-important/

[12]Muhammad Shahid Mehmood, Zhang Jian, Umair Akram, and Adeel Tariq, "Entrepreneurial Leadership: The Key to Develop Creativity in Organizations," *Leadership & Organization Development Journal* (February 2021). DOI:10.1108/LODJ-01–2020–0008

[13]Juan Yang, Zhenzhong Guan, and Bo Pu, "Mediating Influences of Entrepreneurial Leadership on Employee Turnover Intention in Startups," *Social Behavior and Personality: An International Journal* 47, no. 6 (2019): 8117.

a "professional" approach. More than 55% of the business impact achieved by marketing executives is due to leadership factors, and about 15% is due to the contribution of technical marketing skills. Here, we can see that leadership in marketing plays a crucial role in providing value in the form of solutions for customers. It also uses company resources productively to ensure optimal results.[14]

The implementation of marketing strategies also requires strong leadership. Marketing will not function without leadership. The marketing leader's position is growing in importance. This has become increasingly evident during times of uncertainty such as the COVID-19 pandemic. Strong leadership is needed to direct all potential teams within a company to realize a robust customer-centric approach, which will determine the company's market share.[15] By staying focused on these dynamic customers, the leader will direct his team to always be adaptive.[16]

As the responsibilities of marketing leaders expand across a more extensive range of activities, CEOs and CFOs are increasingly inviting them to the executive table. Nearly a third (31.5%) of senior marketers say they participate in earnings calls all or most of the time. More than half (53.5%) say they attend board meetings all or most of the time.[17]

Determining excellent leadership is vital for marketing success, especially in uniting, directing, and motivating the marketing team to move according to the predetermined strategies and tactics. Leadership also has a significant role to play in planning and executing a marketing strategy, which will show financial results and also nonfinancial ones, such as customer loyalty, product leadership, and solid brand equity.[18] Here, we can see the importance of a leader understanding the role of marketing in achieving goals and using the marketing function to ensure growth.[19]

When marketing leaders embrace data and intelligence in the digital era, they become growth leaders. According to a Deloitte survey, 56% of marketers believe that data and intelligence can help them progress their growth plans. By contrast, only 18% perceive that a profound grasp of the product range can help them advance to the next growth stage.[20]

------

[14]https://thomasbarta.com/what-is-marketing-leadership/
[15]https://engageforsuccess.org/strategic-leadership/marketing-strategy/
[16]https://www.forbes.com/sites/steveolenski/2015/01/07/4-traits-of-successful-marketing-leaders/?sh=48796a83fde8
[17]https://deloitte.wsj.com/articles/the-cmo-survey-marketers-rise-to-meet-challenges-01634922527
[18]https://cmox.co/marketing-leadership-top-5-traits-of-the-best-marketing-leaders/
[19]https://www.launchteaminc.com/blog/bid/149575/what-s-the-leader-s-role-in-marketing-success
[20]https://www2.deloitte.com/us/en/pages/chief-marketing-officer/articles/cmo-council-report.html

Leadership and Management

Leadership capabilities in management are crucial, due to rising competition and the increasingly dynamic business environment. The company cannot merely rely on its success on a normative management approach. Management requires a qualified leader, which means having strong leadership. Therefore, companies must devote their attention to ensuring that the leadership capabilities in the company remain relevant for now and in the future.[21]

According to Warren Bennis, leadership is the capacity to translate a vision into reality. We then should translate this vision into several concrete goals. And to achieve these goals, a strategy is needed. We then cascade this strategy into various operational or tactical plans that are more implementable. According to David Garvin, a Harvard Business School professor, properly implementing and executing strategy entails "delivering what's planned or promised on time, on budget, at quality, and with minimal variability—even in the face of unforeseen events and contingencies."[22]

In this new entrepreneurial marketing model, marketing strategy and tactics refer to nine elements held together by positioning, differentiation, and the brand—or the PDB triangle—as their anchors. The nine elements—segmentation, targeting, positioning, differentiation, marketing mix, selling, brand, service, and process—can be grouped into three main marketing management capabilities: customer management, product management, and brand management (see Figure 10.2). The ability to maintain company values in such a way and be able to manifest them in the nine core marketing elements reflects the implementation of leadership.

Management of customers, products, and brands that refer to values is expected for cash flow generation in the short term. It must increase the market value of a brand or company in the future. These are the results that a company should achieve through managing customers, products, and brands.

Customer management, which is part of the marketing strategy, is related to identifying the target market, selecting it, and providing a good customer experience in line with the established positioning. This in turn can lead to customer engagement, the formation of a lock-in mechanism, and strong loyalty. KPMG once surveyed 18,520 customers from more than 20 countries on issues related to customer loyalty. The survey looked at how brands and retailers can attract and retain customer loyalty by improving customer loyalty programs. Per the study, 56% of consumers believe that how companies

[21]https://courses.lumenlearning.com/principlesmanagement/chapter/1–3-leadership-entrepreneurship-and-strategy/
[22]https://online.hbs.edu/blog/post/strategy-implementation-for-managers

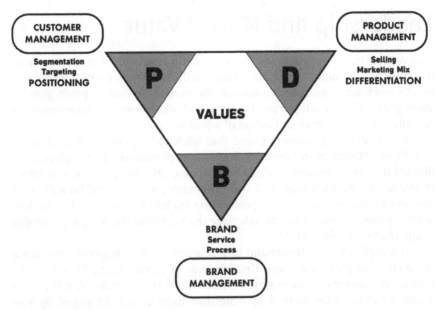

FIGURE 10.2   Values and the PDB triangle

manage their relationships with clients through customer service determines their loyalty.[23]

Product management focuses on managing the product portfolio from development to commercialization for the provision of solutions for the targeted market segment. Included in this is how a level of differentiation will translate into elements of marketing mix tactics followed by sales efforts. When it comes to the importance of a product, in a 2018 Deloitte's holiday shopping habits report, most respondents stated that they look for high-quality items (71%) and product variety (68%).[24]

Brand management ensures the strengthening of brand equity supported by services and processes to enhance customer value. In carrying out effective brand management, we can learn from Apple. Through a branding strategy adept at prioritizing the emotional aspect, Apple has built fanaticism among its customers. Premium services provided through the Apple Store network add customer brand loyalty to its products. In 2021, Apple was considered the most valuable brand worldwide.[25]

---

[23]https://home.kpmg/xx/en/home/insights/2019/11/customer-loyalty-survey.html
[24]https://www2.deloitte.com/content/dam/insights/us/articles/4737_2018-holiday-survey/2018 DeloitteHolidayReportResults.pdf
[25]https://www.statista.com/statistics/264875/brand-value-of-the-25-most-valuable-brands/

Leadership and Market Value

As a capability, we can often see that leadership attached to top management in a company is a qualitative nontechnical skill. Yet the results of top management's work are often assessed quantitatively. The company's profit growth, share price value, employee productivity, and other measures have generally become key performance indicators of a leader.

A 360-degree assessment found that leadership quantitatively makes a significant difference in company financial performance. The leaders were divided into three groups in the study: the top 10% were the best in terms of performance, the lowest 10% were the worst, and the middle 80% were the rest. Consequently, poorest performing leaders lost money. The middle leaders gained money. The top 10% more than doubled the company's profits compared to the other 90%![26]

The application of leadership in a company must adequately oversee a value-creation process to meet the demands of stakeholders. This includes employees, customers, society, and shareholders or investors. The Business Reality Check, commissioned by American Express and developed by The Economist Intelligence Unit, contrasts the perspectives of business leaders with market data gathered from national, international, and specialist data sources. According to the study, 34% of executives believe that shareholder pressure to generate short-term results is a substantial barrier to strategy execution. Moreover, 29% believe that the pressure to be accountable to a larger group of stakeholders is a significant obstacle.[27]

Ulrich and Freed explained that we could no longer determine the value of a company based solely on the traditional approach by exclusively using the financial aspect, which covers only 50% of the company's market value according to their predictions. Investors also consider the intangible value that might be realized because of the vital leadership factor in the company. Therefore, investors need to seriously consider this leadership factor in their decision-making process.[28]

Leadership affects the company's performance by directing, mobilizing, and motivating the management team based on a solid corporate culture. Ouslis's research shows that leadership can contribute to up to 14% of company performance, and CEOs can contribute almost 30% to various

---

[26]https://www.forbes.com/sites/jackzenger/2015/01/15/great-leaders-can-double-profits-research-shows/?sh=3b6094776ca6
[27]https://businessrealities.eiu.com/insights-field-balancing-stakeholder-expectations-requires-communication
[28]https://hbr.org/2015/04/calculating-the-market-value-of-leadership

efforts that can cause differences in company performance. Due to leadership factors, the increase in intangible value has also led to a more significant gap between book value and market value. In recent decades, the gap has become more prominent, and the market value can even reach six times the book value.[29]

According to a research paper published by Deloitte, leadership is an aspect that is still often neglected. Although developing this leadership capability can increase shareholder value and also guarantee long-term sustainability, the percentage of executives who agree that leadership development is very effective is still low. The importance of leadership is in line with Deloitte's findings that analysts consider the senior leadership team effectiveness aspect necessary as a judgment of company success and of more importance than merely looking at the forecast of earnings and ratio analysis. Effective leadership will increase the valuation of a company, but we should note that the effect varies from one industry to another.[30]

Given this description, we can summarize that leadership is essential in executing marketing strategies and tactics through a management process that includes customer, product, and brand management. These are three aspects on the right side of the roof in the omnihouse model. Strong leadership can ensure that all three aspects fully embrace the values—such as honesty, sense of responsibility, commitment to quality, care for the environment, and more—that everyone in a company shares.

Strong leadership is also needed for directing and encouraging the management team to focus on the nine marketing elements included in customer management, product management, and brand management. Strong leadership and support from good management processes for these three aspects will increase the company's market value in the future. This is in line with the increasing intangible value contributed by the leadership (see Figure 10.3).

Good customer management will increase the company's intangible value in terms of stronger customer loyalty. Product management can also expand the company's intangible value through innovative solutions embedded in the products provided to customers. Brand management can strengthen the company's intangible value through higher brand equity.

Management, in the end, must show actual tangible results, both financially and non financially, while maintaining the company's values and culture as well as its social impact. Examples of its application include making

---

[29]https://blog.orgnostic.com/how-can-investors-measure-the-market-value-of-leadership/
[30]https://www2.deloitte.com/content/dam/Deloitte/global/Documents/HumanCapital/dttl-hc-leadershippremium-8092013.pdf

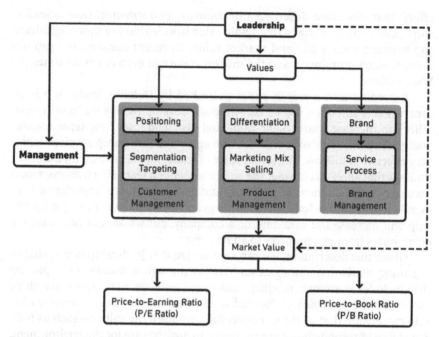

FIGURE 10.3 Leadership and management: From values to market value

an honest profit, ethically increasing the number of customers, expanding the market while paying attention to environmental aspects, and so on.

Leadership means that a person can manifest the company's values in positioning, differentiation, and branding, and then ensure the alignment of those elements with segmentation and targeting, marketing mix and selling, and service and process. Leadership is also related to leading, directing, and motivating the management team as the executor. Therefore, attention to the human aspect is one of the most critical foundations in applying leadership.

A leader must ensure that each member of a team is strongly motivated and mobilizes all their energy and competence to achieve a predetermined goal. Strong leadership will create a positive sentiment that will increase the company's market value in the eyes of investors. We can measure this market value using the price-to-earnings ratio (P/E ratio) and price-to-book ratio (P/B ratio) (see Table 10.1).

By managing three main aspects—namely, customer, product, and brand, which consist of nine core marketing elements—management can ensure that the company's fundamentals are solid. This, in turn, can increase the company's market value, which is very important for acquisition, investment,

TABLE 10.1	Price-to-Earnings Ratio (P/E Ratio) and Price-to-Book Ratio (P/B Ratio)	
	Price-to-Earnings Ratio (P/E Ratio)[31]	**Price-to-Book Ratio (P/B Ratio)**[32]
Definition	Relationship between a company's share or stock price and earnings per share. It calculates (in terms of a ratio) its share or stock price to its earnings per share. The share or stock price is based on the market value.	Relationship between a company's market capitalization (or market value) and the value of its assets. It calculates (in terms of ratio) how the market values a company relative to its book value. The share or stock price is based on the market value.
Formula	$$\frac{Share\ price}{Earnings\ per\ share}$$	$$\frac{Share\ price}{Book\ value\ per\ share}$$
Uses	• To provide a good sense of whether a company's stock or share price is overvalued or undervalued (compared to its earnings) • To provide a basis for comparison or benchmark in a similar industry or a more extensive market (such as S&P Index) • To understand the current market or investors' willingness to pay for shares or stocks by referring to past or future earnings	• To provide a basis for consideration for investors in assessing the potential of an investment • To gauge whether a company is undervalued or overvalued and use it to decide whether an investment in a company can meet the investor's objective or not • To show the market perception of the value of a particular share or stock price or a fair market price for a company

[31]From various sources: Gabriel Hawawini and Claude Viallet, *Finance for Executives* (Mason, OH: Cengage Learning, 2019); https://en.wikipedia.org/wiki/Price%E2%80%93earnings_ratio; https://www.investopedia.com/terms/p/price-earningsratio.asp; https://www.investopedia.com/investing/use-pe-ratio-and-peg-to-tell-stocks-future/; https://www.moneysense.ca/save/investing/what-is-price-to-earnings-ratio/; https://corporatefinanceinstitute.com/resources/knowledge/valuation/price-earnings-ratio/; https://ycharts.com/glossary/terms/pe_ratio; https://www.forbes.com/advisor/investing/what-is-pe-price-earnings-ratio/; https://cleartax.in/s/price-earnings-ratio

[32]From various sources: Gabriel Hawawini and Claude Viallet, *Finance for Executives* (Mason, OH: Cengage Learning, 2019); https://www.investopedia.com/terms/p/price-to-bookratio.asp; https://www.investopedia.com/investing/using-price-to-book-ratio-evaluate-companies/; https://corporatefinanceinstitute.com/resources/knowledge/valuation/market-to-book-ratio-price-book/; https://en.wikipedia.org/wiki/P/B_ratio; https://www.fool.com/investing/how-to-invest/stocks/price-to-book-ratio/; https://groww.in/p/price-to-book-ratio/; https://gocardless.com/en-au/guides/posts/what-is-price-book-ratio/

and even going-public purposes.[33] Market value is also an essential reference for equity investors—private equity, mutual/hedge fund managers, portfolio managers, and venture capitalists—who tend to view the company's value more comprehensively.[34]

Based on the company's current market value or stock price, investors will be able to calculate various ratios as a basis for making investment decisions, such as the price-to-earnings ratio (P/E). This ratio is one of the most used by investors and analysts for determining the stock's relative value. We can use the P/E ratio as a tool to determine if a stock is overvalued or undervalued.[35]

We should note that a leader in a company can consist of more than one person. At every level of the organization there are leaders who are focused on a specific scope of responsibility. They must be able to move the people they lead to achieve a goal that is under their care.

One of the challenges we will face in carrying out a more comprehensive approach to entrepreneurial marketing is how to converge leadership and management. We do not want an over-led but undermanaged condition in a company. This situation is often found in many small- to medium-sized enterprises. We also want to avoid an overmanaged but under-led condition, which can occur in large corporations.

For nearly two decades, Harvard's National Preparedness Leadership Initiative directors Eric J. McNulty and Leonard Marcus have studied and observed public and private sector CEOs in high-stakes and high-pressure scenarios. They've discovered that crises are frequently overmanaged and under-led. Executives must lead and manage effectively in times of crises, which are characterized by both complexity and change. Management's job is to respond to the immediate needs of the moment. Managers must make quick decisions and distribute resources. However, leading entails guiding people to the best potential conclusion across this time horizon.[36]

The relationship between leadership and management is in line with flexibility and rigidity, which has been previously discussed. Leadership often deals with changes or transformations from incremental to radical ones. Management maintains stability and oversees systematic activities.[37]

This idea is also supported by Rita Gunther McGrath, a professor at Columbia Business School. She chose ten corporations from a pool of more than 2,300 significant US companies that improved their net income by at least 5% annually in the ten years leading up to 2009. These high-performing

[33]https://www.forbes.com/sites/martinzwilling/2015/11/03/10-leadership-elements-that-maximize-business-value/?sh=418f3b4568a1
[34]https://www.leaderonomics.com/articles/leadership/market-value-of-leadership
[35]https://www.investopedia.com/terms/p/price-earningsratio.asp
[36]https://hbr.org/2020/03/are-you-leading-through-the-crisis-or-managing-the-response
[37]https://leadershipfreak.blog/2016/04/27/over-led-and-under-managed/

organizations were incredibly stable, with specific organizational traits that remained consistent for long periods. They were also swift innovators, able to quickly transform and readjust their resources.[38]

From our discussion, we can see that leadership cannot stand alone. It must be packaged with qualified management to create a balance that moves the organization through its daily activities and into the future. In addition, entrepreneurial marketing needs to be strengthened with entrepreneurial leadership, as this will strengthen the company's performance. A good combination of leadership and management will positively affect the company's market value in terms of the increasing intangibles, including creating positive sentiment in the eyes of investors. This market value can be seen in various forms, perhaps most notably by calculating the price-to-earnings ratio and price-to-book ratio, which are important indicators for investors.

Key Takeaways

- Leadership is often associated with inspiring and influencing others, having a vision, and guiding a transformation.
- Entrepreneurial leadership can improve a company's performance and drive the development of its people.
- Strong leadership is needed to manage customers, products, and brands.
- Management realizes tangible results in the form of increasing the company's market value through the management of customers, products, and brands.
- Investors will look at aspects related to leadership when evaluating a company; a strong team can help drive market value.

---

[38]Rita Gunther McGrath, "How the Growth Outliers Do It," *Harvard Business Review* (January–February 2012).

CHAPTER 11

Finding and Seizing Opportunities

From Business Outlook to Marketing Architecture

Piyush Gupta, CEO of the Singapore-based DBS Bank, saw significant growth opportunities in Asia by leveraging digital technology. He noticed the younger generation is more digitally savvy. Also, Asian consumers lead the industry in adoption rates of smartphones.

DBS Bank, which provides a full range of financial services in institutional banking, consumer banking, and wealth management, designed a new road map. It invested heavily in technology and undertook radical change to "rewire" the entire organization with digital innovation. It conducted a comprehensive study of emerging technology trends, customer behavior, and technological infrastructure. A team at DBS Bank also visited some of the world's foremost technology companies to acquire valuable insights and learn how to implement best practices in the banking industry.

Based on the findings of the study, DBS Bank's tech infrastructure team changed from 85% outsourcing to 85% insourcing to transform more effectively. It developed a digital business model with five critical capabilities: acquiring, transacting, engaging, ecosystems, and data. With these, it drove business objectives in different segments. In Singapore and Hong Kong, it digitalized rapidly to anticipate challenges. In India and Indonesia, it was the new entrant with Digi Bank, offering an innovative fintech solution.

DBS Bank prepared marketing communication as part of its transformation strategy, with a renewed mission to "Make Banking Joyful" and "Live More, Bank Less." It integrated a perception of simplicity and effortless banking experience with marketing tactics. This campaign encapsulated many factors. DBS Bank intends to enable its customers to live hassle-free with invisible banking, embedding banking in their customer journey, and creating a bank that is ever present for its customers.[1]

DBS Bank strengthened its digital channel by investing in DBS Car Marketplace, the largest direct seller-to-buyer car market in Singapore. It also created DBS Property Marketplace, which connects homeowners and buyers. DBS also invested in Carousell, a platform for buying and selling new or secondhand products, and collaborating with Carousell to offer financial products and payment services on Carousell's platforms.[2]

As a result, investment analysts from Seedly Singapore found that shares of DBS Bank rose about 23%, versus the Straits Times Index (STI), which declined by about 2% in 2020. (STI is an index that measures the 30 largest and most liquid companies listed in Singapore.)[3] DBS Bank received awards such as the Most Innovative in Digital Banking (2021) and Best Bank in the World (2020).[4]

From the DBS Bank case, we learn that consistently understanding a good business environment, determining strategic options, and preparing implementable marketing strategies and tactics up to their execution can affect the competitiveness of the company. We are able to objectively and subjectively measure competitiveness based on multiple financial and nonfinancial indicators.

In previous chapters, we observed the vertical and diagonal interrelationships in the omnihouse model. We will now look at them horizontally. We will discuss the entrepreneurial marketing strategy, which will consist of three parts: the preparation of the strategy itself, the omni capabilities needed to carry out the strategy, and the company's financial management to increase its market value over time.

To do this, we will consider the two roofs in the omnihouse model. These essentially explain that dynamics in a business environment are an essential foundation for the development of a marketing architecture. We can build competitiveness by developing a marketing architecture that will consist of nine core marketing elements (9E) with positioning-differentiation-brand (PDB triangle) as the anchor for those nine marketing elements (see Figure 11.1).

---

[1]https://www.finextra.com/pressarticle/73937/dbs-to-roll-out-live-more-bank-less-rebrand-as-digital-transformation-takes-hold

[2]https://www.dbs.com/newsroom/DBS_invests_in_mobile_and_online_classifieds_marketplace_Carousell

[3]https://blog.seedly.sg/dbs-ocbc-uob-valuations/

[4]https://www.dbs.com/about-us/who-we-are/awards-accolades/2020.page

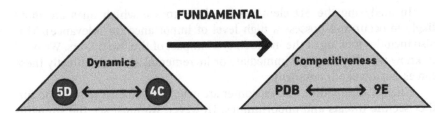

FIGURE 11.1 The dynamics and competitiveness elements in the omnihouse model

From Outlook to Choices

The "dynamics" component consists of five drivers (5D) and—as explained in Chapter 3—includes technology, political/legal, economic, social/cultural, and markets where they are influenced by each other. We refer to these five drivers collectively as *change*. Together with three other elements—namely, competitor, customer, and company—they are all part of the 4Cs (see Figure 11.2).

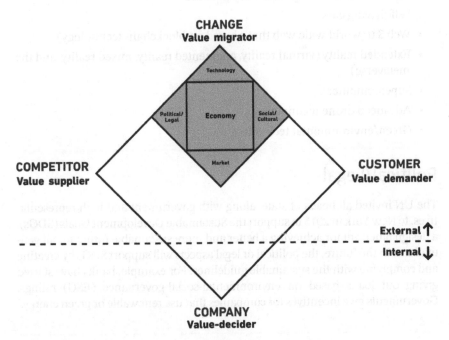

FIGURE 11.2 External and internal sections of the 4C model

In analyzing the 5D elements, we have to see which ones are more likely to occur and possess a high level of importance (or relevance). This also includes looking at the immediacy of impact of the five drivers. We need to know whether they are immediate or incremental and how directly these forces can affect our company.

Change, competitor, and customer are external elements required to further see the threats and opportunities. However, we must see the strengths and weaknesses in the company internally.

Technology

We must see various factors of change originating from the rapid growth of technology, digital advances, and online presence. As mentioned, technological advances are one of the strongest drivers and quickly affect the recent changes in the business environment. Here are ten up-and-coming technologies that are on pace to be mainstream by 2030:

- Advanced robotics
- Sensors and the Internet of Things (IoT)
- 3D printing
- Plant-based and lab-grown dairy products
- Self-driving cars
- Web 3.0 (world wide web that's based on blockchain technology)
- Extended reality (virtual reality, augmented reality, mixed reality, and the metaverse)
- Supercomputer
- Advanced drone technology
- Green/environmental technology

Political/Legal

The UN invited all heads of state, along with government and high representatives, to New York in 2015 to support the Sustainable Development Goals (SDGs), a design blueprint for achieving a better and more sustainable future for all generations. In the future, the political or legal aspects will support SDGs by creating and complying with the sustainable guidelines. For example, banks have started giving out loans based on environmental-social-governance (ESG) ratings. Governments give incentives for companies that use renewable or green energy.[5]

---

[5]https://sdgs.un.org/2030agenda

Economy

The rise of the sharing economy (e.g., content creator, driver ridesharing, and online shop seller), opportunities for remote jobs, and a freelance marketplace has led some professionals to leave behind a 9-to-5 environment. Instead, they are opting for the flexibility offered through the gig economy. The UK government defines the gig economy "as an exchange of activity and money between individuals or companies via a digital channel which actively facilitates matching between vendors and customers, on a short-term and payment-by-task basis."[6]

A gig economy switches the traditional economy of full-time workers, who often focus on their career development, into contract-based workers. In 2017, an estimated 55 million Americans in the workforce were part of the gig economy, or 36% of the workforce.[7] By 2030, American gig workers are forecasted to make up 50% of the entire workforce.[8]

Recently, we have noticed the rise of a circular economy that applies three principles: eliminating waste and pollution, circulating products and materials (at their best value), and regenerating nature. This approach will no doubt positively affect business, people, and the environment. It would also solve global challenges related to biodiversity, waste, climate change, and pollution.[9]

The circular economy will encourage companies to transform their business models as part of their social responsibility to create a better future.[10] According to Accenture, this circular economy is expected to generate an additional US$4.5 trillion in economic output by 2030. The International Labor Organization also projects that 18 million new jobs will be created that year.[11]

Social/Cultural

Activity on social media platforms such as Instagram and TikTok continues to gain traction among users. Virtual reality with the metaverse is the next step

[6]World Economic Forum, "What Is the Gig Economy and What's the Deal for Gig Workers?" (May 26, 2022). https://www.weforum.org/agenda/2021/05/what-gig-economy-workers/
[7]https://www.entrepreneur.com/article/381850
[8]https://www.northbaybusinessjournal.com/article/opinion/outlook-for-the-gig-economy-freelancers-could-grow-to-50-by-2030/
[9]https://ellenmacarthurfoundation.org/topics/circular-economy-introduction/overview
[10]https://www.dnv.com/power-renewables/publications/podcasts/pc-the-rise-of-the-circular-economy.html
[11]https://wasteadvantagemag.com/the-rise-of-the-circular-economy-and-what-it-means-for-your-home/#:~:text=The%20Rise%20Of%20The%20Circular%20Economy%20and%20What%20It%20Means%20For%20Your%20Home,-July%202024%2C%202019&text=According%20to%20research%20by%20Accenture,new%20jobs%20by%20then%20too

in the evolution of social networks and will change how individuals interact. These trends open possibilities for a new culture that has not yet been explored.[12]

Another social and cultural change lies in plant-based food. The University of Oxford and London School of Hygiene & Tropical Medicine reported that surveys from more than 15,000 individuals were analyzed using consumption data from the National Diet and Nutrition Survey 2008–2019. The research found that the proportion of people who reported eating and drinking plant-based alternatives such as plant-based milk (e.g., oat, soy, or coconut), vegan sausages, and vegetable burgers almost doubled from 6.7% in 2008–2011 to 13.1% in 2017–2019.[13]

Market

Amid the fourth industrial revolution, market mechanisms are influenced by technology, global connectivity, and ambitious global goals—such as the Sustainable Development Goals by 2030. Some industries are disrupted already and have started designing digital transformation road maps by embracing technology and supporting the SDGs to be adaptive.[14] For example:

- The automotive industry has developed autonomous electric vehicles to achieve SDG number seven: affordable and clean energy.
- The hospital industry builds telemedicine to achieve SDG number three: good health, well-being, and reaching more people.
- The retail and fashion industry started developing renewable or sustainable materials using recycled content to achieve SDG number twelve: responsible consumption and production.[15]

Changes in the five drivers, which we collectively call *change*, can cause the value proposition we offer to suddenly become obsolete. Therefore, we often refer to change as a value migrator of our products. It can even devaluate the company.

Competitor

On average, companies spend 7–12% of revenue on marketing. Some players spend more, including those in the electronic industry such as Samsung,

[12]https://www.forbes.com/sites/forbesagencycouncil/2021/12/21/what-is-the-metaverse-and-how-will-it-change-the-online-experience/?sh=21a761f52f32
[13]https://www.newfoodmagazine.com/news/158831/plant-based-consumption-uk/
[14]https://www.weforum.org/agenda/2019/09/technology-global-goals-sustainable-development-sdgs/
[15]https://www.fastcompany.com/1672435/nike-accelerates-10-materials-of-the-future

Sony, and Apple. Others budget less, such as Xiaomi Corporation, a Chinese electronic company founded in April 2010. Xiaomi reduced costs by selling through its online channel in the beginning.[16] Its cost leadership model can create affordable products with high-quality specs that make customers love their product. In 2022, Xiaomi was in the top three of global smartphone leaders, beating Sony, LG, and Nokia.[17]

In addition, we have to understand the sources of advantages competitors have, including their resources and capabilities in leveraging those resources. We need to pay attention to the extent to which they have dynamic capabilities, which are the basis for building strong corporate agility. The more unique the resources and capabilities are, the more likely our competitors will form distinctive competencies.

Xiaomi uses unusual marketing in the electronic industry. It creates unique resources called Mi Fans, a huge fan base that engages millions of people worldwide in social media. They invite some fans to watch the new launch of any new product. This strategy gives Xiaomi the dynamic capability to increase sales by relying on advocacy from Mi Fans and keep R&D costs down by getting feedback from customers about bugs and unique ideas.[18]

The number of players in an industry will also determine the level of competition. This will also be determined by the extent to which our competitors can formulate and effectively execute creative strategies. Competitors provide multiple values in response to changes to meet what customers want. Therefore, we may refer to our competitors as value suppliers. If the proposition they offer is valued higher than what we offer in the market, then our customers will likely shift to one of our competitors.

After Xiaomi was quite successful in the smartphone market, some competitors such as Oppo, Vivo, and Realme joined the competition with a similar value proposition and affordable products with high-quality specifications. Oppo and Vivo use advertising and a brand ambassador strategy[19] with campaigns aggressively about "Best Mobile Photography" to grab Xiaomi's market share. In the end, Xiaomi didn't compete with that campaign but focused on building the MiOT Ecosystem to differentiate from competitors.

Customer

We must continuously pay attention to what is happening with our customers, whether these are new or have been with our company for years. We need to

[16]https://www.themarcomavenue.com/blog/how-xiaomi-is-dominating-the-global-smartphone-market/

[17]https://gs.statcounter.com/vendor-market-share/mobile

[18]https://www.themarcomavenue.com/blog/how-xiaomi-is-dominating-the-global-smartphone-market/

[19]https://www.quora.com/Why-are-Oppo-and-Vivo-spending-so-much-on-advertising

monitor if they switch or defect to other competitors. We also have to measure the level of satisfaction and loyalty from our existing customers.

Generation Z (iGen, or a centennial) is associated with those born between 1997 and 2012. These individuals have been raised with an internet network, social media, and smartphones. They tend to be more financially pragmatic and risk-averse. Like Gen Y, Gen Z cares about social causes, corporate responsibility, and being environmentally friendly. Moreover, Gen Z has different values from other generations. They have YOLO, FOMO, and JOMO:[20]

- **You only live once (YOLO).** The present is the only time for them to live life to the fullest. Gen Z will invest and pursue what they love, such as learning a new language, or backpacking across Europe or Africa. For this generation, we might hear, "Life is short; let's buy the bag!"

- **Fear of missing out (FOMO).** The fear or regret of not being part of an activity or something that others are experiencing. Gen Z will buy what their friends or circle have, take a picture at some famous places to be part of society, or exit their current job to pursue their dream.

- **Joy of missing out (JOMO).** They have already experienced FOMO and YOLO. Now they have realized that the answer is JOMO. They do not get involved in certain activities, especially those related to social media or entertainment. They also do not like to compare or compete, and they believe that the source of happiness is from their lives and work.

We must understand how this generation views us. Do they appreciate our value propositions? Do they feel engaged and excited with our various communication efforts? What questions do they often ask, and do they indicate a doubt?

We have to understand the new customer paths in this digital era. In the beginning, customers perhaps will watch advertising on TV or social media ads ("aware" stage). Good advertising will draw the customer's attention to click or explore more information from a website ("appeal" stage). Furthermore, customers can ask friends about their experience or reach out to sales representatives ("ask" stage). If a high value is perceived from the product, they can come to the store and shop or check-out from e-commerce ("act" stage). Finally, customers can evaluate their product quality and share their experience through social media or their circle ("advocate" stage).[21]

Companies must deal with customers looking for better service, personalization, speed, and a streamlined buying process wherever and whenever they want. Among consumers, 71% make purchases online and search their

---

[20]https://www.livemint.com/news/business-of-life/yolo-fomo-jomo-why-gens-y-and-z-quit-1567429692504.html
[21]Philip Kotler, Hermawan Kartajaya, and Iwan Setiawan, *Marketing 4.0: Moving from Traditional to Digital* (Hoboken, NJ: Wiley, 2017).

devices to find the best prices, and 77% of digital consumers expect a personalized experience in their digital purchases. Therefore, a company cannot rely on a product-centric approach anymore; rather, it should become a customer-centric organization.[22]

Company

Every company has internal challenges and advantages. These are often analyzed with the external factors to make a strategic choice. External and internal analysis is what we usually know as TOWS analysis.[23] (Though it is commonly called a SWOT analysis—strengths, weaknesses, opportunities, and threats—we refer to it here as TOWS to emphasize that the spirit is more outward-looking or external-oriented, than inward-looking or internal-oriented.)

Regarding this, we must further investigate three factors in our company:

- **Existing competencies.** What competencies do we have now, and what resources and capabilities can shape these competencies? We have to see if these competencies will remain relevant in the long term. We also have to determine whether these competencies are indeed distinctive. Distinctive competence is defined as a set of unique characteristics that organizations have that enables them to break into desired markets and gain an advantage over winning the competition. A company can develop its distinctive competence in several ways:[24]

  - Produce a high-quality product with specific expertise
  - Hire skilled specialists
  - Discover untapped market niches
  - Be innovative or achieve a competitive advantage through sheer management power
  - Excel at technology, research and development, or have a faster product life cycle
  - Have low-cost production or good customer service

- **Stretch possibilities.** Is the extent to which we can use competence further than what we have managed to do so far? We must explore various options to leverage the competencies that we already have so as to multiply value-creation efforts that are not limited to achieving economies of scale but can also increase economies of scope.

---

[22]https://egade.tec.mx/en/egade-ideas/research/experience-demanding-customer
[23]Here we use the abbreviation *TOWS* instead of *SWOT* just to show that the spirit is more outward-looking (external-oriented) instead of inward-looking (internal-oriented).
[24]https://www.referenceforbusiness.com/encyclopedia/Dev-Eco/Distinctive-Competence.html

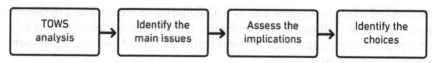

FIGURE 11.3 From TOWS analysis to choices

- **Risk attitude.** What is our perspective in the decision-making process? We may overestimate the various risks that exist and eventually become risk avoiders. Or we may take risks, provided we have calculated these risks. This strategy is called being a risk-taker and differs from a risk seeker, who takes risks, even if they are minor, with no calculation.

After we do the 4C analysis, we must identify what the key issues are and will be. These are determined based on the helicopter view of the TOWS analysis that we have done (see Figure 11.3). We should not be forced to solve each of the problems seen in the TOWS analysis one by one. After we have identified the key issues, we must analyze the extent of the implications for our company. Based on the various implications we discover, we determine our choice to go forward or not.

We can have several strategic choices or intent: the option to invest various resources and efforts to be more competitive, no-go or hold back, harvest, or divest and withdraw or get out of the competition.[25] The choice depends on the available resources and our capability to convert those resources into competency to form a competitive advantage. We can further analyze our resources and capabilities using the VRIO analysis approach (VRIO stands for valuable, rare, inimitable, and organization-wide supported).[26] The fewer the resources that meet the VRIO criteria, the weaker the competitive advantage we can form. If we can fulfill some of the VRIO criteria, then we can create a temporary competitive advantage. We will likely build a sustainable competitive advantage if we can satisfy the VRIO criteria completely.[27]

For example, IKEA offers modular furniture at affordable prices that enables faster assembly, easier maintenance, and improved product longevity over competitors. Customers can replace or add parts through this concept rather than purchase a whole new piece of furniture. If we analyze IKEA using the VRIO framework (see Figure 11.4), we see that this modular design helps IKEA build its competitiveness.[28]

---

[25]The term *strategic intent* was first coined out by Gary Hamel and C. K. Prahalad in the late 1980s.

[26]This VRIO framework was developed by Jay Barney in 1991.

[27]Refer to Jay B. Barney; https://thinkinsights.net/strategy/vrio-framework/

[28]https://www.designnews.com/design-hardware-software/what-can-design-engineers-learn-ikea

Valuable	IKEA provides affordable furniture material enhanced with modular design technology.
Rare	While the competitor creates the whole piece of furniture, IKEA creates a modular design for customers to replace and add furniture parts.
Inimitable	Competitors can also create modular designs, but the parts will not match IKEA products. Competitors cannot imitate because IKEA has a design law/legal patent. Therefore the customer must purchase replacement or additional parts only from IKEA, which functions as a customer lock-in mechanism.
Organization	Many experienced product designers support IKEA.

FIGURE 11.4   Simple VRIO analysis of IKEA

Based on this analysis, we see that IKEA has a great opportunity to sustain its competitive advantage. It strongly fulfills the four VRIO criteria. IKEA can be confident with its vision and mission going forward.

However, if we decide to invest, and there is a gap between what we want to achieve and our choice, then we must try to cover the gap. We might do this by collaborating with other parties in a business ecosystem. If necessary, we can even do coopetition with our direct competitors.

Translating Choice into Marketing Architecture

Once the choice to invest has been made, the marketing architecture needs to be set, which we will describe next. We will then look at each of its components: strategies, tactics, and values (see Figure 11.5).

Marketing Strategy

In the mainstream marketing approach, marketing strategy consists of segmentation, targeting, and positioning (STP). We call it strategy because—in the process of segmentation and targeting in particular—after we have succeeded in mapping out a market into several segments, the next step is to decide which segments we will serve and which ones we will not serve.

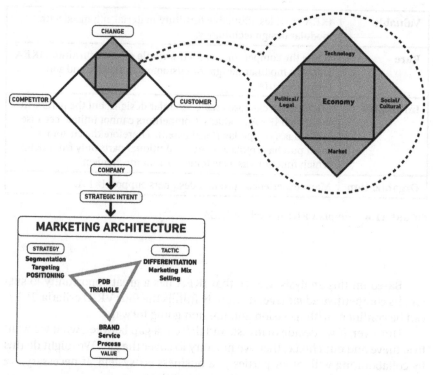

FIGURE 11.5   From outlook to marketing architecture

In developing this concept of marketing, there have been several shifts. One approach is called new wave marketing. It is related to segmentation, targeting, and positioning as shown here.[29]

- **From Segmentation to Communitization**

    We can no longer do segmentation by referring to a static approach, namely, seeing customers as individuals when there is the undeniable fact that customers are social creatures. We are familiar with segmentation using geographic, demographic, psychographic, and behavioral variables, but now we have to strengthen it by including the customer's purpose, values, and identity (PVI) in the segmentation process.

    We cannot see the relationship between the company and the customer only vertically, where we put the customer as the passive target segment. We should also consider a more horizontal approach in which the customer is an active community member. In addition, we must fur-

[29]Several shifts in marketing concepts (so-called new wave marketing) are discussed in Philip Kotler, Hermawan Kartajaya, and Den Huan Hooi, *Marketing for Competitiveness: Asia to the World!* (Singapore: World Scientific, 2017).

ther strengthen customer mapping based on similarities by assessing the community's potential on cohesiveness and influence.

- **From Targeting to Confirmation**

Targeting initially considers how the company devotes its resources to several segments. It considers the size of the segment, its growth rate, competitive advantage, and competitive situation. On top of that, we need further confirmation by looking at three additional criteria: relevance, level of activity, and the total number of community networks (NCNs).

Relevance will refer to the extent of the PVI similarities between a community and our brand. In addition, we must pay attention to how actively community members engage with one another. Rather than a list of names, we have to look at the level of participation from community members in various activities. We must also pay attention to NCNs, namely, the extent to which the community network reaches. This is not limited to its community network but includes parties outside the community across other networks.

- **From Positioning to Clarification**

In line with the rise of customer bargaining power, the effectiveness of the one-sided positioning approach determined by the company is decreasing. Usually, we will develop a positioning statement containing several main elements: the target market, brand, frame of reference, point of differentiation, and reasons to believe. The positioning statement is generally the basis for developing the tagline. However, this kind of emphasis on the positioning is now insufficient. We need a new approach that will clarify for customers to avoid overpromised but, in fact, under-delivered phenomenon.

We are shifting from company-oriented content to customer-oriented content. Positioning, which used to be an attempt to convey a single message, has now involved multidimensional messages. In addition, we must communicate with more than a one-way approach; we must use multiple-way communications.

This marketing strategy is the basis for implementing customer management where we must pay attention to four points related to customers:[30]

- **Get.** Actively seek out potential customers and make them become our customers.
- **Keep.** Build customer loyalty with customer loyalty programs or by creating a solid lock-in mechanism.

---

[30]The get, keep, and grow activities (excluding win back) refer to Steve Blank and Bob Dorf, *The Start-Up Manual: The Step-by-Step Guide for Building a Great Company* (Hoboken, NJ: Wiley, 2020), Figure 3.10 and Table 3.3.

- **Grow.** Add value through cross-sell and upsell so that we are not only pursuing economies of scale but also economies of scope.
- **Win back.** Recapture relevant and significant contributing customers who switched to our competitors.

Marketing Tactic

In the classical marketing concept, tactics consist of three elements: differentiation, marketing mix, and selling. These three elements translate the STP elements into a concrete form. We need to define differentiation in line with positioning, and then translate that differentiation into a marketing mix consisting of product, price, place, and promotion. After that, we must convert what we offer to the market into sales, which are part of our company's selling efforts.

Similar to the STP elements, these three tactical elements have also shifted with today's era of increasingly complex and complicated customers.

- **From Differentiation to Codification**

    The differentiation that has been created so far through content differentiation (what to offer), context differentiation (how to offer), and other enablers (such as aspects of technology, facility, and people) is no longer sufficient. It is limited to only the marketers' point of view. This approach is purely a matter of the marketing department's job. It does not often refer to the organizational culture, which can be the DNA of a brand.

    Therefore, the marketing team must be able to codify the company's DNA to be used as brand DNA. This brand DNA—which refers to symbols and styles, system and leadership, and shared values and substance—must be understood, internalized, and thoughtfully applied by all employees.

- **From Marketing Mix to New Wave Marketing Mix**

    The traditional marketing mix elements also experienced a shift: from product to co-creation, from price to currency, from place to communal activation, and from promotion to the conversation.

    A company is often trapped in a company-centric approach during the new product development stage. From the initial ideation to the realization of a product, the company's role dominates. Customers tend to be passive and can give their opinion only on a product. Now companies must provide opportunities and involve customers in the development of a product. Customers can become co-creators.

    The place element—part of a distribution or marketing channel—is usually a physical platform where people can get products and their supporting services. With the alternative of online distribution, the physical platform becomes unattractive if it only functions for the acquisition of goods or services. Therefore, we must transform this element into a real-world platform for communities to meet and share ideas or experiences. Physical space is essential for strengthening the relationship of a community. The success of this communal activation depends on how a company can effectively combine online and offline approaches.

- **From Selling to Commercialization**

    The traditional selling approach is still needed, but commercialization must now support it by optimizing social networks to get new customers and retain existing ones. The combination of offline and online approaches provides many conveniences for salespeople to build a strong network. The increasing number of customers who use social media makes them more willing to listen to the opinions of others as part of their decision-making process. Commercialization is how we can use these social networks effectively and efficiently to support their sales process.

Marketing Value

The last group of marketing values includes brand, service, and process. A brand is the value indicator that requires service as a value enhancer and process as a value enabler.

In the marketing value section, there are also some shifts to be recognized.

- **From Brand to Character**

    As an identity, we need the brand to form a relationship with its customers. It must provide a functional and emotional benefit. However, there is increasing difficulty in creating customer trust in brands as a company requires us to adopt an approach that emphasizes brand-as-person identity.[31]

- **From Service to Care**

    Despite the rapid development of technology, we can see a paradox. Customers are becoming more human. That is why human-to-human interactions are still more critical than machine-to-human interactions that are technology-based and tend to be mechanistic. In line with that, we cannot serve customers based on a reactive mechanistic approach but must be proactive and humanistic to show that we care. The era of customer service has long ended and been replaced by customer care.

- **From Process to Collaboration**

    The process is an essential part of value creation in a company, from procurement of raw materials to delivering a product to the customers. Companies must manage various processes in the value chain to ensure that everything runs effectively and efficiently. To do this, three indicators are often used as benchmarks: quality, cost, and delivery.

---

[31]David A. Aaker, *Building Strong Brands* (New York, NY: Free Press, 1995).

This marketing value section emphasizes the increasing importance of the brand-as-human approach. Therefore, companies must have highly functioning brand management capabilities.

The Positioning-Differentiation-Brand Triangle

Three main elements integrate the nine core elements of marketing, namely positioning, differentiation, and the brand. This is called the PDB triangle (see Figure 11.6). Positioning is a promise related to the value that a brand will deliver to its customers and is the core of marketing strategy. Differentiation is an effort by a company to understand aspects of products and services relevant to keeping customers satisfied and loyal. Differentiation is the core of marketing tactics. The brand is the core of marketing value.

As an identity, the brand must have a clear positioning. Positioning, a promise to customers, must be realized through strong differentiation to form brand integrity. If we can consistently maintain this differentiation, it will create a strong brand image.

Circling back to the beginning case about DBS Bank in Asia, we can learn that Gupta, the CEO, analyzes macroeconomics to spot opportunities using digital technology and the potential from focusing on the younger generation.

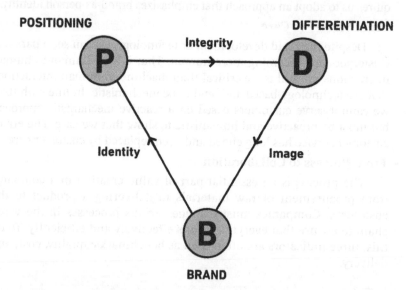

FIGURE 11.6   The PDB triangle

He defines three segments, and each has a different marketing objective. Developing countries (such as Indonesia and India) attract potential users with DigiBank. The rest of the segment reduces cost by implementing technology in its operation. Singapore and Hong Kong's market focus is to self-disrupt and become defensive from the moves of their competitors.

DBS Bank builds its clear positioning based on simplicity and an effortless banking experience. Technology as the core of differentiation supports the positioning and provides the integrity of the brand promise. DBS Bank builds a positive brand image through marketing communication and making sure to fulfill the brand promise. All three elements of DBS Bank's PDB triangle need to be consistent and support one another.

Based on our discussion, we can observe that the preparation of strategy must be consistent and cover all aspects to take advantage of the existing opportunities and create a competitive advantage. Once we understand the landscape, we can choose if we want to move forward into a marketing architecture that consists of strategy, tactics, and value. Finally, the PDB triangle is an anchor for the nine core marketing elements. We must ensure that each element in the PDB triangle can support and be consistent with one another, so that the brand has a strong identity, integrity, and image.

Key Takeaways

- Analyzing the 5D elements (technology, political/legal, economic, social/cultural, and markets) enables us to see which are most likely to occur and are relevant.
- Looking at change, competitors, customers, and the company itself enables us to see strengths and weaknesses, along with threats and opportunities.
- Marketing strategy is moving from segmentation to communitization, from targeting to confirmation, and from positioning to clarification.
- Changes in the marketing tactic include from differentiation to codification, from marketing mix to new wave marketing-mix, and from selling to commercialization.
- In marketing value, there are several shifts to recognize: from brand to character, from service to care, and from process to collaboration.

CHAPTER 12

Building Omni Capabilities

From Preparation to Execution

Shopee, a marketplace built by a Singapore-based company, started out as a team of ten young people in 2015. It grew to 700 people in 2019 and expanded its business activities to places such as Vietnam and Indonesia. This massive expansion pushed Shopee to attract talent to fill managerial, operational, and creative posts.

Shopee faced several challenges in recruiting talent. It had to explain the corporate culture; convince young, fresh talent to build a company with a volatile business landscape; and attract senior talent to establish itself as a professionally run organization.

To tackle these challenges, Shopee created several pathways. First, it communicated its vision, mission, and goals in its online presence. Second, Shopee hosted regular onboarding meetings for newcomers to help them adapt to the fast-paced working environment. Third, Shopee built their "Life at Shopee" page on LinkedIn to show their daily activities and share perspectives on their business moves (such as "Why 9.9 Shopping is important to Shopee").

Now, once the talent market understood Shopee as a company, they could search for an available position. Shopee put the technical details in their vacancies, such as talent officer, legal, finance, creative design, product manager, and employer branding associate. To date, Shopee has 37,774 team members globally and its e-commerce app is currently available in 13 countries, including Mexico and Chile.[1]

---

[1] https://hrmasia.com/talent-search-shopee/; https://www.linkedin.com/company/shopee/about/; https://careers.shopee.co.id/; https://careers.shopee.co.id/job-detail/6078; https://medium.com/shopee/the-role-of-brand-design-in-cultivating-a-powerful-employer-brand-6bc574143bca; https://www.reuters.com/article/us-sea-mexico-idUSKBN2AM2BS

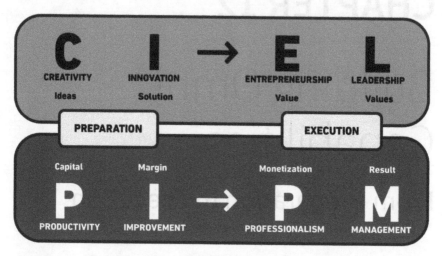

FIGURE 12.1 Horizontal relationship of CI-EL and PI-PM elements

The Shopee case shows that a company can no longer rely solely on one or two capabilities. It must build several capabilities and leverage them simultaneously for rapid expansion. Converging, balancing, and leveraging those capabilities aligns with the idea of building omni capabilities. This—in addition to referring to the name of the primary model that we use—means an organization has all the necessary capabilities and can use them in value-creation processes to shape powerful competitiveness. Therefore, we need to include people who have these capabilities, shape them, and keep them in our organization.

In the following discussion of the omnihouse model, we will look horizontally at the elements of CI-EL and PI-PM (see Figure 12.1). We will explore the omni capabilities needed to carry out the strategy.

Preparation and Execution

We have the "preparation" section (which includes CI and PI elements) on the left section of the omnihouse model and the "execution" section on the right side (which includes EL and PM elements) (see Figure 12.2).

We can see the summary of what we have to do in the preparation section in Figure 12.3.

And, Figure 12.4 shows what we have to do in the execution section.

A company that wants to be successful must identify what capabilities are required for its operational, managerial, or strategic positions. After that, the firm should invite talent with different capabilities and competencies to join and carry out an integrated value-creation process with maximum results.

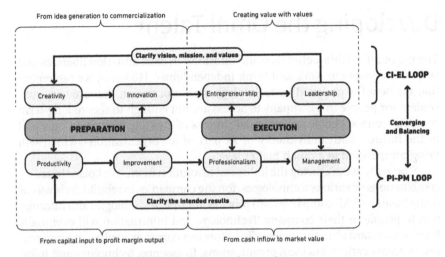

FIGURE 12.2   Framework of preparation and execution

CREATIVITY	Follow all developments and understand the driver elements that serve as references or triggers for creativity. Then prepare technically feasible creative ideas based on several customer problems the company should solve while also referring to the company's strategic intent.	From idea generation to commercialization
INNOVATION	Understand the four elements consisting of change, competitor, customer, and company, then prepare concrete forms of various market-winning products with several supporting services that are problem-solving in the eyes of customers and value-creating for the company.	
PRODUCTIVITY	Prepare sufficient and relevant capital that can be traced in the company's asset records in the balance sheet to support the creative process optimally. In addition, the company must prepare various methods to calculate the productivity regarding that capital.	From capital input to profit margin of output
IMPROVEMENT	Prepare various processes to detect, identify, and improve multiple operations to reduce profit margins for further innovation. We must trace the profit margin improvement in the company's income statement.	

FIGURE 12.3   Summary of the preparation section

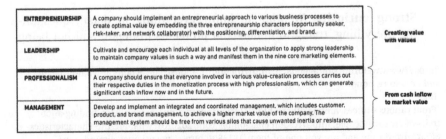

ENTREPRENEURSHIP	A company should implement an entrepreneurial approach to various business processes to create optimal value by embedding the three entrepreneurship characters (opportunity seeker, risk-taker, and network collaborator) with the positioning, differentiation, and brand.	Creating value with values
LEADERSHIP	Cultivate and encourage each individual at all levels of the organization to apply strong leadership to maintain company values in such a way and manifest them in the nine core marketing elements.	
PROFESSIONALISM	A company should ensure that everyone involved in various value-creation processes carries out their respective duties in the monetization process with high professionalism, which can generate significant cash inflow now and in the future.	From cash inflow to market value
MANAGEMENT	Develop and implement an integrated and coordinated management, which includes customer, product, and brand management, to achieve a higher market value of the company. The management system should be free from various silos that cause unwanted inertia or resistance.	

FIGURE 12.4   Summary of the execution section

Developing the Omni Talent

The use of affordable technology and information dissemination liberates and empowers people to work and think independently. However, we remember that the benefits provided by technology and information that are very convenient for people in a company to access are not enough to secure long-term competitiveness. People are potential sources of creating disruption now and in the future—both individually or as part of an organization—which will bring competition to a much higher level.

Currently, we are facing the industrial revolution in the workplace based on combinations of various technologies, forcing companies to rebuild their way of doing business.[2] All companies will provide multiple technologies and information to people in their company. Technology and information will eventually become standard elements or generic factors in a company's value-creation processes across various business organizations. In essence, technology and information are necessary but insufficient for creating long-term competitiveness.

The critical factor distinguishing between competitive and noncompetitive companies lies in how the company recruits, develops, and retains talented people. In the current fourth industrial revolution era, many senior executives and business leaders in an organization should understand the challenges the business operations team faces in the changing environment due to technological advancement.[3] Companies especially need people who understand how to leverage various technologies and have the skills to analyze information and interpret it well to be used as a strong basis in the decision-making process. This situation will force companies to abandon conventional staffing approaches and shift to more sophisticated methods that focus on acquiring and developing talented people.

Building Creative Capability

What is the character of the people we call creative whom we should involve in our business processes? Here are some traits to consider:[4]

Strong curiosity. Wanting to know everything in detail, questioning everything, trying to understand problems in-depth, and not being

---

[2]https://www.weforum.org/agenda/2016/01/the-fourth-industrial-revolution-what-it-means-and-how-to-respond/

[3]Ibid.

[4]From various sources, among others: https://www.indeed.com/career-advice/finding-a-job/traits-of-creative-people; http://resourcemagonline.com/2020/01/what-are-the-characteristics-of-creative-people-and-are-you-one-of-them/181380/; https://www.verywellmind.com/characteristics-of-creative-people-2795488; https://www.tutorialspoint.com/creative_problem_solving/creative_problem_solving_qualities.htm; https://thesecondprinciple.com/understanding-creativity/creativetraits/

satisfied with what they already know. Curiosity is a gray area of human knowledge. It is about getting to learn more about something outside our expertise.[5]

Open-minded. Able to quickly understand reasons and be ready to argue, dare to test diverse opinions, try all possibilities, share adjustments, and be prepared to fail but immediately look for replacement ideas. This includes being flexible, objective, and collaborative.

Fun to work with. Communicative, uses language that is easy to understand, can express thoughts clearly, treats others as horizontal partners. Attitude tends to be playful, energetic, and passionate.

Out-of-the-box thinking. Uses high intelligence and strong intuition to read complex patterns, has a strong imagination, stays focused on the main goal, and doesn't forget reality. Doesn't tire of spawning ideas because they can think divergently and convergently to obtain the ultimate idea.[6]

Dare to accept challenges. Individuals who are highly motivated by challenges are willing to learn new things, respond quickly to difficult questions, motivate themselves to not give up quickly, and motivate others.[7]

There are several efforts companies must make to accommodate creative people:[8]

Banish the silos. Silos can hinder talent from connecting with others, resulting in unproductive collaboration.[9] Companies must be able to embed a variety of diversity. The organization needs to be utterly fluid to allow open communication through multiple channels. Communication is also horizontal, without being hurdled by the level of position in the organizational structure.

Give autonomy. Companies can provide clear guidelines but not restrict the freedom necessary for the seeds of creativity to grow. Providing autonomy to talent in an organization shapes a sustainable flow of trust.[10]

---

[5]https://www.fastcompany.com/90683974/how-and-why-to-train-your-brain-to-be-more-curious-at-work

[6]https://www.inc.com/martin-zwilling/how-to-grow-your-business-by-thinking-outside-the-box.html

[7]https://hbr.org/2016/10/help-employees-innovate-by-giving-them-the-right-challenge

[8]From various sources, among others: https://kantaraustralia.com/what-stands-in-the-way-of-creative-capability/; https://www.googlesir.com/characteristics-of-a-creative-organization/; https://slideplayer.com/slide/14881811/; https://www.slideshare.net/gdpawan/creative-organisation; https://www.iedp.com/articles/managing-creativity-in-organizations/; https://hbr.org/2017/05/how-to-nourish-your-teams-creativity

[9]https://www.forbes.com/sites/forbescoachescouncil/2019/05/13/how-to-break-down-silos-and-enhance-your-companys-culture/?sh=41f35a5d4ab1

[10]https://www.forbes.com/sites/forbeshumanresourcescouncil/2020/09/09/how-autonomous-teams-enhance-employee-creativity-and-flexibility/?sh=66cf7415538e

Offer a tolerance of failure. Companies can create a safe environment to fail and foster a willingness to try.[11] A company should allow a trial-and-error approach, encouraging experimentation and exploring possibilities. Credit should be given to brilliant ideas.

Provide an appropriate allocation of resources. Resources are needed to build multiple facilities or infrastructure (including technology) to support the creative process.[12]

Support flexibility. Companies must have a clear plan and room to improvise if necessary. In addition, the company can balance idealism with practical commercial goals, support people to express themselves both individually and in groups, and provide enough time to work. Flexibility allows talent to have the desire to create something new and generate ideas.[13]

Offer clarity of strategic intent. Companies should place creativity as part of their corporate values and recognize creative people as their essential capital. The company must explain a challenging vision and mission that will attract creative people to be called on to contribute their thoughts and commit to supporting the company in achieving its goals.[14]

Building Innovation Capability

For innovation to occur, we need talent with the following characteristics:[15]

Solution-oriented. A great imagination to provide solutions in different, challenging, even risky ways because they introduce entirely new, authentic, non-mainstream ideas. They take advantage of resources that are sometimes limited by looking at the multiple complexities and the potential or opportunities in the market. Innovation can be a problem-solver or problem prevention.[16]

---

[11]https://hbr.org/2019/01/the-hard-truth-about-innovative-cultures

[12]https://www.workamajig.com/blog/creative-resource-management-basics

[13]https://www.flexjobs.com/employer-blog/companies-use-flexibility-foster-creativity/

[14]https://hbr.org/2019/03/strategy-needs-creativity

[15]From various sources, among others: https://www.forbes.com/sites/rebeccabagley/2014/01/15/the-10-traits-of-great-innovators/?sh=192e0b7f4bf4; https://dobetter.esade.edu/en/characteristics-innovative-people?_wrapper_format=html; https://ideascale.com/blog/10-qualities-of-great-innovators/; https://inusual.com/en/blog/five-characteristics-that-define-successful-innovators; https://hbr.org/2013/10/the-five-characteristics-of-successful-innovators

[16]https://www.forbes.com/sites/larrymyler/2014/06/13/innovation-is-problem-solving-and-a-whole-lot-more/?sh=301612c233b9

Continuous innovation. Ongoing innovation from a company can keep customers loyal.[17] Continuous innovation relies on people who are aware that they must get out of their comfort zone and make a breakthrough to stay competitive and sustainable.

Perform iterations. These talents carry out an iterative process between ideas and concrete forms for the best result. In the process, they seek information or arguments, ask critical questions, are not fascinated and fixated on one innovation, dare to experiment, and are open to different alternatives, always perfecting them and realizing them.

Mentally strong. These talents are thorough, patient, and not prone to giving up. Falling and getting up is daily, but they're always ready to race against time and the ongoing competition.

Spread positive energy. These talents are self-motivating, passionate, and intense. They are always ready to be a team player and willing to share knowledge, pass on skills, and transmit an innovative mindset to others for the common good.

Attention to detail. These talents have the ability to see minor points that are relevant. They use high intelligence in making detailed observations. They are innovators who understand a process thoroughly.[18]

Companies cannot simply accept the creative power of a group of genuinely innovative individuals. They must build an environment to foster capabilities while also developing them. Here are some characteristics of innovative companies:[19]

Innovation-based strategic intent. A company must instill an innovative spirit in its vision, mission, and strategy. The company also has to communicate it well to understand it easily. The organization's value-creation processes must reflect the concept of innovation, which triggers excitement.

---

[17]https://www.techfunnel.com/information-technology/continuous-innovation/
[18]https://www.forbes.com/sites/forbestechcouncil/2019/10/17/innovation-starts-with-ownership-how-to-foster-creativity-internally/?sh=58de6d3d4087
[19]From various sources, among others: https://www.fastcompany.com/90597167/6-habits-of-the-most-innovative-people; https://hbr.org/2002/08/inspiring-innovation; https://quickbooks.intuit.com/ca/resources/uncategorized/common-characteristics-innovative-companies/; https://innovationmanagement.se/2012/12/18/the-seven-essential-characteristics-of-innovative-companies/; https://smallbusiness.chron.com/top-three-characteristics-innovative-companies-10976.html; https://www.linkedin.com/pulse/eight-traits-innovative-companies-ashley-leonzio; https://innovationone.io/six-traits-highly-innovative-companies/; https://www.forbes.com/sites/marymeehan/2014/07/08/innovation-ready-the-5-traits-innovative-companies-share/?sh=69c83bd01e28; https://miller-klein.com/2020/06/15/what-are-the-characeristics-of-innovative-companies/

Provide a consistent, innovative culture. The company demonstrates commitment to ongoing real and implemented innovations. It creates the right conducive environment, supported with proper recognition and appreciation, to encourage people to innovate.

Provide broad opportunities. The company offers room to express opinions and applies a control approach that is not too tight. This shows trust and provides autonomy to individuals, empowering and encouraging them to innovate through training programs. Failure is not taboo.

Promote collaboration. Open-mindedness and transparency are imperative for cooperation in a highly diverse environment. The leaders should exemplify this attitude.

Offer strong knowledge management. Open access to knowledge and data can help a company find a solution to its problem.[20] Knowledge helps understand risk so that firms are more informed and can execute.

Building Entrepreneurial Capability

We need people with an entrepreneurial mentality who have several characteristics:[21]

Resource allocator. Are knowledgeable and can use the available resources and tools, have an awareness of their strengths and weaknesses, and a focus on creating value with their capabilities for the organization.

Opportunity seekers. Have a high curiosity, a genuine interest in the learning process, and aren't resistant to the development of science and technology. They never get satisfied with what is already known. Instead, they ask new questions.[22]

---

[20]https://www.forbes.com/sites/forbestechcouncil/2019/03/28/spur-innovation-by-sharing-knowledge-enterprisewide/?sh=1d03e0b55ce0

[21]From various sources, among others: https://www.babson.edu/media/babson/site-assets/content-assets/about/academics/centres-and-institutes/the-lewis-institute/fund-for-global-entrepreneurship/Entrepreneurial-Thought-and-Action-(ETA).pdf; https://online.hbs.edu/blog/post/characteristics-of-successful-entrepreneurs; https://www.forbes.com/sites/theyec/2020/05/11/six-personality-traits-of-successful-entrepreneurs/?sh=505d02470ba9; https://www.forbes.com/sites/tendayiviki/2020/02/24/the-four-characteristics-of-successful-intrapreneurs/?sh=5546a5b17cad

[22]https://www.forbes.com/sites/forbesbusinesscouncil/2021/07/29/three-steps-to-find-the-best-opportunities-for-your-business/?sh=1dc8f6e34d87

Risk-taker. Approach risk like exercising; they try to mitigate the risk to generate value.[23] Entrepreneurs feel comfortable with failure and are able to learn from past mistakes, determine tolerable affordable loss, reduce the risks faced, and have the ability to experiment.

Self-starter. Are motivated, not dependent on rewards from others, understand the passion that can encourage more optimal activities, and have a clear purpose in running their duties.

Network collaborators. Able to build meaningful relationships with others, are oriented to teamwork, like to do things together, and can involve other parties with multiple competencies to support a common goal.

Companies need an entrepreneurial approach to identify opportunities in the market and offer multiple solutions resulting from the innovations carried out in a company. Here are some characteristics of companies that intend to develop an entrepreneurial mindset within the organization:[24]

Facilitate experimentation. The company encourages employees to dare to try new things and provides constructive input on the successful and unsuccessful results. The company inspires employees to daringly test their ideas directly on the market or with customers, including through prototyping.

Nurture learning culture. The company encourages employees to use the lessons from their past activities. The definition of learning also needs to be expanded through books or written sources and experiences and interactions with customers. Every interaction with customers needs to be a valuable lesson to improve the solutions in the company's products and services repertoire. Learning opportunities should be available for everyone.[25]

Increase sense of ownership. Entrepreneurial employees will grow when they have a sense of belonging to the company. Companies can encourage this by providing incentives in partial share ownership to

[23]https://www.forbes.com/sites/chriscarosa/2020/08/07/why-successful-entrepreneurs-need-to-be-calculated-risk-takers/?sh=17d917142f5b
[24]From various sources, among others: https://www.inc.com/peter-economy/7-super-successful-strategies-to-create-a-powerfully-entrepreneurial-culture-in-any-business.html; https://www.fastcompany.com/90158100/how-to-build-an-entrepreneurial-culture-5-tips-from-eric-ries; https://hbr.org/2006/10/meeting-the-challenge-of-corporate-entrepreneurship; https://medium.com/@msena/corporate-entrepreneurship-in-8-steps-7e6ce75db88a; https://www.business.com/articles/12-ways-foster-entrepreneurial-culture/
[25]https://www.forbes.com/sites/forbesbusinesscouncil/2021/03/11/three-lessons-on-creating-a-culture-of-learning/?sh=6e03101a5d13

eligible employees. Giving specific authority to lead a program or project will also increase the sense of belonging in employees.[26]

Provide autonomy. Companies need to involve employees when setting goals or targets. They must avoid micromanagement in the process of achieving these goals and give employees the freedom to make decisions independently. Companies still need to establish an effective evaluation method without much intervention. Giving a space where talent can showcase their achievements and work progress is a valuable reward from the company to keep the talent loyal and consistently contributing to the value-creation process.[27]

Strengthen cross-functional collaboration. Companies need to facilitate the formation of cross-functional teams. They must optimize the use of technology to encourage collaboration between physically far apart teams.

Building Leadership Capability

Here are some common characteristics of strong leaders:[28]

Act strategically. Ready to adjust according to the challenges and opportunities faced. Must have a helicopter view of problems, not just focus on the issues at hand.[29]

Good communicator. Have the ability to influence others and convey ideas clearly and persuasively, both for issues related to strategic goals and technical tasks. Listen to other people's opinions. Able to communicate in an interpersonal context (one-on-one) and public communication (one-to-many). Good listening skills build effective communication.[30]

Visionary. Have the ability to predict future situations and relate them to the organization's strategies. They can motivate team members to look ahead to the future with optimism. In addition, they balance stability and growth.

---

[26]https://www.forbes.com/sites/forbesfinancecouncil/2020/04/15/how-an-ownership-mindset-can-change-your-teams-culture/?sh=4b1987434b8b

[27]Ibid.

[28]From various sources, among others: https://www.forbes.com/sites/deeppatel/2017/03/22/11-powerful-traits-of-successful-leaders/?sh=5fe70ebc469f; https://online.hbs.edu/blog/post/characteristics-of-an-effective-leader; https://www.gallup.com/cliftonstrengths/en/356072/how-to-be-better-leader.aspx; https://asana.com/resources/qualities-of-a-leader; https://www.briantracy.com/blog/personal-success/the-seven-leadership-qualities-of-great-leaders-strategic-planning/

[29]https://www.pmi.org/-/media/pmi/documents/public/pdf/learning/thought-leadership/pulse/pulse-of-the-profession-2017.pdf

[30]https://www.forbes.com/sites/theyec/2021/01/19/nine-communication-habits-of-great-leaders-and-why-they-make-them-so-great/?sh=1c87617b6ec9

Delegate and empower others. Not doing everything alone, but instead involving team members according to their abilities. Delegation of tasks does not mean a leader escapes responsibility. They are still present to empower team members, both technically and psychologically.[31]

Show integrity and responsibility. Conveys consistency between words and actions. Gives orders or instructions and is a role model for team members. Even though they involve other team members in completing the task, a leader does not let go of their responsibilities.

The following describe several characteristics of a company that is serious in encouraging the development of leadership capabilities within its organization:[32]

Recognize potential candidates. Companies need to identify the potential of each employee from the very beginning of the hiring process. Routine evaluations carried out by the company can also be a source of reference.

Provide coaching and mentoring. Coaching will encourage employees to reflect on their leadership potential. Meanwhile, mentoring will assist them in overcoming personal issues.[33]

Offer new challenges. Companies need to provide a variety of jobs to employees. Those who can handle new, higher challenges will likely get more significant responsibilities. Those new challenges will also be a test of leadership for employees.

Measure progress. Companies need to evaluate the development of each employee, especially related to their leadership abilities. Evaluation can be based on routine responsibilities that have become part of the job description or through special assignments. Companies also need to reward those who deserve it.

Facilitate personal development. Systematic training will help increase the understanding and skills of employees regarding leadership. In a team, every talent should have the same opportunity to develop a personal relationship with each other and experience the process of gradually taking on more responsibilities in order to be the future leader.[34]

For a summation of how to build CI-EL capabilities, see Table 12.1.

---

[31] https://www.forbes.com/sites/forbescoachescouncil/2021/07/27/achieve-more-success-by-leading-from-your-helicopter/?sh=681b362d57e8

[32] From various sources, among others: https://www.entrepreneur.com/article/335996; https://learnloft.com/2019/07/24/how-the-best-leaders-create-more-leaders/; https://www.inc.com/tom-searcy/4-ways-to-build-leaders-not-followers.html; https://hbr.org/2003/12/developing-your-leadership-pipeline; https://www.themuse.com/advice/5-strategies-that-will-turn-your-employees-into-leaders

[33] https://www.forbes.com/sites/forbesbusinesscouncil/2021/08/05/three-ways-you-can-be-a-leader-and-mentor-to-those-on-your-same-path/?sh=738f6f8044ad

[34] https://hbr.org/2019/03/as-your-team-gets-bigger-your-leadership-style-has-to-adapt

TABLE 12.1   Summary of CI-EL Capability Building

| | **Capabilities** | | | |
	Creativity	Innovation	Entrepreneurship	Leadership
Individual	• Strong curiosity • Open-minded • Fun to work with • Out-of-the-box thinking • Dares to accept challenges	• Solution-oriented • Continuous innovation • Performs iterations • Mentally strong • Spreads positive energy • Attention to details	• Resource allocator • Opportunity seeker • Risk-taker • Self-starter • Network collaborator	• Acts strategically • Good communicator • Visionary • Delegates and empowers others • Shows integrity and responsibility
Corporate	• Banishes the silos • Gives autonomy • Tolerates failure • Provides appropriate allocation of resources • Supports flexibility • Provides clarity of strategic intent	• Practices an innovation-based strategic intent • Provides a consistent innovative culture • Provides broad opportunities • Promotes collaboration • Has strong knowledge management	• Facilitates experimentation • Nurtures learning culture • Increases sense of ownership • Provides autonomy • Strengthens cross-functional collaboration	• Recognizes potential candidates • Provides coaching and mentoring • Offers new challenges • Measures progress • Facilitates personal development

Building Productivity Capability

The following list describes some of the characteristics of productive individuals:[35]

Focus on goals. The ability to point out essential goals that must be achieved every day and prioritize them. They can break goals into minor to-dos.[36]

Create priority lists. Can divide their tasks according to importance in their personal or professional lives (even blending and balancing). They can understand the work that needs to be accomplished and what can be postponed or eliminated.

Excellent scheduling. Managing a calendar (including to-do lists) is one way to divide time properly. Productive people have priorities and organize their time to complete them one by one.

Plan some rest. Able to manage time to rest but are not trapped in procrastination, the origin of the accumulation of workload. Allocating resting time can help boost concentration after rest and manage time more precisely.[37]

Monotask. Single tasking helps individuals reduce distractions at work and complete tasks efficiently, ranging from major assignments to minor activities such as checking email and text messages.

Companies should also accommodate productive people to maintain and even increase their skills. Following are some of the ways this can be done:[38]

Attention to time allocation. Effective time allocation is an impactful way to reduce stress during work.[39] Companies should provide sufficient

---

[35]From various sources, among others: https://scienceofzen.com/productivity-state-mind-heres-get; https://hbr.org/2020/05/want-to-be-more-productive-try-doing-less; https://sloanreview.mit.edu/article/own-your-time-boost-your-productivity/; https://www.nytimes.com/guides/business/how-to-improve-your-productivity-at-work; https://news.mit.edu/2019/how-does-your-productivity-stack-up-robert-pozen-0716; https://www.cnbc.com/2019/04/11/mit-researcher-highly-productive-people-do-these-5-easy-things.html
[36]https://hbr.org/2020/05/want-to-be-more-productive-try-doing-less
[37]https://www.inc.com/samira-far/5-monotasking-tips-that-will-save-your-brain-and-make-you-more-successful.html
[38]From various sources, among others: https://www.forbes.com/sites/theyec/2021/09/20/five-tips-to-increase-productivity-in-the-workplace/?sh=49f09626257b; https://www.businesstown.com/8-ways-increase-productivity-workplace/; https://www.forbes.com/sites/forbeslacouncil/2019/09/18/12-time-tested-techniques-to-increase-workplace-productivity/?sh=4a7d6b9c274e; https://www.forbes.com/sites/theyec/2020/07/13/want-a-more-productive-focused-team-encourage-these-10-habits/?sh=2d64cc5f2ef9; https://www.lollydaskal.com/leadership/6-powerful-habits-of-the-most-productive-teams/; https://blogin.co/blog/7-habits-of-highly-productive-teams-74/
[39]https://clockify.me/blog/productivity/team-time-management/

space to complete tasks. They can implement a culture of short meetings, provide space for individuals to organize their to-do lists, and offer short breaks amid busy times.

Regulate meetings. Companies can provide guidelines for conducting meetings so that each team can run meeting sessions more regularly. A meeting time limit can be established and the meeting agenda sent out beforehand. The number of meetings, and their duration, should be regulated.

Emphasize goals. Every team that can work productively knows the expected result. Team members then work quickly because they already understand specific objectives, tasks, and plans.

Smooth communication. Every productive team has a habit of open discussion to solve problems and obstacles to work better.[40]

Provide enabler tools. Companies and teams can use productivity hacks according to their needs. These might include collaborative workspaces for remote teams, measuring work achievement, and tracking work in process and completed tasks.

Building Improvement Capability

The following list covers characteristics of individuals who want to make continuous improvement:[41]

Never stop asking questions. Continually question the status quo and work every day to find loopholes for better operations. They ask the right questions and know about the system operations to identify areas that can be made better.[42]

Problem-solver. Individuals can find room for improvement by first searching for a problem. Bringing solutions to the current problem is the first and most common reason for improvement.[43]

Clarify process. Find what to do with the process: improve, eliminate, or disrupt.[44] Individuals can view the current processes and seek possible adjustments.

---

[40]https://www.fearlessculture.design/blog-posts/pixar-culture-design-canvas
[41]From various sources, among others: https://www.spica.com/blog/kaizen-principles; https://createvalue.org/blog/tips-creating-continuous-improvement-mindset/; https://mitsloan.mit.edu/ideas-made-to-matter/8-step-guide-improving-workplace-processes; https://hbr.org/2012/05/its-time-to-rethink-continuous; https://hbr.org/2010/10/four-top-management-beliefs-th
[42]https://www.velaction.com/curiosity/
[43]https://hbr.org/2012/09/are-you-solving-the-right-problem
[44]https://hbr.org/2012/05/its-time-to-rethink-continuous

Never stop learning. Individuals need to upgrade their knowledge from time to time so that they can find improvement gaps.[45]

Know where to start. Defining the problem and identifying the root cause is usually the best starting point in dealing with a challenging situation.[46]

The company must maintain a continuous improvement spirit in each employee. For this reason, here are some characteristics of companies that can encourage continuous improvement:[47]

Create a base for improvement. Every company can start continuous improvement from existing work standards by reviewing what goals they could not achieve with the current standards. This method can then be used as a new standard for people in the organization.

Ensure flow of ideas. Companies can provide a simple platform for individuals to submit ideas for improvement in their respective functions. Companies can build a horizontal approach for managers and other workers to work together and improve. Anyone in the organization can contribute a great idea, such as the front-liners who better understand customers' main problems.[48]

Make a habit. Companies can create a routine to pursue improvement and manage an exemplary communication environment so that everyone in the organization can develop their teams.

Encourage. Companies need to understand the barriers affecting organizational members in their contribution to continuous improvement. Companies must identify and minimize fears so individuals can contribute.[49]

Provide learning space. Companies need to provide suitable learning opportunities to prepare employees with the knowledge and skills required for continuous improvement.[50]

---

[45]https://hbr.org/2021/05/break-down-change-management-into-small-steps

[46]https://au.reachout.com/articles/a-step-by-step-guide-to-problem-solving

[47]From various sources, among others: https://tulip.co/blog/continuous-improvement-with-kaizen/; https://www.mckinsey.com/business-functions/operations/our-insights/continuous-improvement-make-good-management-every-leaders-daily-habit; https://sloanreview.mit.edu/article/americas-most-successful-export-to-japan-continuous-improvement-programs/; https://theuncommonleague.com/blog/2018618/creating-a-mindset-of-continuous-process-improvement; https://hbr.org/2019/05/creating-a-culture-of-continuous-improvement; https://www.zenefits.com/workest/top-10-ways-to-improve-employee-efficiency/

[48]https://www.viima.com/blog/collect-ideas-from-frontline-employees

[49]https://www.industryweek.com/talent/education-training/article/21958430/action-learning-key-to-developing-an-effective-continuous-improvement-culture

[50]https://hbr.org/2021/05/break-down-change-management-into-small-steps

Building Professionalism Capability

When looking for individuals with professional capabilities,[51] companies often seek out the following attributes:

Well prepared and punctual. Get everything ready for a meeting, presentation, or phone call by practicing in a mirror or creating a script. Arrive 15 to 30 minutes early to prepare.

Good communication skills. Use the right words when writing or speaking in the work environment. The words and terms used, comments, the choice of the topic of conversation, and the style of speech will form an opinion regarding a person's professionalism.

Suitable appearance. Appearance is not only about how to dress but includes how to use the working desk and organize files. Presentable attire shows that the individual is ready to work and professionally engage with others.[52]

Always accountable. Shows a high commitment to carrying out various duties according to the agreement, hence, being someone you can count on. Being accountable means that a person can receive credit for successes, and vice versa: take the blame for failures.[53]

Demonstrates integrity. Being honest and having strong moral principles.[54] Because professionals are ready to be seen and judged by others, they need to display their honesty in their words, acts, and in the work they deliver.[55]

Companies can strengthen professional capabilities systematically and institutionalize these capabilities by implementing the following:

Establish workplace rules and culture. Small-sized organizations need a strong leader. Medium-sized organizations require company

---

[51]From various sources, among others: https://smallbusiness.chron.com/build-professionalism-709.html; https://www.robinwaite.com/blog/7-ways-to-develop-and-practice-professionalism/; https://www.umassglobal.edu/news-and-events/blog/professionalism-and-workplace-etiquette; https://www.conovercompany.com/5-ways-to-show-professionalism-in-the-workplace/

[52]https://www.robinwaite.com/blog/7-ways-to-develop-and-practice-professionalism/

[53]Ibid.

[54]https://www.oxfordlearnersdictionaries.com/definition/american_english/integrity#:~:text=noun-,noun,a%20man%20of%20great%20integrity

[55]https://www2.deloitte.com/content/dam/Deloitte/sk/Documents/Random/sk_deloitte_code_ethics_conduct.pdf

regulations or standard operating procedures (SOP). Large companies must have rules, regulations, and culture to direct how people work.

Provide a performance management system. In addition to the regulations, a company should provide a fair measurement method for all parties to form professional behavior. Feedback and performance management systems are relevant so everyone can understand their work.

Encourage coworkers to attend training or seminars. Companies must be able to adapt to current conditions. For this reason, employees need to update their knowledge and skills through training and education programs to carry out their work, create value, and maintain company competitiveness.[56]

Building Managerial Capability

The following list describes those who demonstrate managerial capabilities:[57]

Helicopter view analysis. Able to make programs by looking at macroeconomics, industry, and competitor movements. A helicopter view enables a manager to lead their team to do the technical work by providing vision, mission, and the broader context of a project.[58]

Effective decision-making. Able to see the advantages and disadvantages of several alternatives to make timely decisions and take actions that align with business objectives.[59]

Proficient in managing projects. Ability to plan (make goals, resource planning, and time lines), execute (make work processes or conduct training), check (audit or monitor), and act (take preventive or corrective actions) is needed to be able to carry out the organization's operations.[60]

---

[56]https://www.forbes.com/sites/forbesbusinesscouncil/2021/03/11/three-lessons-on-creating-a-culture-of-learning/?sh=6e03101a5d13
[57]From various sources, among others: https://www.pmi.org/learning/library/core-competencies-successful-skill-manager-8426; https://bizfluent.com/info-8494191-analytical-skills-management.html; https://distantjob.com/blog/helicopter-manager-remote-team/; https://www.lucidchart.com/blog/plan-do-check-act-cycle; https://www.teamwork.com/project-management-guide/project-management-skills/
[58]https://www.forbes.com/sites/forbescoachescouncil/2021/07/27/achieve-more-success-by-leading-from-your-helicopter/?sh=681b362d57e8
[59]https://www.pmi.org/-/media/pmi/documents/public/pdf/learning/thought-leadership/pulse/pulse-of-the-profession-2017.pdf
[60]Ibid.

Team-building ability. Able to encourage and enable anyone to work as a team to complete projects or routine work. Managers don't have to work alone. They can form solid teams and use their collective strengths to achieve challenging organizational goals.[61]

Adaptive. Quick changes in the business environment require a manager who can adapt to external and internal changes.

Companies must be able to maintain a management system that is constantly evolving and relevant. Following are some strategies to build and maintain management capabilities:[62]

Clear succession plan. A good organization is not only led by one person but several people. Therefore, it is necessary to plan for the replacement or rotation of the management team to ensure the continuity of the management process. Succession plans in an organization can come from ranking talents' scores in their feedback, performance management reviews, and interviews to assess communication skills and strategic thinking.[63]

Provide performance feedback. Managers can create opportunities for every team member to give feedback, forming a habit of constructive feedback.[64] Periodic performance feedback is needed to inform the expectations of each job and provide suggestions to make the team's work better in the future.

Open communication. Companies can implement two-way communication between managers and their teams through town hall meetings, weekly or monthly meetings, or a whistleblower system.

For a summation of PI-PM capabilities, see Table 12.2.

---

[61]https://www.forbes.com/sites/brianscudamore/2016/03/09/why-team-building-is-the-most-important-investment-youll-make/?sh=1657a771617f
[62]From various sources, among others: https://www.investopedia.com/terms/s/succession-planning.asp; https://www.vital-learning.com/blog/how-to-build-better-manager; https://thepalmergroup.com/blog/the-importance-of-open-communication-in-the-workplace/
[63]https://hbr.org/2016/10/the-performance-management-revolution
[64]https://hbr.org/2014/06/how-to-give-your-team-feedback

TABLE 12.2 Summary of PI-PM Capability Building

			Capabilities		
		Productivity	Improvement	Professionalism	Management
Individual		• Focuses on goals • Creates priority lists • Excellent scheduling • Plans some rest • Monotasking	• Never stops asking questions • Problem-solver • Clarifies process • Never stops learning • Knows where to start	• Well prepared and punctual • Good communication skills • Suitable appearance • Always accountable • Demonstrates integrity	• Has helicopter view analysis • Effective decision-making • Proficient in managing projects • Team-building ability • Adaptive
Corporate		• Attention to time allocation • Regulates meetings • Emphasizes goals • Smooth communication • Provides enabler tools	• Creates a base for improvement • Ensures flow of ideas • Makes a habit • Encourages • Provides learning space	• Establishes workplace rules and culture • Provides a performance management system • Encourages coworkers to attend training or seminars	• Clear succession plan • Provides performance feedback • Open communication

In Practice

It's infrequent, if not impossible, for an individual to have all CI-EL and PI-PM capabilities at once. Having two or three of the eight is sufficient. However, one can also learn about other capabilities to understand other partners who have strengths in different capabilities.

Strategic talent management is essential to convert a business strategy into tangible results.[65] Companies must have a clear plan to find, unite, develop, assign, and retain people in the organization. They'll need to have talent aligned and integrated with the goals and strategies of the organization. Such an approach is the essence of strategy-driven talent management and is imperative for today's environment.

Key Takeaways

- When bringing in talent, companies can review their CI-EL and PI-PM loops to see what type of workers are needed.
- Companies will want to build capabilities in these areas: creative, innovative, entrepreneurial, leadership, productivity, improvement, professionalism, and managerial.
- Understanding the mix needed and filling in positions can help everyone bring their strengths and contribute to a company's performance.

---

[65]Rob Silzer and Ben E. Dowell, *Strategy-Driven Talent Management: A Leadership Imperative* (San Francisco, CA: Jossey-Bass, 2010).

CHAPTER 13

Securing Future Trajectory

From Balance Sheet to Market Value

Louis Vuitton, the world's top luxury goods company, reported €64.2 billion of revenue in 2021. This figure was up 44% from 2020 and 20% from 2019.[1] Also in 2021, Louis Vuitton was named the most valuable luxury company in Interbrand's Top Global Brands study. It was ranked 13th overall in the study and was the only fashion company to make the top 20 in the list.[2]

Bernard Arnault, chairman and CEO of Louis Vuitton, explained the reasons behind the outstanding performance of the brand in 2021 during the gradual recovery from the pandemic. He credited the results to a highly efficient team. He also noted exceptional adaptability amid a difficult business environment.

These financial and nonfinancial accomplishments emerged from the company's commitment to placing customers in the center of all operations. Amid a prolonged crisis, Louis Vuitton maintained a relationship with its customers, and the brand continues to inspire.[3]

From the Louis Vuitton case, we can learn how a considerable concern for financial results must accompany market orientation and the application of customer-centricity by the marketing team. When that happens, nonfinancial outcomes lead to financial performance. High awareness of our product or brand is a first step. However, it is not enough before customers are interested in our product or brand.

---

[1]https://www.lvmh.com/news-documents/press-releases/new-records-for-lvmh-in-2021/
[2]https://fashionunited.uk/news/fashion/louis-vuitton-ranks-as-most-valuable-luxury-company-in-interbrand-s-2021-top-global-brands/2021110258951
[3]https://www.lvmh.com/news-documents/press-releases/new-records-for-lvmh-in-2021/

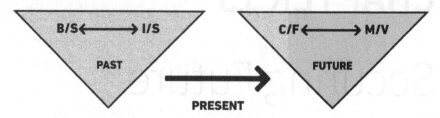

FIGURE 13.1 The financial components of the omnihouse model

In this chapter, we'll study the very bottom of the omnihouse model, which will briefly discuss the financial aspect for marketers (see Figure 13.1). We will also discuss the relationship between balance sheets (B/S), income statements (I/S, also called profit-and-loss statements), cash flow (C/F), and market value (M/V). All these terms are essential for marketers, especially when applying an entrepreneurial marketing approach.

Cash Is Still King

In general, a company's revenue comes from the sale of products—goods, services, and supporting services—which are part of the company's core business. Other sources such as investments and bank interest can also contribute. Sales transactions are usually in cash or noncash. Noncash sales will increase account receivables, and we must convert this into cash as soon as possible. A company's assets cannot produce anything if we are unable to leverage them.

One of the crucial measures to maintain cash inflow is to convert the noncash payments into cash immediately. However, if the business environment is not conducive, the condition may disrupt cash flow. A break is troubling because cash is the lifeblood for a company's operational continuity and is often needed for financing and investing activities. Given this, companies of all sizes should prioritize having an ongoing cash flow.

After the company converts revenue into cash, it will increase the cash amount on the balance sheet. This cash will be used to make payments or cover activities such as R&D, the supply or procurement of raw materials, production processes, and marketing and sales processes. It will support customer services and pay for retention (loyalty) programs. Cash will cover operating expenses such as overhead and salaries. In addition, the company needs cash for investing and financing activities.

Some companies are cash rich. In 2022, 13 companies held nearly 40% (about US$1 trillion) of the total US$2.7 trillion held by all companies in the S&P 500. In early 2022, Apple, one of the most extreme examples, had

Equity + Liabilities = Assets

FIGURE 13.2   The formula of assets

US$202.5 billion in cash and investments, up nearly 4% from the year before. That equates to 7.4% of all the cash held by S&P 500 companies. Alphabet had US$169.2 billion in cash and investments, equivalent to 6% of all S&P 500 cash. Microsoft held US$132.3 billion, the same as 5% of all cash in the S&P 500.[4]

Revenue minus the expenses is equal to the net profit. At the end of the financial year, the company produces an income statement. In the case of a net profit, the board of directors will propose how much to distribute as dividends and how much to allocate for retained earnings. This is usually presented at the general meeting of shareholders. Once it is approved, dividends and retained earnings are allocated.

Any retained earnings will increase equity and improve the company's ability to add new debts or funding from investors if necessary to expand its business. We will later record these borrowings as liabilities, and funding from investors will be part of the equity in our company's balance sheet. With increasing equity and liabilities, assets will also increase, so companies must up their sales and ultimately their net income. This simple explanation summarizes the formula that equity plus liabilities equal assets (see Figure 13.2).

Thus, we can see a relationship between the income statement and the company's balance sheet. Shareholders are typically more concerned with net income at the bottom of the company's income statement. This is because the figure is used to determine the dividends to distribute.

Past, Present, and Future

Under certain conditions, if a company's bottom line is negative, it can still finance activities from investors rather than borrowed money (debts). From the investors' perspective, the balance sheet and income statement are reflections of the past. Hence, it is more important for investors to see what the company currently owns, what its managers will do now, and its future business prospects.

Potential investors will carefully look at the as-is condition of the company and its ability to generate cash. They will examine the extent to which

[4]https://www.investors.com/etfs-and-funds/sectors/sp500-companies-stockpile-1-trillion-cash-investors-want-it/

the company's value-creation process can guarantee a sufficient return for them, increasing the market value as reflected in the P/E ratio and P/B ratio (as discussed in Chapter 10). Investors will evaluate how the company strives to remain superior and relevant in the industry. They will also consider the company's internal conditions, including tangible and intangible resources, capabilities to manage multiple resources, an establishment of its core competence, and possibly distinctive competences. In short, investors want to know how a company can handle external factors such as dynamics of the macro environment, market, competition, and changes in behavior or customer preferences.

The company's ability to generate cash is an essential measure of the value-creation processes. Investors see the cash flow statement as an indicator of profitability and long-term prospects. It can assist in determining whether the company has sufficient cash to cover its expenses. A cash flow statement, in other words, represents a company's financial health.[5]

A start-up, if able to show a promise of disrupting an industry, can often attract investors to fund its business development. Even if the income statement shows a loss position for several years, investors may believe the start-up has the potential to become a market leader over time. They might be convinced its market value will increase significantly and give them an outstanding future return.

The Balance Sheet and Income Statement Loop

The value of dividends paid divided by the net income is called the payout ratio. The higher it is, the stronger the company balance sheet is (see Figure 13.3). According to Demmert, the payout ratio of attractive companies is usually 35–55%.[6] However, the amount of dividends also depends on the company's condition. If the company is in a mature and stable stage, it will usually have a high payout ratio. Aggressively expanding companies tend to withhold profits (as retained earnings) to be reinvested in the company.[7]

Retained earnings will increase shareholder equity. More equity can strengthen the company's leverage ability to obtain loans, which will increase

---

[5]https://www.kotaksecurities.com/ksweb/articles/why-is-the-cash-flow-statement-important-to-shareholders-and-investors
[6]James Demmert is the founder and managing partner at Main Street Research in Sausalito. Please refer to https://money.usnews.com/investing/dividends/articles/what-is-a-good-dividend-payout-ratio
[7]https://www.investopedia.com/articles/03/011703.asp

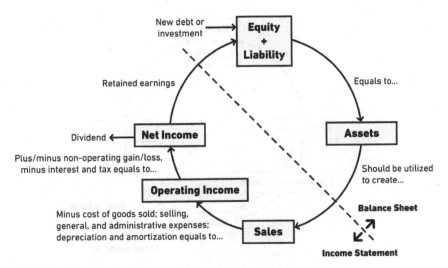

FIGURE 13.3   The balance sheet and income statement loop[8]

the amount of debt. Consequently, assets will also rise, and therefore the company will need to increase its sales. We must continue to maintain this cycle on an ongoing basis to ensure business growth over time.

If the cycle is divided by two, the picture on the top right of Figure 13.3 shows the balance sheet, and the bottom left shows the income statement. We can now clearly see the relationship between the balance sheet and the income statement from this cycle. This also explains why we depict a two-way arrow between balance sheet and income statement in the omnihouse model.

Financial Ratios: The Counterclockwise Approach

The explanation starts with equity and liabilities and ends with net income, cycling clockwise. To make it easier for marketers, we can use this loop to understand the concept of return. We will work backward to see the financial ratios that show a company's profitability. We will start with operating income and work counterclockwise to calculate return on sales (ROS) and net profit margin.

[8]Adapted from Gabriel Hawawini and Claude Viallet, *Finance for Executives: Managing for Value Creation* (Mason, OH: South-Western College Publishing, 1999).

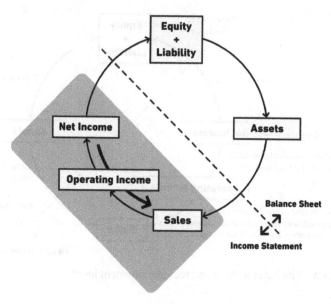

FIGURE 13.4   Components to calculate return on sales and net profit margin

The Overlooked ROS and Net Profit Margin

If we put operating income over sales (that is, operating income divided by sales), it will produce a financial ratio called ROS.[9]

$$ROS = \frac{Operating\ Income}{Sales}$$

ROS reflects profitability, that is, how much operating income is generated from a sales result (see Figure 13.4). If the ratio is a relatively small number, it indicates the company's operations are not running efficiently. This means there are unnecessary costs incurred.

We must look further to see if these costs are due to marketing and sales operations or not. Sales results may reach or surpass the target, but if this is achieved by "selling-at-any-cost" efforts, there could be an underlying problem. For example, if we offer someone to buy one product and get three for free, it could sell well. A price discount that causes a 1% decrease in sales will reduce the net profit by up to 12% because we cannot automatically reduce

---

[9]Operating income (or also referred to as operating profit) is sales (or as a whole with various other income called revenue) minus all operating expenses that consist of cost of goods sold (COGS); selling, general, and administrative expenses (SGA); and depreciation and amortization.

| TABLE 13.1 | The Impact of Discount on Unit Sales Increase to Maintain Same Gross Margin[10] | | | |

Gross Margin / Price Decrease	−5%	−10%	−15%	−20%
30%	+20%	+50%	+100%	+200%
35%	+17%	+40%	+75%	+133%
40%	+14%	+33%	+60%	+100%
45%	+13%	+29%	+50%	+80%
50%	+11%	+25%	+43%	+67%

all costs according to the discount rate. It is nearly impossible to ask everyone in our value chain to lower their bills when the company runs a customer discount program.

If we decide to give a price discount, we have to sell more units of our product to maintain the same gross profit. With a gross margin of 40% and a sale discount of 20%, we need to sell 100% more product units than usual for the same profit margin. The larger the gross margin we want to achieve and the higher the price discount given, the higher the unit sales increase we have to deal with, as explained by GrowthForce in Table 13.1.

According to McKinsey's research on the average income statement of S&P 1500 companies, we can see that price has a tremendous impact on operating income. A 1% increase in prices will result in an increase of about 8% in operating income. This is almost 50% greater than the 1% reduction in variable costs and three times greater than the 1% increase in sales volume.[11]

Waste can arise quickly in other areas. Goods shipped to the wrong address can be costly when they are redirected. Large inventories that don't sell accrue maintenance expenses. If they are financed with debt, the interest will incur further charges. Printed brochures, if not read, drain the budget, as do sales tools that aren't used appropriately. Digital advertising can also produce waste. According to *Marketing Week*, more than 90% of digital ads are viewed for no more than a second.[12]

[10]https://www.growthforce.com/blog/how-giving-discounts-can-destroy-your-business-profits
[11]https://www.mckinsey.com/business-functions/marketing-and-sales/our-insights/the-power-of-pricing
[12]https://www.marketingweek.com/marketers-continue-to-waste-money-as-only-9-of-digital-ads-are-viewed-for-more-than-a-second/?nocache=true&adfesuccess=1

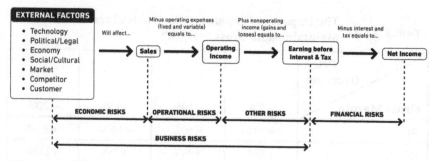

FIGURE 13.5   Various types of risks that affect profitability[13]

In the income statement, there can be hidden costs that reduce profitability. This includes waste related to marketing and sales. If costs are high, it can affect the operating income, which is listed between sales and net income. If the operating income improves, the net income will improve.

To gauge performance, we can calculate what is generated from sales. By dividing net income by sales, we will get a net profit margin ratio. This is an essential indicator of the company's financial health.[14]

$$Net\ Profit\ Margin = \frac{Net\ Income}{Sales}$$

In addition to internal factors, sales are dependent on external forces, as discussed in the 4C concept. These external factors pose multiple risks to companies, known as *economic risks*. Combining these economic risks with operational risks results in a term known as *business risks* (see Figure 13.5).

There are other risks (nonoperational risks) that will affect the value of nonoperating gains and losses. These come from foreign exchanges, investment losses and gains, and inventory write-offs. They can also include damages to assets and unexpected costs.[15]

....

[13]Adapted from Gabriel Hawawini and Claude Viallet, Finance for Executives: Managing for Value Creation (Mason, OH: South-Western College Publishing, 1999).
[14]Chris B. Murphy, "What Is Net Profit Margin? Formula for Calculation and Examples," *Investopedia* (October 2021). https://www.investopedia.com/terms/n/net_margin.asp
[15]https://www.theactuary.com/features/2020/07/08/joining-dots-between-operational-and-non-operational-risk; https://corporatefinanceinstitute.com/resources/knowledge/accounting/non-operating-income/; https://www.accountingtools.com/articles/non-operating-income-definition-and-usage.html#:~:text=Examples%20of%20non%2Doperating%20income%20include%20dividend%20income%2C%20asset%20impairment,losses%20on%20foreign%20exchange%20transactions.

The Forgotten Asset Turnover

Continuing around the circle, we come to the sales and assets components (see Figure 13.6).

Dividing sales by assets produces a ratio known as asset turnover. This can be used to measure how effectively company assets are being used to generate sales.

$$Asset\ Turnover = \frac{Sales}{Assets}$$

Here, marketers must calculate the actual value of the assets they use to achieve a specific sales result. If the assets directly related to marketing are large and the sales are small, it could be assumed that the assets are not effective. This could be due to assets that aren't suitable or an error in the strategy and execution by the sales team.

In marketing, assets tend to be intangible, such as brands, logos, customer databases, positive public perceptions or associations for brands, customer loyalty, social media and website content, infographics, brand guidelines, and service blueprints. However, there are also tangible assets to consider. These

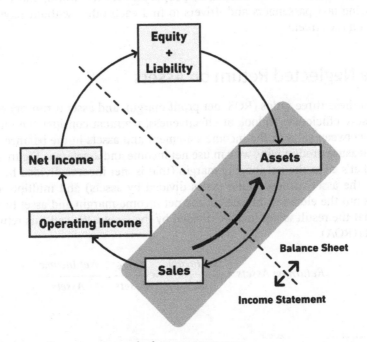

FIGURE 13.6   Components to calculate asset turnover

include physical marketing and sales infrastructure, training facilities, equipment and supplies, warehousing, and inventory.[16]

In addition to leveraging intangible assets, we must pay attention to our productivity level in using these tangible assets to create sales. If salespeople promise to achieve sales higher than their targets, first check how many assets or resources they will use to achieve the level of sales they have pledged. Suppose they aim to sell a certain number of units of a specific product per month at a rate above the industry average. Check the value of fixed assets (e.g., vehicles, production machines, land, buildings, and many others) directly related to marketing and sales. What if there is a competitor with the exact product, but the business model is different in such a way that the fixed assets turn out to be very small? How can we compete?

The two-sided marketplace is one of the most basic online business concepts that requires few tangible assets. The business model connects a group of buyers and sellers via a technical intermediary, such as a website or mobile app, and charges a fee for each transaction. eBay was the first significant two-sided marketplace success. The model is now more popular than ever, thanks to start-ups like Airbnb and Uber. Each company in this space has improved the experience and economics of the "old school" system it has replaced: eBay, by allowing people to buy and sell almost anything to almost anyone; Airbnb, by enabling rooms to be booked by people all over the world; and Uber, by allowing taxi passengers and drivers to find each other without relying on luck on the street.[17]

The Neglected Return on Assets

From these three ratios (ROS, net profit margin, and asset turnover) we can measure efficiency. To look at effectiveness, we must consider the relationship between sales in the income statement and assets in the balance sheet. To measure productivity, we can use net income and assets (see Figure 13.7).

Let's align the net income margin (that is, net income divided by sales) with the asset turnover ratio (sales divided by assets) and multiply it. We cross out the elements of sales in the net income margin and asset turnover so that the result is net income divided by the assets. We call this return on assets (ROA).

$$Return\ on\ Assets = \frac{Net\ Income}{Sales} \times \frac{Sales}{Assets} = \frac{Net\ Income}{Assets}$$

---

[16]https://valcort.com/assets-marketing-assets/
[17]https://www.cbinsights.com/research/report/how-uber-makes-money/

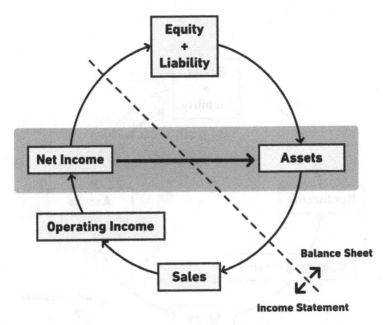

FIGURE 13.7   Return on assets as a measure of productivity

What makes a strong ROA? Usually, the higher the ROA, the more profit-generating efficiency the company has. However, we must compare the ROA of any given company to its competitors in the same industry and sector. An asset-heavy company, such as a manufacturing firm, might have an ROA of 6%. An asset-light company, such as a telemedicine app, might have an ROA of 15%.

If we compared the two based on return on investment, we would probably choose the app. However, if we compare the manufacturing firm to its nearest competitors, all of whom have ROAs below 4%, we may discover it is outperforming its peers. By contrast, if we compare the telemedicine app to similar tech firms, we could find that most of them have ROAs closer to 20%. This would indicate that the company is underperforming compared to similar firms.[18]

The Incomprehensible Equity Multiplier Ratio

Let's continue our counterclockwise journey in the loop by looking at assets and equity (see Figure 13.8).

---

[18]https://www.forbes.com/advisor/investing/roa-return-on-assets/

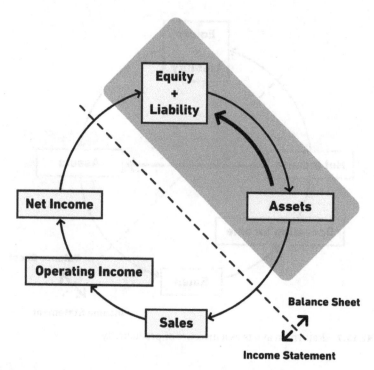

FIGURE 13.8 Components to calculate equity multiplier ratio

Putting assets above equity (assets divided by equity) results in the equity multiplier ratio, which indicates the share of assets financed by equity as opposed to debt. This ratio shows the "leverage," meaning the company's ability to obtain funding from other parties.

$$Financial\ Leverage = \frac{Assets}{Equity}$$

If we have a large number ratio, the company's assets are financed mainly by debt. This could indicate higher financial risks. The asset element can include tangible and intangible assets related to sales and marketing.[19]

Maersk Line, a logistics company, is one of the main arteries of the world's supply chain and plays a crucial role in supporting global trade. Its intangible assets include a competent workforce that can deliver a high level of service.[20] Its tangible assets consist of resources such as its fleet of ships.

----

[19]Some of the intangible assets that can usually be listed on the balance sheet are patents, copyrights, franchises, licenses, and goodwill. Please refer to Hawawini and Viallet (1999).
[20]https://investor.maersk.com/static-files/b4df47ef-3977–412b-8e3c-bc2f02bb4a5f

The Unthinkable Return on Equity

The return on equity (ROE) is the last ratio in our journey around the circle that connects the income statement to the balance sheet (see Figure 13.9).

This ratio is one of the most crucial productivity indicators, especially for shareholders and potential investors. The calculation relates to the ratios discussed (ROS, net profit margin, asset turnover, and equity multiplier). The formula includes a sales element.

If the net profit margin ratio multiplied by the asset turnover ratio (after crossing out the two sales elements and producing the ROA ratio) is then aligned and multiplied by the equity multiplier ratio and crossed out by the two asset elements, the result is the ROE ratio (see Figure 13.10).

Income statements are used for more than just the top-line indicator of sales. They display details of expenses, including those related to marketing and sales. Top management pays close attention to marketing expenses, especially when creating the corporate income statement and aligning salespeople's remuneration with revenue levels. These are costs incurred by a firm to offer its goods and services. Marketing expenses are included in a company's operational expenses, and accountants report them separately in the "selling, general, and administration expenses" portion of the income statement.[21]

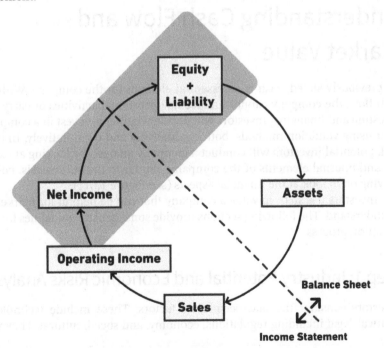

FIGURE 13.9   The components of return on equity

[21]https://bizfluent.com/info-8221377-types-income-statements-marketing-expenses.html

$$\underbrace{\frac{Net\ Income}{Sales} \times \frac{Sales}{Assets}}_{\substack{Net\ Profit \\ Margin\ Ratio}} \underbrace{}_{\substack{Assets \\ Turnover}} \times \underbrace{\frac{Assets}{Equity}}_{\substack{Equity \\ Multiplier\ Ratio}} = \frac{Net\ Income}{Equity} = \textbf{Return on Equity}$$

FIGURE 13.10   How to calculate return on equity

Companies can use financial statements, particularly income statements, to improve their day-to-day marketing operations and discover the types of products that could create future growth potential. Managers can use them to plan budgets, measure efficiency, analyze product performance, and build short- and long-term objectives.[22] Best practices for marketers include understanding the balance sheet and linking it to the income statement, knowing what the ratios mean, and using them to make marketing and sales decisions.

Understanding Cash Flow and Market Value

As previously stated, cash is an essential element for the company. Without cash flow, the company cannot finance its operational activities or carry out investing and financing. Investors will decide whether to invest in a company after using valuation methods, both qualitatively and quantitatively. In general, potential investors will conduct a company analysis by looking at external and internal elements of the company, similar to the 4C analysis, before moving on to look at the financial aspects (see Figure 13.11).

Investors use steps to value a company that can be helpful for marketers to understand. The following sections provide some general guidelines for the valuation process.

Step 1: Industry Potential and Economic Risks Analysis

Investors consider the macroeconomic factors. These include technology, political/legal including regulations, economy, and social/cultural. They will

---

[22]https://www.investopedia.com/ask/answers/041515/how-does-financial-accounting-help-decision-making.asp

STEP-1
Industry potential
and economic
risks analysis

STEP-2
In-depth
company
analysis

STEP-3
Historical financial
performance
evaluation

STEP-4
Financial
projection
development

STEP-5
Investment
decision
making

FIGURE 13.11   General stages of corporate valuation

also observe microeconomic indicators such as future market conditions, industry growth, competition between players, customer behavior, and potential developments.

For instance, in the banking industry, macro trends like the emergence of blockchain technology, new regulations, economic contraction, and lifestyle changes will create opportunities and threats for companies. At the micro level, there is the increasingly cashless lifestyle of customers and the shift to digital banking. The initial identification of these shifts will become input for determining the company's strategic intent. From the investors' point of view, they will see how the company can respond to these dynamics.

Step 2: In-Depth Company Analysis

Potential investors will learn more about a company's condition by reviewing its business model. They will see whether it is consistent with its core competency (even distinctive competence) and can guarantee an ongoing revenue stream long term. In other words, companies must have a competitive advantage built on sufficient resources supported by capabilities and managed under corporate governance. Investors will see whether the company has a clear strategy that is consistent in its application to the operational level. They will look at short-term and long-term operational risks.

Investors will also evaluate the extent to which technology plays a role in shaping their competitive advantage, how strong the company's digital orientation is, how well integrated their marketing and sales teams are, and how strong their market orientation and level of customer-centricity are. They will be interested in the implementation of talent management and the culture in the company. They will also consider creativity and innovation capabilities.

Step 3: Historical Financial Performance Evaluation

Investors will study the company's financial statements to understand its performance in recent years:

- Achievable operating margin
- Products and services that make a significant profit contribution

- Net income, dividends, and retained earnings
- Profitability ratios or returns generated
- Equity and liabilities
- Tangible and intangible assets
- Cash flow, including the allocation of cash in operating, investing, and financing activities
- The company's current market value (P/E ratio and P/B ratio)

Investors will pay close attention to operating cash flow to see if it is allocated in investments that create value. They will view a company's journey. They will want to see if it is newly formed or a start-up. The company could be growing with aggressive expansion or it may have reached its sunset years. Investors will compare company performance indicators with similar companies or its closest competitors and industry averages.

Step 4: Financial Projection Development

Because cash is king for investors, it is necessary to make a realistic operating cash flow projection for the next few years. This projection must be based on a robust business model that can show the company's ability to compete in a dynamic business environment. The business model must clearly show the company's revenue stream, which is then projected for the next few years. Investors study the operating cash flow (which has been deducted from all operational expenses) and capital expenditures (which are part of the company's investing activity) that will happen in the next few years.

We can obtain a free cash flow projection from the projected operating cash inflow that has been deducted from operating expenses and capital expenditures (CAPEX). This free cash flow is then discounted, which is known as the discounted cash flow (DCF). Investors use this indicator to determine the company's current market value based on the fair market price and estimate the potential for increasing market value in the future.

Step 5: Investment Decision-Making

Investors will decide whether the calculation of the DCF minus their total initial investment shows a significant positive difference. The initial investment amount will also determine how much of the company's ownership belongs to investors. If there is a positive net income at the end of the financial year, and it is decided it will be distributed in the form of a dividend (partially or in whole), then each investor will get a share of the dividend according to the portion of the shares they hold. Investors will see whether the P/E ratio is satisfactory. In addition, if the market value increases significantly from time to time and the value is above the book value (meaning the P/B ratio is favorable), then investors can sell it to obtain a capital gain. For this reason, investors will look at the current market and book value of the company, the predicted market value, and the actual market value.

Anticipating Investors

Understanding the steps taken during the valuation process can help an organization prepare for investors. This could occur when a company aims to raise money. In other instances, obtaining investors might be part of a strategy to help the company gain value for future purposes. Among family businesses, there could be a desire to become "fit for sale," even if the objective is not to sell the company.[23] The process could help a family firm appear more professional in its industry. Table 13.2 lays out guidelines to keep in mind before undergoing a valuation.

TABLE 13.2   Summary: Preparation to Anticipate Investors

Company's Preparation Checklist	
STEP 1 Industry potential and economic risks analysis	• Management understanding the macro environment well • Having a strategic flexibility • Keep up or be even more advanced compared to the industry • Clear competition cluster • Clear market position supported by differentiation • Be a part of the business ecosystem • Minimize risk (risk mitigation)
STEP 2 In-depth company analysis	• Vision, mission, corporate values, and corporate culture • Robust business model • Consistent strategies and tactics up to the execution/ implementation • Know what the core competency (or even its distinctive competence) is • Qualified corporate governance • Identify various company resources that are indeed valuable • Have capabilities (technology, creative and innovative talents, and others)

(Continued)

[23]https://www.pwc.com/sg/en/publications/assets/epc-transform-family-businesses-201805.pdf

TABLE 13.2 *(Continued)*

Company's Preparation Checklist	
STEP 3 Historical financial performance evaluation	• Ensure high productivity (efficiency and effectiveness) • Good customer management (from acquisition to loyalty) • Solid and well-managed product portfolio • Sound financial management; no cash flow problems • Complete and easily accessible documentation of various financial reports • Identify various valuable intangible resources that are unique and valuable • Identify the stage of the company (start-up, expansion/growth, or mature)
STEP 4 Financial projection development	• Medium- and long-term growth plan • Product development plan • Market development plan • Diversification plan
STEP 5 Investment decision-making	• Prepare for the negotiation process • Select the compatible investors • Ready to review all legal terms

Cash Flow and Market Value Loop

There is a reciprocal relationship between cash flow and market value that we can illustrate in a virtuous upward cycle of cash flow and market value. However, it could be used to describe the opposite effect (i.e., a vicious cycle) if a company's external and internal conditions are not as good as expected. We can divide the cycle that links cash flow and market value into three domains: monetization, cash flow, and market value (see Figure 13.12).

Within the monetization domain, improvements and innovations can significantly aid the multiple value-creation processes and ultimately increase sales achievement. After that, we enter the cash flow domain. In this phase, sales deducted by operating expenses (including depreciation and amortization) will generate operating income. After combining it with nonoperating gains or losses and deducting interest and taxes, it will produce net income. This will then be distributed in the form of dividends and retained earnings.

Next, we turn to the market value domain, where increasing dividends will improve the P/E ratio. This elevates share prices so that the P/B ratio will further grow. Then we go back into the cash flow domain, where companies

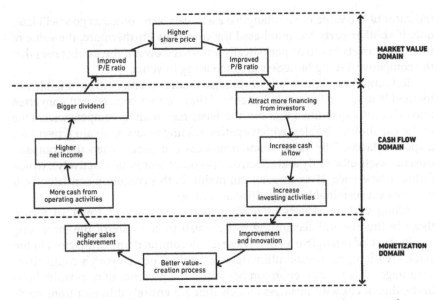

FIGURE 13.12   Simple illustration of cash flow and market value virtuous cycle

with better market value will be more attractive to investors for investment. If that happens, the company's cash inflow will increase due to the financing activity. The company will allocate a portion of this cash to investing activities, namely CAPEX, and investments involving intangible assets such as brands, processes, and people. This investment is expected to increase the company's ability to make improvements and innovations. Then the cycle continues.

Grasping this loop enables marketers with an entrepreneurial perspective to see the significant role that marketing and sales plays in the monetization, cash flow, and market value domains. It also shows how marketing and sales are an integral aspect of securing the company's long-term trajectory.

It's worth noting that the balance sheet does not accommodate intangible assets other than patents, copyrights, franchises, licenses, and goodwill. Suppose there is substantial brand equity that would generate a high selling price. If the company has not been acquired, it is not possible to record the brand's value as a company asset on the balance sheet. The value of this valuable intangible asset can result in a significant difference between the company's book value and the company's market value. The more valuable an intangible asset, the higher the company's market price compared to its book value.

Companies must also carefully identify and acquire other intangible assets—apart from brands, copyrights, franchises, patents, and other intangible assets—such as innovation capabilities, a strong corporate network, unique corporate culture, solid managerial capabilities, and a customer database. The variance between book value and market value, which is an indicator of the value of an intangible asset, can be recorded as goodwill later only if another party has purchased the company. Furthermore, the value of intangible assets has to be periodically amortized even if the market sees that the company's intangible assets are increasing in value.

Relating these discussions to strategic management, neither tangible nor intangible assets will provide benefits if they cannot be used and converted into relevant capabilities that are the basis for creating competencies. One of the capabilities is sales, which applies existing assets to obtain a result for a specific target. The value-creation process can occur when the company uses its assets efficiently and effectively (in other words, productively), which forms competence. If a company can maintain this condition consistently, it will create a sustainable competitive advantage.

Along with marketers increasing their awareness of financial terms, those in finance and accounting will do well to be aware of the increasing significance of intangible assets. These are becoming dominant factors in the value-creation process and ultimately determine the company's competitive advantage. This phenomenon can be seen in the presence of companies born in the digital era with business models that are entirely different from traditional versions. In some cases, the digital start-ups' performances have been stronger. This presents an opportunity for companies using traditional models to reexamine them. It could be an opportune time to learn new approaches to increase their value.

Key Takeaways

- Cash is the lifeblood of an organization, and is used to cover operating expenses, investments, and financial activities.
- When marketers understand key financial terms, they can communicate on a strategic level with other executives and better assess how to budget, fund, and measure projects. Financial savvy marketers will have a positive impact on a company's productivity.
- To value a company, investors will carry out analyses to determine industry-related and economic risks, look in-depth at the company, review historical performance, create financial projections, and make a decision.
- Having an awareness of what investors prioritize can help a company prepare for a valuation.

CHAPTER 14

Uniting Marketing and Finance

From Separation to Integration

In 2013, Raja Rajamannar, chief marketing officer of Mastercard, wanted to elevate the marketing division and give it a more strategic role. At that time, Mastercard was already a well-known brand. Rajamannar saw that marketing efforts had been successful in raising brand awareness. However, they hadn't led to increased revenue.

Rajamannar also observed that the CFO did not work directly with the CMO, even though marketing expenses were among the top three expenses listed in the income statement. To change course, Rajamannar asked the CFO to work with him and integrate the departments.

For this integration to work, Rajamannar added a finance team member into his marketing team. He asked the newly formed group to use a formula to measure ROI for marketing activities. The goal was to set up a common knowledge to measure marketing's impact on the broader business goals.

As a B2B2C brand, Mastercard's strategic plans included engaging directly with the end customer. The company wanted the individual cardholder to recognize the brand. To achieve this, Rajamannar carried out experiential marketing executed by Mastercard in regional offices. He wanted every region to find the right way to communicate directly with the individual customers. He then asked the regional offices to measure the impact of the campaign using the ROI measurement. As a result, Mastercard's brand value rose from US$69 billion in 2013 to US$112 billion in 2021.[1]

---

[1] https://www.marketingweek.com/the-top-100-most-valuable-global-brands-2013/; Sunil Gupta, Srinivas Reddy, and David Lane, "Marketing Transformation at Mastercard," *Harvard Business Review Case 517–040* (2019); https://www.kantar.com/campaigns/brandz/global

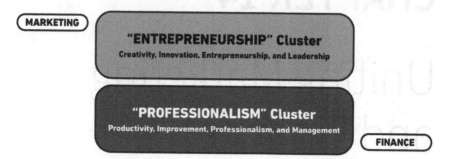

FIGURE 14.1 Marketing and finance elements in the omnihouse model

The Mastercard example shows that an integrated relationship between marketing and finance can significantly affect competitiveness and sustainability. In reality, there is often a lack of harmony between the two departments. For this reason, we listed it as a blind spot previously in this book.

In this chapter, we'll look at overcoming established barriers to unite marketing and finance. We'll explore the mutual benefits that can come from integrated departments. We'll also study how the two can be brought together through a step-by-step process (see Figure 14.1).

Historically Important but Separate Pillars

Despite being in one management ecosystem, traditionally the marketing and finance departments often are unconnected. The common practice among marketing leaders is to make decisions regarding budgets primarily based on current business strategy. Marketing leaders are less likely to determine their budget calculation based on the measurements of financial returns. This practice can potentially bring misunderstanding to both marketing and finance teams because apparently, although they both have the same goal—supporting the company's business strategy—they think differently.[2]

Usually, the finance team will measure the cost and return of marketing activity. However, according to marketing leaders, numeric formulas to measure marketing campaigns might not always be the right approach. Most of the marketing strategy aims for long-term impact. In the short term,

---

[2]https://cmosurvey.org/wp-content/uploads/2021/08/The_CMO_Survey-Highlights_and_Insights_Report-August_2021.pdf

marketing activities can bring a quantitative return. However, for long-term impact, marketing activities get more qualitative results, such as the brand image.[3]

Uniting the two provides an opportunity for better performance. Sarah Allred and Timothy Murphy, in an article published by Deloitte, revealed that a partnership between marketing and finance is needed for growth. Their research showed that executives at the highest growing companies are strongly aligned on measuring marketing's impact.

This alignment provides an essential basis for harnessing the strengths of CMOs and CFOs. Deloitte's research also found that trends are changing: there are indications that some CMOs and CFOs are finding ways to collaborate more effectively. A close and harmonious relationship between the CMO and CFO can significantly help business performance.[4]

Marketing and finance divisions can and should create value for each other. Finance gives a budget to fuel marketing activities, and marketing activities can bring valuable revenue or brand value. Both the marketing and finance divisions need a common language and agreeable way to report to each other. As two very decisive departments, both should work together in line with their company's mission to achieve its vision.[5]

Efficiency, Effectiveness, and Productivity Revisited

In Chapter 13, we discussed efficiency, effectiveness, and productivity using a balance sheet and income statement loop (see Figure 14.2). In general, if marketers want to know the efficiency level, they can review the income statement and calculate the return on sales (ROS) and net profit margin ratios. All of these reflect profitability.

Generally speaking, a "no-margin-for-error" approach does matter to avoid losses due to inefficiency. By understanding the income statement up to operating income, we realize we must avoid any potential inefficiencies. These include unnecessary costs related to non-value-creating activities and errors that could be prevented.

As seen in Chapter 13, marketers can calculate the asset turnover ratio to see how effectively they are running as a team and business. If the company's assets are growing but there is not an adequate increase in sales, it could be

[3]Ibid.
[4]https://www2.deloitte.com/us/en/insights/topics/strategy/impact-of-marketing-finance-working-together.html
[5]https://smallbusiness.chron.com/accounting-marketing-work-together-38276.html

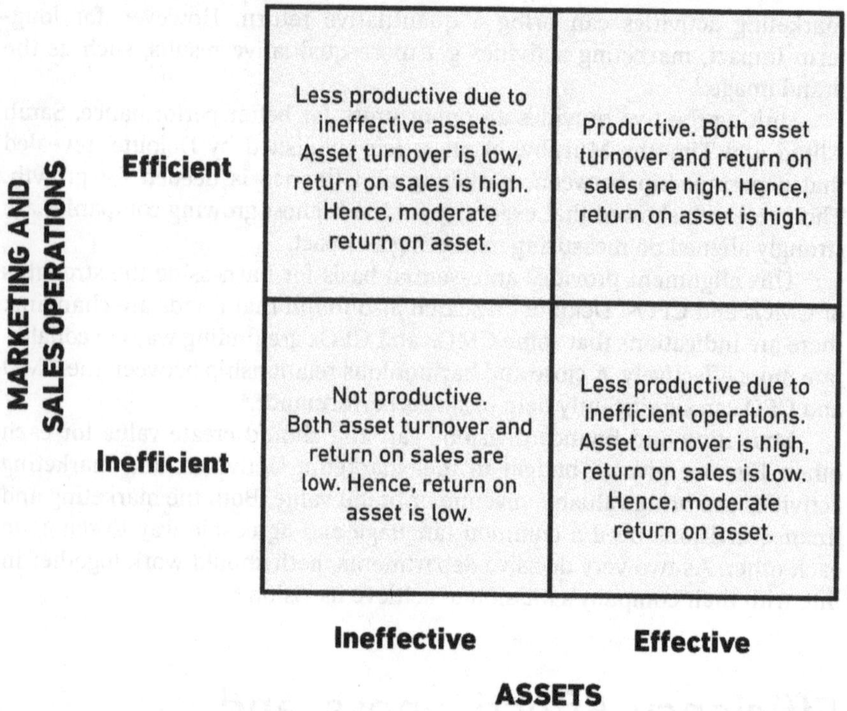

		Ineffective	Effective
MARKETING AND SALES OPERATIONS	**Efficient**	Less productive due to ineffective assets. Asset turnover is low, return on sales is high. Hence, moderate return on asset.	Productive. Both asset turnover and return on sales are high. Hence, return on asset is high.
	Inefficient	Not productive. Both asset turnover and return on sales are low. Hence, return on asset is low.	Less productive due to inefficient operations. Asset turnover is high, return on sales is low. Hence, moderate return on asset.

ASSETS

FIGURE 14.2 Productivity matrix

due to using the incorrect assets. Or vice versa. Perhaps the company has the right assets, but the problem lies in sales efforts. There could also be other fundamental mistakes, such as targeting the wrong segments, inappropriate positioning, commoditization of value propositions (as manifested in products and prices), weak marketing communications, or a misaligned sales strategy.

Combining efficiency and effectiveness leads to a measure of productivity, as reflected in the return on assets (ROA) ratio. If there is an issue with productivity, the source can be investigated. Low productivity could be caused by the following:

- Marketing and sales operations are inefficient even when they have the suitable assets.
- Marketing and sales operations are efficient, but they don't have the right assets.
- There is inefficient marketing and sales operations as well as ineffective assets.

Standard Financial Statements Are Not Enough

A handful of marketing metrics are relevant to financial calculations. These include marketing ROI, cost per action (CPA), customer acquisition cost (CAC), customer lifetime value (CLV), and revenue attribution. Although critical, not all marketers or companies use these key performance indicators (KPIs). Let's review each:

- **ROI.** In a marketing perspective, this is a way to calculate the effectiveness of any marketing activity. ROI is calculated by subtracting marketing cost and sales growth and dividing it by the marketing cost. The result is a percentage of ROI. For example, if the ROI of any marketing activity is 20%, it means the investment of the marketing activity creates 20% of the profit.[6]
- **CPA.** As the total cost of the campaign divided by the number of converted customers, the figure describes how much money we have to spend to get one new customer coming from a marketing campaign activity. The lower the CPA, the more efficient a marketing campaign is.[7]
- **CAC.** This refers to how much it costs to persuade one customer to purchase a product or service. It is found by taking the sales and marketing expenses and dividing them by the number of new customers.
- **CLV.** The formula calculates the total income a company can expect to receive from a typical customer as long as that individual purchases from the company. It is a measure of customer value and loyalty throughout the relationship.
- **Revenue attribution.** This term involves matching customer sales to a specific advertisement to see where the revenue is coming from. It is often used when deciding how to calculate future advertising budgets.

Some of these metrics are vital for measuring marketing performance. However, they are not usually included in standard mandatory financial statements. The financial statements are not typically marketing specific.

There are also marketing-specific nonfinancial metrics to evaluate marketing performance. These provide insight into strategic and tactical decision-making processes. Many of the common ones are listed in Table 14.1.

---

[6]https://www.investopedia.com/articles/personal-finance/053015/how-calculate-roi-marketing-campaign.asp
[7]https://www.bigcommerce.com/ecommerce-answers/what-is-cost-per-acquisition-cpa-what-is-benchmark-retailers/

TABLE 14.1 Marketing-Specific Nonfinancial Metrics

General Marketing Metrics		Digital Marketing Metrics	
• Multiple touchpoint attribution	• Customer satisfaction index	• Likes	• Email click-through rate
• Marketing qualified lead (MQL)	• Repeat purchase	• Subscribe	• Unsubscribe rate
	• Number of new customers	• Forward/share	• New subscribers
• Sales qualified lead (SQL)	• Number of customers	• Social media engagement	• Unengaged subscribers
• MQL to SQL conversion rate	• Cross- and upsell ratio	• Pageviews	• Click-through rate (CTR)
• Lead-to-customer conversion rate	• Number of complaints	• Unique pageviews	• Automate Leads with Chatbots
• Sales team response time	• Number of advocacy (positive/negative)	• Retention rates	• Leads Acquisition via live chat
• Purchase action ratio (PAR)	• Brand advocacy ratio (BAR)	• Engaged time	• Lead-to-customer conversion rate
• Units sold	• Net promoter score	• Pages per session	• Landing page conversion rate
• Market share	• Customer churn	• Bounce rate	• Capture versus conversion rate
• Share of wallet (SOW)		• Website traffic	• Multiple touchpoint attribution
• Top-of-mind		• Website conversion rate	• Number of complaints
• Brand equity		• Email marketing performance (overall)	• Number of advocacy (positive/negative)
• Brand awareness		• Email open rates	• Engagement metrics
• Brand association		• Email bounce rate	• Reach
• Brand loyalty			• Impressions
• Perceived quality			• Number of followers
• Brand experience			• New followers and follower growth rate
• Brand preference			• Traffic (mobile and social media)
• Customer retention rate (CRR)			• Leads (mobile and social media)
			• Conversion rates (mobile and social media)
			• Brand mentions
			• Abandon rate

These metrics are not always shared with non-marketing divisions because they are often viewed as insignificant. Sometimes, the performance looks optimal based on these metrics. Unfortunately, with no or few financial results, they are deemed irrelevant. The difficulty in converting those nonfinancial results into financial results often raises skepticism from other departments, especially finance. Metrics that look solid but do not have meaning attached to them are often referred to as vanity metrics.

Marketing-specific financial metrics are essential and should be presented in meetings, especially with the C-suite. Despite their usefulness, many of the financial metrics in Table 14.2 are not used. If they do exist within a company,

TABLE 14.2   **Marketing-Specific Financial-Related Metrics**

| General Marketing Metrics | | Digital Marketing Metrics |
Marketing-Based	Standard Finance-Based	
• Sales	• Revenue	• Cost per click
• Cost of goods sold	• Depreciation and amortization	• Cost per action (CPA)
• Sales growth	• Operating expenditure	• Cost per lead (CPL)
• Discount	• Operating margin	• Customer acquisition cost (CAC)
• Return on sales (ROS)	• Cash flow	
• Gross margin (segment, category, product, brand, territory, etc.)	• Account receivables	• Digital ad spending
• Sales and marketing expenditures	• Turnover	• Return on [digital] ad spend (ROAS)
• Marketing ROI	• Inventory	
• Cost per lead (CPL)	• Inventory write-off	
• Cost per acquisition (CPA)	• Net profit margin	
• Cost-to-serve per customer	• Asset turnover	
• Average revenue per account/user/customer (ARPA/ARPU/ARPC)	• Return on assets (ROA)	
• Revenue growth rate of existing customers	• Financial leverage	
• Revenue churn	• Return on equity (ROE)	
• Monthly recurring revenue (MRR)	• Price-to-book ratio (P/B ratio)	
• Customer lifetime value (CLTV)	• Price-to-earnings ratio (P/E ratio)	
• Marketing ROI or ROMI		
• Brand value		

they are usually not part of the standard mandatory financial statement (with the exception of common ones such as sales and costs of goods sold).

It is ideal for entrepreneurial marketing organizations to combine finance and marketing teams and set agreeable metrics to interpret marketing activities financially. Without a good analysis and interpretation of these metrics, marketing decisions perhaps will be based on best guess, estimates, or assumptions. If we refer only to the standard mandatory financial statements, which are not marketing-specific, our marketing decisions will be misleading and ineffective.

Using marketing-specific financial and nonfinancial metrics that have been approved by finance counterparts, marketers can increase accuracy in measuring the efficiency, effectiveness, and productivity of their efforts. Teams should measure their marketing activities in all stages, from creating awareness to maintaining customer loyalty. It is important to select the appropriate marketing-specific metrics based on the specific marketing objective.

Stages of Unification

There are five stages that can be used to indicate the relationship between marketing and finance. They range from two separate groups to full integration (see Figure 14.3). We'll look at each stage next.

Stage 0: Entirely Separated

Marketing and finance departments function and develop independently. The two share almost no meaningful information. Communication, even at an informal level, rarely occurs. The two only connect for urgent matters, problems, or issues.

Each person in the two departments focuses on their respective goals based on the KPIs of their department. They have separate routines and agendas and are not interested in collaborating to solve problems. The two departments have yet to show signs of coexistence.

In this stage, occasionally marketing and finance clash, primarily over budget allocation. Their relationship is full of "tug-of-war". Marketers see that the finance team deliberately makes it difficult to disburse budgets. The finance team observes that the marketing group wastes money on ambiguous purposes without clear direction.

Stage 1: Basic Communication

In this phase, the relationship between the marketing and finance departments is still separated but has opened meaningful and essential communication

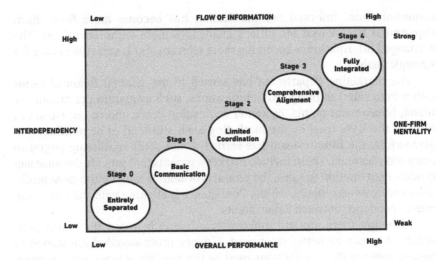

FIGURE 14.3   From separation to integration of the marketing and finance departments

lines. Information interaction has also begun. The information shared is not usually regarded as valuable. Each department functions strategically on its own.

Similar to the previous stage, each person in the two departments still focuses on their respective goals based on the KPIs of their given department. While maintaining their routines, they have begun paying attention to the agenda of one another. They recognize that these could have implications for other functions. Both departments have shown signs of coexistence but don't collaborate to solve internal problems.

Differences of views are evident between the two departments, especially regarding budget allocations, how to use them, and what they want to achieve. However, both departments intend to adjust to enhance suitability in operational matters. Financial professionals do not fully believe most assumptions that marketers use when submitting the marketing budgets. Yet the finance team has started to share information with marketing about their expectations regarding the budget allocation. Marketers have started to consider the financial team's concerns in using this budget.

Stage 2: Limited Coordination

In this second stage, the relationship between the marketing and finance departments has shown significant progress, marked by better coordination efforts. The two departments have more formal lines of communication to exchange more helpful information. Apart from scheduled formal communication, informal communication has become more fluid. Each department has viewed the other's challenges more comprehensively. The exchanged information is becoming more relevant and is sometimes used for strategic goals.

The marketing department has started to use general financial terms (other than sales) to bridge communications, such as margin per product or brand, break-event points, customer acquisition costs, and so on. However, most of the KPIs used by the marketing team still tend to be nonfinancial. Meanwhile, the finance team has started to use some marketing jargon in discussion sessions. These include market segments that provide the most significant contribution to sales, the products or brands that are the most profitable, and customer lifetime value. Coexistence is aligning with the increasing interdependence between departments.

Although there are still differences in views between the two departments, they can be better reconciled. Finance professionals have started to believe some of the assumptions used by the marketing team when submitting their budgets.

The marketing team has become more dedicated to meeting some of the expectations of the finance team. The relationship is becoming harmonious due to the openness of communication and better information exchange. Physically, the workspace of the marketing and finance department in an office is adjacent or at least closer to one another. They hold regular monthly meetings to review business growth, budget use, and the results, both non-financially and financially. They resolve different expectations, problems, and issues in formal and informal meetings. Each department has appointed its liaison to facilitate better coordination. Both collectively establish policies and regulations to avoid disputes or unproductive conflicts.

Stage 3: Comprehensive Alignment

In the third stage, the relationship between the two departments progresses beyond limited coordination to become more comprehensively aligned toward common goals. In addition to strengthening the established communication lines, the two departments have started to use a shared information platform that both departments can update in real time. Both parties increasingly align their activities in terms of objectives they should achieve, KPIs agreed on and used, the division of tasks, decision-making processes, implementation, and monitoring by a joint team of the two departments. There is more collaboration in almost every process, resulting in a growing interdependence.

There are no more obstacles regarding informal communication between departments. Even formal communication can run on a day-to-day basis. Each department sees problems in other departments more comprehensively and starts to discuss and resolve issues together. The information exchanged is no longer just relevant but always up-to-date, well disseminated, and quickly responded to by multiple parties from the two departments, for both strategic and tactical matters.

Information becomes a vital foundation because the two departments have entered the data-driven alignment stage. The data is used to make accurate predictions. Inter-departmental conflicts still occur, but only at a moderate level. Both departments are more focused on facing challenges together to ensure the best results for the company.

The marketing department has begun to use financial information fluently to make decisions regarding the budgets. They aim to effectively use company assets to increase sales. The marketing team uses several financial KPIs to complement and justify the outcomes measured by different non-financial KPIs.

The finance department team has also increasingly understood the marketing processes down to the operational level. They provide input on increasing efficiency and improving profit margins. The finance department has come to appreciate many aspects in marketing, such as the customer database, product innovation capability, and brand equity. The finance team believes that those intangible assets can affect financial results and the company's market value.

The ideal coexistence is becoming a reality, and interdependence is strong. Financial staff members have started to believe and are even involved in determining assumptions used by the marketing team. The fact-based approach has become commonplace, enhancing objectivity in the budgeting decision process for the marketing department.

Marketing personnel have become more involved in setting marketing financial goals that are objective and achievable by the marketing team. Both departments have the same expectations. The relationship is harmonious because both communicate in an understandable language and refer to the same information platform that they can access in real time. The information is accurate and up-to-date. Financial people are fluent in using the lingo of the marketing person and vice versa; the marketing team understands and uses the language of the financial people.

The two departments hold regular weekly meetings to review the overall productivity. They look for available opportunities to grow the business. Both departments strive to avoid issues that could hinder the performance of either one.

Stage 4: Fully Integrated

The fourth stage is when the full integration of the marketing and finance departments occurs. Even though the boundaries are clear, all collaborative processes between the two departments are flexible and accommodative.

Communication is carried out through offline and online platforms, allowing for a seamless relationship.

With the support of AI technology, management can use dynamic information to make predictions and contextual solutions, including customization and personalization. KPIs for both marketing and finance are monitored minute by minute on a dashboard that both departments can access. The decision-making process is also swift and in line with the pace of changes in the business environment. Interdependence reaches its peak so management can reduce the margin for error to the lowest level.

Formal and informal communication occurs effortlessly. The unnecessary bureaucracy, which often slows down the company's managerial process, no longer exists. Each department further broadens its horizons by discussing operational and tactical matters related to strategic issues. Hence, the two departments always refer to the relationship between achievements of two different KPIs. For instance, they discuss the relationship between market share and profitability, the sensitivity of selecting market segments to profit margins, the relationship between customer data platform (CDP) use on customer loyalty and sales, and the influence the acquisition of a brand can have on the company's market value. This strategic relationship ultimately refers to one goal, namely, the company's sustainability, beyond the conventional KPIs of each department.

The integration of the marketing and finance departments is characterized by data- and tech-driven decision-making processes. Computational analysis of data, including big data, or extensive statistics is commonplace. This systematic analysis (or what is known as analytics) will produce meaningful information and insights that form the basis for joint decisions of the two departments. This simultaneously strengthens the integration of the two departments, both at strategic and tactical levels.

The use of company resources under the control of the marketing and finance department has been optimal for its effectiveness and efficiency, focusing on economies of scale and optimizing economies of scope. Full integration with the help of technology can eliminate conflicts and enhance a one-firm mentality. There are no more communication problems because one department already understands the language of the other department and vice versa.

The finance department team sees the marketing department as a strategic business unit that requires budget allocation for operational needs (OPEX) and investment (CAPEX). The difference in perspectives is minimal, because processes tend to be fact-based and data-driven. If it is necessary to use some assumptions, the two departments will jointly develop them. This total interdependence also causes the two departments to create a "success and fail together" mentality, which shows strong cohesiveness and coexistence.

The finance department channels the operational budget and investment to the marketing department. Marketing provides returns to the finance department. Any value for money spent will have an obvious purpose for what it is, and it will also be clear about the results. The two departments have the same vision, develop a joint strategy consistent with the corporate strategy, and use the system or platform together. Coordination at C-suite, especially among the CEO, CFO, and CMO, is becoming more harmonious, and the "tug-of-war" phenomenon is no longer visible.

To see an integration in action, consider the case of ABB Group, which appointed a double-headed CFO. This position oversaw the global marketing team along with finances. This ensured the connectivity required to run business operations.[8]

The Finance–Marketing Loop

The finance–marketing looping runs flawlessly in a fully integrated condition. With the support of technology, it will strengthen the marketing and finance integration platform. Figure 14.4 relates this relationship.

FIGURE 14.4 Simplification of finance–marketing loop

---

[8]https://hbr.org/2014/12/why-corporate-functions-stumble

The looping process begins when the two departments set goals and strategies to achieve these goals before the budget allocation. In addition, the two departments outline and agree on technical or operational matters to ensure a smooth execution stage. Both departments do all their work through an integrated offline and online platform.

The marketing department will allocate the budget for marketing operational activities and investment on at least three elements: customer, product, and brand (see Table 14.3).

TABLE 14.3	Examples of Financial Activities on Customer, Product, and Brand	
	Operational (Short Run)	**Investment (Long Run)**
Customer	• Brick-and-mortar store operations (store staffing, store merchandising, store administration, store audit, etc.) • Store maintenance (electricity, facilities, furniture, etc.) • Online store management (order management, user experience or Interface management, etc.)	• Building omni-channel platform and experience • Building new brick-and-mortar stores • Installing new technology in offline stores (artificial intelligence, face recognition, augmented reality, etc.)
	• Market research (survey, focus group discussion, in-depth interview, ethnographic research)	• Market development • Resegmentation and retargeting
	• Customer acquisition program	• Building customer data platform (CDP)
	• Customer loyalty program	• Developing customer loyalty platform
	• Customer service operations • After-sales service	• Building customer care center (with a chatbot)
	• Collecting customer database • Running customer community programs/sites	• Personalization and customization platform • Building customer analytics process (big data software, etc.)

TABLE 14.3   *(Continued)*

	Operational (Short Run)	Investment (Long Run)
Product	• Production cost (raw material procurement and manufacturing cost) • Product packaging • Research and development for products[9]	• Building new product development systems and facilities • Building new manufacturing facilities • Product innovation (create differentiation) • New product patents and rights
	• Sales activities • Brochure/promotional tools production • Salesperson compensation • Product samples and freebies • Travel cost for salespersons' activities • Teleselling activities	• Installing sales force management software (i.e., salesforce.com) • New server and website for online stores
	• Sales training	• Building a new learning center
	• Distributions/logistics activities • Warehousing • Storage and transportation • Inventory management and control • Channel member relationship management (channel acquisition, development, evaluation, and termination)	• Distribution network (i.e., new outlets, new distribution hub, online platform, warehouses, etc.) • Developing new channel system (i.e., developing franchise system)

(Continued)

[9]Based on "Condensed Consolidated Statement of Operations (Unaudited) of Apple." Apple considers R&D as operational expenses. Please see more at https://www.apple.com/newsroom/pdfs/FY20-Q3_Consolidated_Financial_Statements.pdf

TABLE 14.3 *(Continued)*

	Operational (Short Run)	Investment (Long Run)
Brand	• Co-branding • Brand deals with brand ambassadors	• New brand acquisition
	• Developing new product line (complementary/supplementary products)	• New brand development
	Offline brand activation: • Advertising • Event management • Sales promotion • Direct marketing • Community marketing activities • Public relations Online brand activation: • Social media marketing (Facebook marketing, Instagram ads, YouTube ads, etc.) • Search engine marketing • Content marketing • Email marketing	• Brand equity enhancement • Brand extension • Brand rejuvenation • Brand repositioning

The marketing team must deliver to the finance department a demonstrable result from these operational and investment activities. First, the marketing department will achieve several nonfinancial goals by creating product or brand awareness in the eyes of prospective customers or their specific target market. If the market sees a clear value proposition, non-overpromised positioning, strong differentiation, and the chance to receive real solutions, this will create a strong appeal for the product or brand and ultimately generate customer loyalty.

Later, the sales team will convert these nonfinancial achievements into financial results, step-by-step from a preference to an interest in buying, and finally, purchase. Purchases in cash will immediately generate cash inflows for the finance department, whereas noncash purchases will result in account receivables that will become cash and will be received by the finance department. If the nonfinancial KPIs achieved are strong enough, but the financial results are not satisfactory, it will be concluded that something is awry. Both departments will work to find the root cause and solve it quickly.

With tangible results in the form of returns, trust will be built between the finance and marketing departments. This accelerates the finance–marketing loop cycle. In essence, the marketing department must always link its efforts with actual value creation as reflected in both nonfinancial and financial metrics.

Marketing investments, usually in intangible assets such as brands, sales networks, loyal customers, and product differentiation, cannot be recorded in a balance sheet. However, these intangible assets have value at a certain range of prices, as indicated by the variance between book value and market value. If we find that the market value is higher than the book value, then the value of intangible assets, including those created through marketing investments, will have a higher value. The high value of intangible assets can be used as an indicator to show that the company's future financial performance is promising.[10]

Based on these explanations, marketing teams should not be lulled by the view that only marketing is everyone's job. Now finance is also everyone's job, especially for marketing people themselves. As such, marketers can understand and master the language of finance. With those tools in hand, the department can better communicate with other functions and show up at C-suite meetings, ready to carry its own weight in strategic conversations.

Therefore, it is necessary to develop a focused finance course for marketers. This could be offered through educational institutions as well as in-house training programs at companies. The lessons could demonstrate the key ratios to know, explain how to communicate with finance, and lay out the process to integrate both functions.

Key Takeaways

- A partnership between marketing and finance can reduce friction, lead to integration, and propel the company toward growth.
- The relationship between marketing and finance can be identified as five stages on a spectrum, ranging from both departments operating as separate groups to being fully integrated. These stages are: entirely separated (stage 0), basic communication (stage 1), limited coordination (stage 2), comprehensive alignment (stage 3), and fully integrated (stage 4).
- When fully integrated, there is a loop that runs flawlessly between finance and marketing; it can be continually strengthened and upleveled.
- Both marketing and finance knowledge are needed throughout an organization. To raise awareness, companies can hold internal training sessions to teach basics.

---

[10]https://knowledge.wharton.upenn.edu/article/non-financial-performance-measures-what-works-and-what-doesnt/

CHAPTER 15

Technology for Humanity

High Tech, Higher Touch[1]

Today, a customer who wants to schedule a haircut at a salon can do so through Google's AI-based duplex assistant service feature. This simulation, first announced in 2018, gives a human impression. It uses tone, language, and even filler worlds such as "mm-hmm," to the extent that customers may not even realize they are talking to a robot.[2]

The Google duplex service, now available in the US and other countries, frees its users from directly interacting with other parties. It enables customers to make a variety of transactions, including restaurant reservations and online movie ticket purchases. Its scope of services is expected to expand further in the coming years.[3]

The feature is symbolic of just how far AI has come. Gone are the days of robotic voices and limited vocabulary. The advancement also marks a shift from mobile-first to an AI-first world. AI enables technology to become more accessible, friendly, and solution-oriented.[4] No longer perceived as "cold," AI can serve as a human interaction tool.

As AI and other technologies continue to develop, considering the human context is essential (see Figure 15.1). Stakeholders will be looking for the assurance that advancements are used humanely. Moreover, they will want to see technology provide tangible benefits, like an improved quality of life.

---

[1]This subtitle borrows the term *high tech high touch*, which was put forward by John Naisbitt in his book with Nana Naisbitt and Douglas Philips, *High Tech High Touch: Technology and Our Accelerated Search for Meaning* (London: Nicholas Brealey Publishing, 1999).
[2]https://www.youtube.com/watch?v=D5VN56jQMWM
[3]https://www.androidauthority.com/what-is-google-duplex-869476/
[4]https://blog.google/technology/ai/making-ai-work-for-everyone/

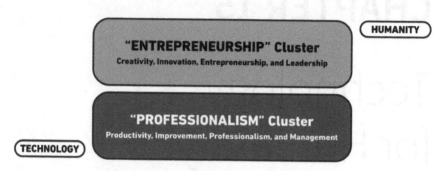

FIGURE 15.1 Technology and humanity elements in the omnihouse model

In Chapter 6, we discussed that technology and humanity are a dichotomy. In this chapter, we will look at how to converge technology and humanity to achieve higher revenue, build stronger brand awareness, and increase customer satisfaction. In Chapter 16, we will consider what benefits can be provided to employees, society, stakeholders, and the company itself.

The New Level of Touch

The discussion about high technology and high touch has been going on since John Naisbitt first described the concept in the early 1980s. Frequently, the topic has focused solely on the customer as the most crucial goal. However, there are other elements to consider, including the well-being of society. The application of corporate social responsibility (CSR) may not always be embedded into a business process or model.

Furthermore, societal marketing tends to overlook the people in the company as a vital element. If we want to deliver benefits for humanity, the starting point lies with how employees are treated. Next, we can focus on customers as the source of the company's profitability. Finally, we can consider society, which is essential for long-term sustainability.

One of marketing's blind spots is ignoring the humanity aspect. When this happens, marketing is merely a tool for the company's interest, which is solely profit-oriented. Companies "persuade" the wider community to buy their products without paying attention to employees, the environment, or other stakeholders.

Despite its huge and rapid development, Amazon ran into troubles regarding the well-being of its workers. In Christmas 2019, the Amazon "Faster Shipping" campaign led to more than US$87 billion in revenue. This achievement might have been excellent news for the shareholders, but to employees, who were only given two 15-minute breaks, it may have seemed like a disaster.

Reports of injury rates at one facility were also in the spotlight, resulting in a petition made by 600 workers at the Amazon warehouse, demanding that the company improve the working conditions and give more breaks.[5]

Amazon has also faced environment-related challenges. A former employee mentioned pushing Amazon to develop its climate change policy at its annual board meeting.[6] Amazon was promoting customer conveniences such as faster shipping, one-day shipping, and 2-hour grocery delivery, especially during high season or on specific days like Christmas. This campaign often didn't measure its worker loads and the impact on the environment from so many orders and fast shipments. The consequences included significant waste and pollution while rushing out deliveries.[7]

In response, Amazon stated it would promote the use of renewable energy in its business processes.[8] The efforts may inspire other companies to follow suit and initiate environment-focused programs. Doing so would align with the UN's SDGs in the years to come.[9]

In situations with few competitors, the customer sometimes does not have much say in how a company behaves. In recent years, as we have discussed, these conditions have changed. There has been a shift of bargaining power from producers to consumers, which is why companies need to be more customer-centric. Customers are now more sophisticated, connected, educated, informed, challenging to satisfy, and disloyal. As such, companies today try to insert social elements into their business models, rather than promoting weak CSR efforts.

One company that has shown success is Cassava Bags Australia, who created a 100% natural biodegradable bag. It will dissolve entirely in water, deteriorate in landfills, and break down in other environments. The bag is safe for the environment because it is nontoxic, contains no palm oil, and is not harmful to marine life. The company was formed on the belief that businesses can be a force for good and that the singular actions of individuals, collectively, have the potential to transform the world.[10] These bags generate a profit, protect the environment, and support SDG number 13, climate action.

It is important to underscore that every company also has a social responsibility. Companies must base their marketing efforts on values established by the leadership. Hence, tech-driven marketing's goal for humanity is to create value through values.

---

[5]https://www.theguardian.com/technology/2020/feb/05/amazon-workers-protest-unsafe-grueling-conditions-warehouse
[6]https://www.bbc.com/news/business-56641847
[7]https://www.wbur.org/onpoint/2021/07/09/the-prime-effect-amazons-environmental-impact
[8]https://www.bbc.com/news/business-56641847
[9]https://www.wbur.org/onpoint/2021/07/09/the-prime-effect-amazons-environmental-impact
[10]https://cassavabagsaustralia.com.au/

Bitwise Industries, a tech ecosystem company, has developed digital programs that help underserved populations access their basic needs. The company built an app that manages grocery orders and tracks food deliveries. It also launched a network to connect workers with jobs.[11] Its efforts showcase a strategy to integrate and align business with social affairs.

Implications of Tech-Driven Marketing

Indeed, we cannot separate the new entrepreneurial marketing genre from the technology support that will affect marketing in a company, both for B2B and B2C. The marketing application within a company can no longer only refer to the marketing dimension itself. It must be transcendent and collaborative, banish existing silos between departments, and converge existing functions. For this purpose, technology will play a crucial role as an enabler.[12]

In line with strengthening the tech-driven marketing approach, marketers may need to get out of their comfort zone to understand new technologies. If they don't, they could quickly become incompetent and, ultimately, irrelevant. For example, Borders at one time was a national book and music retailer. Once a very popular location, Borders eventually went into massive debt and invested in retail locations without realizing that customer habits were changing rapidly. Entering the digital era, Borders was late to accommodate the technology that provided e-books and music streams. With too much spent on real estate and not enough on technology innovation, Borders could not maintain its business.[13]

Facing the future, we must combine technology with the marketing discipline. To trailblaze versus merely catch up, a company should hire a marketing technologist, a new type of marketer who can design and operate the necessary technologies to carry out marketing-related efforts and understand the technological context. A new breed of these marketers can see and realize the application of marketing in an already digital world.[14]

In 2020, internet users worldwide reached 4.83 billion, with more than 60% of the global population connected to the internet. This number will continue to escalate, and by 2030 it has been estimated that 90% of people will

[11]https://www.npr.org/2022/02/04/1078050740/irma-olguin-why-we-should-bring-tech-economies-to-underdog-cities
[12]Please refer further to https://hbr.org/2019/07/building-the-ai-powered-organization
[13]https://www.collectivecampus.io/blog/10-companies-that-were-too-slow-to-respond-to-change
[14]As disclosed by Scott Brinker and Jason Heller. Please refer to https://www.mckinsey.com/business-functions/marketing-and-sales/our-insights/marketing-technology-what-it-is-and-how it should work

be connected online.[15] Advertising on mobile ads is growing to coincide with these trends.[16]

This opportunity aligns with where our marketing technology is heading. Marketing has become more digitalized and advanced. For example, big data, blockchain, and social media advertising tools like Facebook ads and chatbots enable marketers to provide customers with more customization and personalization.[17] Although the effectiveness varies among industry sectors, many companies, both B2C and B2B, have used social media platforms such as Instagram, TikTok, and LinkedIn. These tools, combined with technology, will help marketers to know their customers, their shopping preferences, and the specific keywords they use when searching.

For the best application of new technology to a brand or product, marketers need the support of other departments in the company, such as information technology and legal. The more insights companies can collect, the more strategies they can build. The challenge is not about the data collected but how to use it.[18]

A tech-driven marketing approach goes beyond installing new technologies. It affects the entire company by integrating departments and establishing a new mentality. Research by McKinsey shows that a few keys to the success of digital transformation include hiring tech-savvy executives, developing future workforce capabilities, empowering employees to work in new ways, offering day-to-day tools a digital boost, and frequently communicating via traditional and digital methods.[19]

In general, the application of technology-based marketing will have implications for marketing management, including customers, products, and brands.

Customer Management

Companies can better manage customers with the help of technology, which focuses attention on several components, as discussed in the next sections.

More Attention on Community

In the era of connectivity, we see that community is becoming increasingly important for companies to understand the market better, build relationships,

[15]https://www.currentware.com/blog/internet-usage-statistics/
[16]https://www.statista.com/statistics/303817/mobile-internet-advertising-revenue-worldwide/
[17]https://www.ama.org/journal-of-marketing-special-issue-new-technologies-in-marketing/
[18]https://www.digitalmarketing-conference.com/the-impact-of-new-technology-on-marketing/
[19]https://www.mckinsey.com/business-functions/people-and-organizational-performance/our-insights/unlocking-success-in-digital-transformations

understand customers, and carry out an exchange of value. Intimacy with the community—both offline and online—will enable companies to better support customers. Shoppers can get acquainted and interact with each other as well as the brand.[20]

More Contextual Approach

With the support of technology, a company can and should manage customers in a one-on-one manner. It can enable customers to interact anytime and anywhere as long as they are connected online. Companies can provide personalization and vice versa; customers can customize products and services to meet their preferences.

AI-based interactions can provide a better customer experience and robust engagement. This can occur through digital platforms such as chatbots. For example, Mastercard, a leader in global payments, launched a chatbot, mainly for customers' inquiries. These bots can answer questions related to an account balance, money managing tools, and transaction records.[21]

Content marketing—primarily through social media platforms that are entertaining, inspiring, educating, and convincing—will play a more significant role. These efforts can create awareness, generate interest, and increase customer advocacy. It can lead customers to discover information, make purchases, and continue using the products and services.

Testimonials, case studies, and content featuring real customers are crucial components to gain customer trust. This is often referred to as "social proof." We can use customer-generated content, put it on social media, and let the community discuss and share an honest opinion about the products. Hence, it will be easier for everyone to find more helpful information and share it with friends. This platform can also enable marketers to get feedback on their products or see whether their marketing strategies work.[22]

Customer-generated content can provide direct contact and help our brand recognition within the customer community. Ultimately, a positive experience will resonate with the brand's credibility. It could lead to repurchase, resulting in increased customer retention. The more content relates to the real-life experience of a customer, the easier it will be to gain customer satisfaction.[23]

---

[20]https://seths.blog/2012/02/horizontal-marketing-isnt-a-new-idea/

[21]https://www.retaildive.com/ex/mobilecommercedaily/mastercard-unveils-chatbot-platform-for-merchants-and-banks-along-with-wearable-payments

[22]https://www.socxo.com/blog/5-ways-customer-advocacy-will-enhance-content-marketing/

[23]https://blog.usctada.com/win-the-market-with-customer-advocacy

More Realistic Positioning

Customers and the wider public have more access to determine if a company keeps its promises. They are value- and purpose-driven, willing to alter their purchasing patterns to support a cause. They apply the "trust, but verify" approach, and check more than the information on the packaging. As shown by research from IBM in 2020, up to 75% of customers who already trust a brand will still do extensive research before making purchases.[24]

Because customers are getting smarter and understand our company inside and out, it is not uncommon for a "consensus" to surface among customers to accept a company's positioning. Therefore, companies must ensure promises align with reality. Customers and the public will know if messages contain the truth, which is the foundation for building customer trust.

Fast-fashion brands such as Zara, H&M, and M&S are launching green and sustainable clothing lines. H&M became one of the big players in this trend when it implemented a new green clothing line called "Conscious" in 2019.[25] They claimed to use more sustainable materials, such as organic cotton and recycled polyester, to help reduce environmental waste. However, customers started to investigate the claim and found that it was misleading, with a lack of existing evidence to support it. We often refer to this phenomenon as "greenwashing," creating a false impression or presenting incorrect information about how a company's products are more ecologically friendly.[26]

In August 2021, climate activists protested by sitting in the window display of an H&M store in the UK that displayed posters claiming the brand as an "Eco Warrior & Climate Crusader." Their purpose was to show their disagreement with advertising techniques compared to the actual product that H&M sold. This reaction to greenwashing shows that customers are now more critical than ever when receiving positioning messages from brands.[27]

Product Management

In line with the increasingly mainstream customization and personalization, managing products and matters related to these products has become more challenging. Companies will do well to carry out the actions described in the following sections.

---

[24]https://www.ibm.com/downloads/cas/EXK4XKX8
[25]https://a-little-insight.com/2021/05/09/hm-are-greenwashing-us-again-can-fast-fashion-ever-be-ethical/
[26]https://www.investopedia.com/terms/g/greenwashing.asp#:~:text=Greenwashing%20is%20the%20process%20of,company's%20products%20are%20environmentally%20friendly
[27]https://www.bigissue.com/news/environment/hm-greenwashing-is-disguising-the-reality-of-fast-fashion/

Codify Authentic Differentiation

The solution platform is crucial to strengthening differentiation, which can become the basis for establishing a lock-in mechanism. For instance, the Ritz-Carlton brand is known for its "gold standards," which are the foundation of its culture and services. Its philosophy, "We are ladies and gentlemen serving ladies and gentlemen," pertains to how visitors and coworkers alike are treated.[28] The service, supported by its loyalty program, has led Ritz-Carlton to become one of the world's top destinations for patrons seeking a luxury and high-quality experience.

An organization can also identify elements of its corporate DNA to develop an authentic differentiation. It must communicate these stand-out features to customers. The elements will need to be relevant so that customers who appreciate them are willing to pay for them. The solution platform then should reflect this authenticity.

Reinvent Marketing Mix

Companies can expand opportunities for using their customers' input to improve product development. Involving customers in this co-creation process on different technology-based platforms enables customization, reduces the company's R&D costs, and minimizes the opportunity for product failure to occur.[29] For instance, Starbucks launched My Starbucks Ideas to focus on what customers want and gather ideas regarding products, in-store experiences, and the company's involvement on social issues.[30] The platform provides space for customers to share ideas and discuss what improvements they want to see. Their input has helped the company create new flavors, led to Wi-Fi in all its stores, and even the development of a mobile app.[31]

Consumer prices are dynamic, similar to currency exchange rates. A company can no longer set and fix prices unilaterally. Instead, the customer and company can work together to determine the value. Uber's base fare is typically lower than a taxi, but it can fluctuate depending on variables such as time and distance, traffic, and rider-to-driver demand. This information enables customers to evaluate the prices and decide if they are reasonable for them.[32]

[28]https://ritzcarltonleadershipcenter.com/about-us/about-us-foundations-of-our-brand/
[29]Refers to the concept of C.K. Prahalad and Venkat Ramaswamy in their book *The Future of Competition: Co-Creating Unique Value with Customers* (Boston, MA: Harvard Business Review Press, 2004).
[30]https://digital.hbs.edu/platform-digit/submission/my-starbucks-idea-crowdsourcing-for-customer-satisfaction-and-innovation/
[31]https://skeepers.io/en/blog/customer-loyalty-increases-starbucks-profits
[32]https://www.forbes.com/sites/forbestechcouncil/2019/01/08/dynamic-pricing-the-secret-weapon-used-by-the-worlds-most-successful-companies/?sh=3eadac2a168b

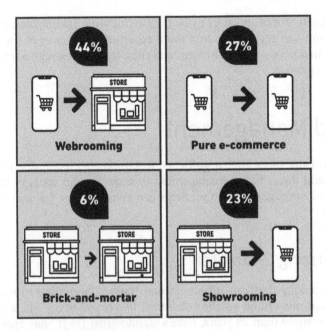

FIGURE 15.2   The phygital lifestyle[33]

Promotion must be two-way in nature to become a conversation in line with a company's increasingly horizontal position with its customers. For instance, Paradigm Life, a banking and solutions supplier based in the US, created an interactive financial literacy quiz. The arrangement informed customers of their level of financial expertise. It also unconsciously made people perceive they needed Paradigm's services if they did not achieve high scores.[34]

Redesign Sales Channel

Selling should be solution-centric by leveraging omni-channel capabilities. Brick-and-mortar companies must also exist online, and vice versa (see Figure 15.2).

In the figure, *webrooming* refers to consumers researching products online first and then buying the products in a physical store. *Showrooming* is when the customer tries out the products in a physical store before buying them online.[35] The omni-channel sales process maintains an effort to meet

---

[33]Philip Kotler, Hermawan Kartajaya, and Iwan Setiawan, Marketing 5.0: Technology for Humanity (Hoboken, NJ: Wiley, 2021).
[34]https://paradigmlife.net/perpetual-wealth-strategy
[35]https://www.techopedia.com/definition/31036/webrooming

customer preferences and actively involve them. With the help of technology, a salesperson can get a closer and more accurate perspective of the customers' individual needs, offer solutions, and close the sale through a transparent transaction process.

Brand Management

In line with the more robust guidance to humanize customers, an organization should direct brand management to show human traits in the brand identity and messaging. To do so, firms can adhere to the following in their messaging.

Build Strong Character

Using technology that can mimic human traits is becoming more critical. Management must build a strong character in a brand to become alive like a human. For more than 20 years, Nike's tagline "Just Do It" has appeared on their products. It is simple yet direct, powerful, and competitive. Nike has also used this to inspire female empowerment in sports. The company considers the line to be more than just a slogan, but rather a philosophy.[36]

Instill a Sense of Caring

Technology can help create a more proactive approach to customer care. Analytics may reveal common pain points and desires of customers. Adjustments on how to handle situations can be made based on the findings.

In 2018, Spotify patented speech recognition technology that observed patterns. The arrangement enabled the company to combine speech recognition with other information, such as previously played songs. It could then recommend new songs as suggestions to listeners.[37]

Open Up Collaboration

Some interactive processes can be done by collaborating with customers and enabling them to do it themselves, similar to outsourcing. Assigning roles

---

[36]https://hbr.org/1992/07/high-performance-marketing-an-interview-with-nikes-phil-knight
[37]https://www.bbc.com/news/entertainment-arts-55839655

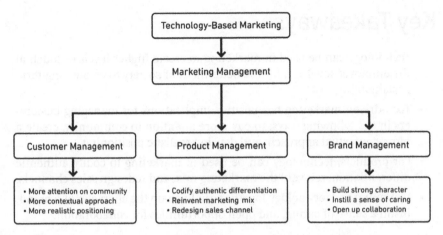

FIGURE 15.3   Implications of technology-based marketing on marketing management

in these processes makes customers an inseparable part of the company. Furthermore, in doing so, companies can collaborate with multiple partners in a specific digital business ecosystem.

Singapore Airlines collaborates with its passengers by providing several check-in options online through its official website, its app, the check-in service kiosk, or the check-in counter. In addition, at specific terminals at Changi International Airport, travelers can take advantage of the automated bag drop where they can print baggage tags at the self-service kiosk, attach the tags, and put their luggage on the conveyor belt, all by following the instructions on the screen.[38] This method frees passengers from the queue and, at the same time, eases the burden on Singapore Airlines officers.

Through collaboration, the company invites customers to participate in the value-creation process. Customers can monitor all stages of delivery of the product or service they need. When waiting for a food delivery, for example, customers often want to know where their meal is. With a tracking system, they can watch its progress and prepare for its arrival.

Together, technology and the right marketing strategies can create a positive impact for everyone involved (see Figure 15.3). Tech-driving marketing leads to better customer management, product management, and brand management. In Chapter 16, we'll look at further benefits that come from combining the powerful forces of technology and humanity.

---

[38]https://www.singaporeair.com/en_UK/sg/travel-info/check-in/

Key Takeaways

- Technology can be used in marketing to create higher levels of touch at the employee level and for the betterment of society to create long-term sustainability.
- Tech-driven marketing has positive implications for managing customers in the following ways: to pay more attention to community, create a more contextual approach, and develop realistic positioning.
- For products, technology can be used in marketing to codify authentic differentiation, reinvent the marketing mix, and redesign sales channels.
- Marketing and technology together can liven up the character of a brand, instill a sense of caring, and open opportunities for collaboration.

CHAPTER 16

Technology and Stakeholders

Leveraging Tools to Increase Value

I f we use technology for the common human good, customers, and society, we know it as technology for real humanity. This is not just high touch but higher-touch because it holistically accommodates all stakeholders' perspectives and broader implications. Therefore, this book's discussion about technology does not comprise the technical details about the technology, but how companies use technology and the resulting implications. In this chapter, we'll look at technology for the people, customers, and stakeholders. Then we'll consider its effect for a company.

Technology for People

Companies can leverage technology to assist talent in optimizing their efficiency. The exact technology to use depends on the industry. In the next sections we will explore several that can make the workforce more productive and humane.

Compensation Management Software

Compensation-related digital tools can help companies manage salaries. All payrolls can be seen on a dashboard and adjustments made based on an employee's achievements. The company can adopt policies that optimize the existing budget and are fair to its people.[1]

Capterra, an online marketplace vendor, uses Paycom to manage its workforce. Its approach enables it to onboard new workers, handle time-off requests, and keep on top of HR tasks. These solutions accommodate flexible scheduling, which boosts productivity.[2]

Cloud Computing

This technology enables employees to connect via the cloud to a centralized server to view files, data, and other functions. Thus, people can do their work remotely.[3] Cloud computing also increases transparency and, at the same time, strengthens collaboration between divisions in a company.[4]

In a survey, 55% of respondents agreed that cloud computing data could provide collaboration breakthroughs. In addition, 64% said that cloud computing collaboration tools help them execute business tasks faster. Moreover, 58% of respondents, of which 90% are leaders, agreed that cloud computing could improve the business process.[5]

Collaboration Platforms

Collaboration platforms facilitate communication between people virtually as they carry out their work. They can easily share documents and exchange information. With more workers logging in remotely, collaboration tools have become more critical than ever.

Data Analytics

Data analytics enable us to process data based on specific algorithms to answer what is happening (descriptive) and why (diagnostic). They can make predictions based on historical data. For instance, Amazon uses data gathered from

---

[1]https://www.g2.com/categories/compensation-management#:~:text=Compensation%20
management%20software%20helps%20organizations,report%20on%20company%20
compensation%20data
[2]https://www.paycom.com/resources/blog/paycom-recognized-for-helping-businesses-
thrive-in-2020/
[3]https://www.cobizmag.com/the-future-of-work-how-technology-enables-remote-employees/
[4]https://www.careermetis.com/ways-cloud-computing-improve-employee-productivity/
[5]https://www.forbes.com/sites/forbespr/2013/05/20/forbes-insights-survey-
reveals-cloud-collaboration-increases-business-productivity-and-advances-global-
communication/?sh=295bd24d2a50

customers while browsing to provide targeted recommendations. The more the customers search, the better Amazon can predict what they want to buy and provide recommendations. The analytics also build a profile based on user information compared with other similar profiles. Amazon will then offer the same products that similar users have purchased.[6]

Augmented Reality and Virtual Reality

Augmented reality (AR) and virtual reality (VR)—collectively called mixed reality (MR)—are emerging technologies used to make it easier for people to do their work.[7] AR can be used directly on tablets or smartphones and does not require additional headsets or consoles like VR does. The technology can be used in teaching sessions. For instance, CAE Healthcare uses compatible devices such as Microsoft HoloLens to train its physicians and practice complex medical procedures in a three-dimensional setting.[8]

3D Printing

This technology—also known as additive manufacturing—can make three-dimensional solid objects through a layer-by-layer process. It is used in a variety of industries, including construction, automotive, fashion, and medical science. It can make bone replacement, joints, and skull plates—often customized. More than 100 types of implants and clinical devices are 3D printed and have the Food and Drug Administration's endorsement in the US.[9]

With conventional methods, a company developing a product would make a basic mock-up to send to another professional prototype developer. This process of sending the design and prototype back and forth takes time. When using 3D printing, the process is more efficient. ABB robotics, for instance, uses 3D printing to reduce prototype time from five weeks to just one hour.[10]

---

[6]https://bernardmarr.com/amazon-using-big-data-to-understand-customers/
[7]https://www.ibm.com/thought-leadership/institute-business-value/report/ar-vr-workplace
[8]https://www.cae.com/news-events/press-releases/cae-healthcare-announces-microsoft-hololens-2-applications-for-emergency-care-ultrasound-and-childbirth-simulators/#:~:text=and%20childbirth%20simulators-,CAE%20Healthcare%20announces%20Microsoft%20HoloLens%202%20applications,care%2C%20ultrasound%20and%20childbirth%20simulators&text=CAE%20Healthcare%20announces%20the%20release,physiology%20into%20its%20patient%20simulators
[9]https:// //www.nytimes.com/2020/03/18/business/customization-personalized-products.html
[10]https://3duniverse.org/2020/10/26/how-3d-printing-can-reduce-time-and-cost-during-product-development/

Robotics/Automation

Certain industries, such as manufacturing, have leveraged the use of robotics in their processes for a long time. Many believe that it can help people carry out their duties ergonomically and provide higher safety and productivity. Tedious work can be left to the robot to be completed automatically.[11]

This technology is the answer to the challenge of achieving high productivity growth rates along with superior and consistent product quality. However, we cannot rule out the potential for excesses that lead to poor conditions. In Amazon's warehouses, an automated management system monitors workers to see how fast they work and gives them a rate based on the number of items they process in an hour. Employees have reported being pushed to work nonstop or risk getting fired for not being fast enough. The situation became so bad that almost 10% of full-time workers sustained severe injuries in 2018.[12]

Industrial Internet of Things

Industrial internet of things (IoT) is the essence of the industrial revolution that we know as Industry 4.0. Its application enables machine-to-machine (M2M) communication, automation, and wireless control. Sectors using this technology include automotive, health care, manufacturing, transportation, logistics, and retail, all of whom can benefit from IoT.[13]

From these, staff in a company will experience these advantages:

Quality of work life. Employees will focus their attention on issues in the value-creation process, which technology cannot handle. An Intel survey showed that more than one-third of respondents said IoT solutions for public safety, health care, and transportation are in place or coming in their communities.[14]

Cost-efficiency. Technology can help a company reduce operating costs and increase profits. In the manufacturing industry, IoT monitors equipment and uses predictive applications to lower maintenance costs.[15] General Electric is forecasted to create around US$19 trillion in profits and cost savings by 2026 through adopting IoT.[16]

---

[11]https://www.techrepublic.com/article/3-ways-robots-can-support-human-workers/
[12]https://www.theverge.com/2020/2/27/21155254/automation-robots-unemployment-jobs-vs-human-google-amazon
[13]https://www.oracle.com/internet-of-things/what-is-iot/
[14]https://www.forbes.com/insights-inteliot/connecting-tomorrow/iot-improving-quality-of-life/#4add0b2717a5
[15]https://www.machinemetrics.com/blog/industrial-iot-reduces-costs
[16]https://medium.datadriveninvestor.com/how-manufacturers-use-iot-to-improve-operational-efficiency-2c9192cc9725

More flexibility. Technology enables workers more say in how they will work while simultaneously increasing productivity. Airbus, an aerospace company, has implemented IoT in all its sites in Spain to streamline their production process. Most of their aircraft components are now fitted with sensors that can monitor the plane's behavior in real time, enabling employees to check for faults and maintenance requirements remotely and efficiently.[17]

Technology for Customers

The main intention in using technology is to humanize employees so they, in turn, can humanize their customers. However, a company can also use those technologies to humanize their customers, not exploit them. Following are some technologies that can make customers' quality of life even better.

Customer Data Platforms (CDPs)

An integrated database that multiple systems can access enables a company to understand customers at different touchpoints. Personalized products and services can be offered to shoppers in a relevant way. For example, Next Big Sound has sorted out ways to use the information from Spotify streams, iTunes purchases, SoundCloud plays, Facebook likes, Wikipedia online visits, YouTube hits, and Twitter mentions to anticipate the next big trend in music. The company's investigation gives insights into social media fame, the impact of television appearances, and data that is priceless to the music business.[18]

Online Payment Systems

Electronic payments are increasingly replacing conventional cash payment methods. Indeed, we are moving toward a cashless society, and now we are increasingly relying on electronic financial transactions based on digital technology supported by the internet network. Online payment development is also in line with the online shopping and internet banking trends.

[17]https://ati.ec.europa.eu/sites/default/files/2020–07/Industry%204.0%20in%20Aeronautics%20%20IoT%20Applications%20%28v1%29.pdf

[18]https://www.icas.com/news/10-companies-using-big-data

Chatbots and Virtual Assistants

We've already discussed how AI can be used as a virtual assistant. Robots like this can help user requests to do multiple tasks, from answering questions quickly and accurately to pointing out the way to a specific place and even making reservations at a restaurant or salon.

For example, Sephora, a leading beauty retailer, uses chatbots to improve customer experience. The Sephora Reservation Assistant makes appointments with beauty specialists by sending a message to the chatbot. Sephora is also equipped with intelligent learning technology to understand customer language and have more interactive communication.[19]

Internet of Things

The IoT connects everyday physical objects with the internet to live life intelligently. We can control devices or appliances at home through smartphones. Alexa and Siri can respond to voice commands.

Tata Consultancy Services is a worldwide leader in IT service, counseling, and business solutions. Through IoT, it monitors swimming pools and allows owners to remotely control pool settings and change the temperature and lighting. Customers can use the system to contact a support team. If there are issues, an engineer will solve the problem remotely.[20]

Community Platform

This tool can be a center of information for many people, especially consumers. For example, BabyCenter by Johnson & Johnson became a community platform made to accommodate new moms who wanted to discuss pregnancy and parenting. Many features and information are provided based on their needs, such as a baby names finder and a tutorial on baby diapering. BabyCenter also features websites based on customers' countries to fit in with their language.[21]

Brands can strengthen customer engagement by using online community platforms to build more open and horizontal interactions. This can include even videos and gamification. Through this engagement, the company can understand its customers and get input for improving its products and services.

[19]https://digitalmarketinginstitute.com/blog/chatbots-cx-how-6-brands-use-them-effectively
[20]https://www.iotworldtoday.com/2021/02/24/how-iot-devices-can-enhance-the-connected-customer-experience/
[21]https://www.babycenter.com/

Augmented Reality and Virtual Reality

The use of AR/VR will benefit customers in many segments. For example, in the fashion industry, with the help of AR, customers can see things in "the real world," which fuels their trust in the buying process. In the hospitality and tourism industry, a hotel can provide a virtual visit through their rooms. Travel firms may offer an example of what travelers will see when they book a tour.[22]

Facial Recognition

Facial recognition technology can help confirm a person's identity based on biometrics, either in real time or through photos or videos.[23] Apple uses face recognition to verify payments connected to the Apple ID. This feature helps to secure any payment made in the Apple environment. It also provides auto-filled passwords through facial recognition to improve efficiency.[24]

This technology is widely used for digital transactions in the banking industry. Approximately 11,000 financial institutions in the United States use face recognition to verify their customers. It is often applied to single-use transactions such as logging in to the account. Such a user-friendly system could increase customer loyalty.[25]

Thanks to these technologies, customers will have more positive experiences:

Higher customer touch. Individuals who receive more personal attention will feel more valued. This might include live customer service rather than an FAQ page. Every customer needs a quick solution, and we could handle this by prioritizing customer service. Automated systems such as chatbots could help with a deep analysis of FAQs from the customers.[26]

More relevant offerings. By understanding customers, marketers and companies can give customers what they want when they want it. If a company can maintain this, it will have a positive impact on customer lifetime value.

---

[22]https://www.forbes.com/sites/forbesagencycouncil/2020/09/04/10-industries-likely-to-benefit-from-arvr-marketing/?sh=f0461522ed2a
[23]https://www.kaspersky.com/resource-center/definitions/what-is-facial-recognition
[24]https://www.americanbanker.com/news/facial-recognition-tech-is-catching-on-with-banks
[25]Ibid.
[26]https://www.meetbunch.com/terms/high-touch-support; https://www.providesupport.com/blog/faq-page-customer-self-service-choose-questions-cover/; https://www.forbes.com/sites/theyec/2020/11/12/four-easy-ways-to-increase-customer-loyalty/?sh=3b3edc1e55a1

Seamless customer experience. Connecting customers with information and interactions digitally and physically at different touchpoints according to their wishes could win their patronage. According to a study, 73% of customers think good experience is the key to influencing their brand loyalty.[27]

Technology for Society

An organization cannot ignore virtues in order to maintain the well-being of its surrounding communities. As such, companies must allocate their investments for technology intended for the best interest of society. This technology generally refers to green technology, which encompasses the following categories.

Green Material

It is becoming increasingly common for companies to use more environmentally friendly materials, both natural and artificial. The goal is to reduce harmful waste in the ecosystem, which can be damaging for society and cause health problems. For example, Seventh Generation has provided eco-friendly products such as personal care and baby care for more than 30 years. It values creating a healthier, sustainable, and equitable generation. Seventh Generation believes we have a responsibility to this generation and the next seven as well. For this reason, the company uses plant-based products and packaging that can be recycled.[28]

In addition to benefiting the community, companies can reduce costs related to handling waste that is not environmentally friendly. Hazardous waste is essentially replaced with biodegradable matter. Kalundborg, a city in Denmark, carried out industrial symbiosis to value the waste from each company. The industrial symbiosis tends to make nearly zero waste, which helps the environment and reduces waste handling costs for the companies.[29]

Green Manufacturing

Using recycled materials in manufacturing processes is in line with the growing public concern for the environment. It can reduce waste piles and turn

---

[27]https://hbr.org/2007/02/understanding-customer-experience; https://www.forbes.com/sites/blakemorgan/2019/09/24/50-stats-that-prove-the-value-of-customer-experience/?sh=1484d99f4ef2
[28]https://www.seventhgeneration.com/values/mission
[29]https://www.symbiosis.dk/en/

garbage into valuable products. A company recycling policy brings the benefits of reducing soil, water, and air pollution.

The Global Environmental and Safety (EAS) team from Estée Lauder has a record of limiting waste. Since 2003, more than 20 company-owned manufacturing and distribution facilities claim to have sent no waste to landfills. Any waste that cannot be reused is incinerated and converted over to energy.[30]

Apart from being beneficial for society, recycled materials can provide significant savings for the company. This policy will reduce the demand for raw materials, reducing energy use. For example, Unilever launched a "Reuse. Refill. Rethink" campaign. This campaign was started to reduce plastic waste by encouraging customers to refill their bottles instead of buying a new one. From this campaign, Unilever reduced their need to produce new plastic bottles, leading to production cost reduction for plastic bottles.[31]

Implementing the current recycling policy is no longer enough, and companies are raising the bar by implementing procedures to use renewable energy resources in running their business. This is especially the case in the manufacturing processes of products. This policy can also reduce pollutants generated from unclean energy sources.

Almost every sector of manufacturing systems uses electricity. In the US, at least 29% of the carbon footprint stems from the electricity sector with fossil fuels as the power generator. We can note the difference in emissions created between each resource. Natural gas for electricity releases approximately 0.6 to 2 pounds of carbon dioxide per kilowatt-hour. Renewable energy such as wind and hydroelectric only emits 0.02 to 0.5 pounds of carbon dioxide per kilowatt-hour.[32]

Through the implementation of green technology, even though not everyone in a community buys products from a company that implements this policy, consumers can benefit from the company's existence. They receive the following advantages:

Better environment quality. Technology enables the formation of a more livable community environment because cleaner air, land, and water can help prevent harmful health conditions.

Lower social cost. An increasingly healthy society will reduce the government's burden on social costs. Coal or natural gas power plants release greenhouse gases that cause harm. The cost accumulates up to billions of tax dollars spent each year in the US to deal with the harmful effects of wildfires, floods, and insurance costs. When companies start using green

---

[30]https://www.forbes.com/sites/justcapital/2018/04/20/these-5-companies-are-leading-the-charge-on-recycling/?sh=7a1727d423ec
[31]https://www.unilever.com/reuse-refill-rethink-plastic/
[32]https://www.ucsusa.org/resources/benefits-renewable-energy-use

technology and reducing the environmentally damaging effects, the government can allocate those funds to other priorities.[33]

Embedded CSR. CSR efforts are no longer seen separately from a company's business process. The company should deliver its CSR efforts to the community as an integrated part of its various value-creation processes. Royal Dutch Shell, known as Shell, is an oil and gas company with embedded CSR. Shell's CSR supports youth with entrepreneurial skills to promote their business ideas into a sustainable business. Shell provides training, workshops, and mentoring for these young people.[34]

The Impact on a Company

Discussions related to technology have noted multiple impacts on a company's three main stakeholders: people, customers, and society. The next question is, What is the effect on the company itself? What is the impact on shareholders?

We will answer this question using the technology for humanity model shown in Figure 16.1, which shows technology's role as an essential catalyst.

- **Self-Actualization and Competency**

    Using technology for people, companies can help their employees achieve self-actualization, not just monetary compensation. Technology that supports the quality of work life will increase people's productivity so that they are eager to devote all relevant competencies to the company.

- **Solutions and Profitability**

    The company can provide solutions beyond products and services by using technology for customers. Technology enables customers to get the most from the company with an excellent customer experience. In turn, shoppers will make the company a preferable entity, creating profitability.

- **Goodwill and Sustainability**

    The public will see the company as an admirable business organization. Based on environmentally friendly technologies, the company can show concern for the community's well-being. If this goodwill is well communicated, the community will appreciate the company and provide support, which will help ensure the company's sustainability.

---

[33]https://theconversation.com/what-is-the-social-cost-of-carbon-2-energy-experts-explain-after-court-ruling-blocks-bidens-changes-176255
[34]https://www.emg-csr.com/sdg-4-8-shell/

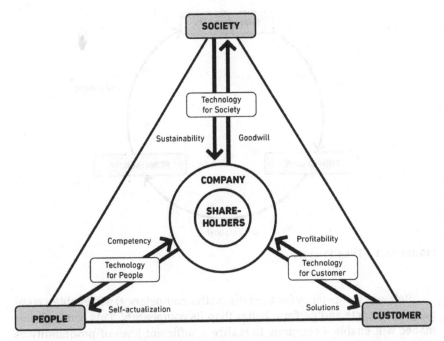

FIGURE 16.1   Technology for humanity model

Besides being the most innovative place to work, Google has earned a reputation for being environmentally friendly. The company uses 50% less energy in their data centers than others in the world. Google has also committed over US$1 billion to projects related to renewable energy, and their service (e.g., Gmail) plays a role in reducing the amount of paper used.[35]

If a company is compatible with talents, preferable in customers' eyes, and well respected by society, it will also garner respect and support from stakeholders. What could be better than this? Those three main stakeholders will function as a propeller to move the company forward. In the end, the company's goal of marketing efforts will be for the good of society.

There is an interesting cycle among the three elements in the technology for humanity model—competency, profitability, and sustainability; CPS in short—as depicted in the CPS cycle shown in Figure 16.2.

[35]https://digitalmarketinginstitute.com/blog/corporate-16-brands-doing-corporate-social-responsibility-successfully

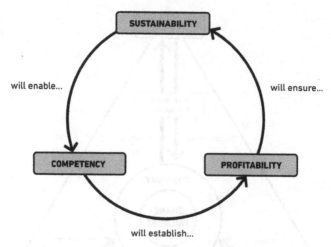

FIGURE 16.2 The CPS cycle

Relevant competency (or even distinctive competency) will enable a company to compete and perform better than its competitors. This better performance will enable a company to realize a sufficient level of profitability as expected. If the company treats its customers properly (and, of course, other relevant stakeholders), it will maintain or even increase its profitability over time. If the company can consistently maintain its profitability, it will ensure its sustainability, which in turn gives a chance to develop the next level of competency. The question is, How to keep your company profitable and sustainable?

Let's review a "classic" 60-year-old company like Walmart. CEO Doug McMillon once stated that Walmart continues to build its capabilities and move aggressively and rapidly. The company has strong supply chain management, supporting its cost leadership proposition. In addition, Walmart uses technology, including automation, in almost all aspects, including distribution centers and when interacting with its customers. Walmart has also succeeded in achieving economies of scale and has diversified to go beyond retail, because it believes retail alone is not enough to continue to exist in the future.[36]

On top of that, Walmart has a solid plan for the environment. It aims to use 100% renewable energy by 2035 and zero out emissions by 2040. It has a

[36]https://www.cnbc.com/2021/02/18/why-an-emboldened-walmart-is-looking-to-beyond-retail-for-future-growth.html; https://www.tradegecko.com/blog/supply-chain-management/incredibly-successful-supply-chain-management-walmart#:~:text=Walmart's%20supply%20chain%20management%20strategy,competitive%20pricing%20for%20the%20consumer; https://querysprout.com/walmarts-competitive-advantages/; https://www.thestrategywatch.com/competitive-advantages-wal-mart/

goal to transition to low-impact refrigerants for cooling and electrified equipment for heating by 2040.[37]

Walmart has continued to innovate to build its agility. It has ensured it is using the right strategy to form competitive advantages to maintain profitability and become a sustainable company. As such, Walmart serves as a company to illustrate the CPS cycle.

A company should always pay attention to all elements in the CPS cycle to become virtuous; if one of the elements is disturbed, it will trap the company in a vicious cycle. If a company is to establish this virtuous cycle, then it must win the hearts of all stakeholders through interactions and integrations facilitated by technology. Companies must demonstrate that technology is authentically designed for humanity.

Going forward, firms will do well to think about technology and apply it toward the well-being of everyone involved. First and foremost, employees will feel appreciated and empowered to be more productive. Societies at large will benefit from well-applied technologies. Stakeholders will value a company that is giving back to its surroundings. When a company monitors its efforts and keeps an eye on the future, it can continue its virtuous cycle.

Key Takeaways

- Companies can use technology to optimize talent management through compensation software, cloud computing, data analytics, virtual reality and augmented reality, 3D printing, robotics/automation, and the industrial internet of things.
- Technologies to improve the way of life for customers include customer data platforms, online payment systems, chatbots and virtual assistants, the internet of things, community platforms, augmented reality and virtual reality, and facial recognition.
- When it comes to society, technology enables companies to improve the well-being of lives and the planet with green material and green manufacturing initiatives.

---

[37]https://corporate.walmart.com/purpose/sustainability

CHAPTER 17

The Post-Operational Excellence

Balancing Rigidity and Flexibility

Taiwan Semiconductor Manufacturing Company (TSMC), a manufacturing company that focuses on producing semiconductors according to the designs requested by its customers, has an operating approach known as the TSMC way. It consists of two main aspects. First, TSMC allocates an order volume from its 1,000 customers to all its factories to achieve a specific level of efficiency (use of scale). Second, TSMC operates using a unique modular design in producing these orders. This enables the company to dynamically allocate its production capacity to meet these orders.[1]

In addition, TSMC has a cyber shuttle, a design verification and testing tool for chips that can accommodate customers' sudden needs. Through the TSMC way, the company can fulfill emergency orders while still adhering to rigid manufacturing operational principles. It operates on the principle of intelligent manufacturing. This is a machine learning-assisted manufacturing process applied to optimize quality, productivity, efficiency, and operating flexibility, maximize cost-effectiveness, and accelerate overall innovation.[2] As a result, TSMC can respond to a wide variety of market demands and very diverse product requirements for customers worldwide.[3]

Due to its ability to balance rigid processes with the flexibility that customers demand and increasingly need, TSMC has become the world's largest

---

[1] Willy C. Shih, Chen-Fu Chien, Chintay Shih, and Jack Chang, "The TSMC Way: Meeting Customer Needs at Taiwan Semiconductor Manufacturing Co.," *Harvard Business School Case 610–003* (2009).
[2] https://www.tsmc.com/english
[3] Shih, Chien, Shih, and Chang, "The TSMC Way."

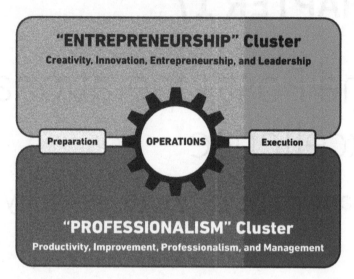

FIGURE 17.1 Operations element in the omnihouse model

semiconductor manufacturer. It plays a vital role in the global supply chain. Among its most prominent clients are Apple and AMD.[4]

In this chapter, we'll discuss the element of the omnihouse model that is in the middle, namely, *operations*, which is a very strategic element in business (see Figure 17.1). On the one hand, operations must be able to run without significant obstacles. On the other hand, it must be capable of keeping up with a dynamic environment.

The operations element is one of the direct influences on a company's profit margin. Improving the operations aspect is essential for increasing company efficiency, reducing costs, and directly affecting the income statement's operating margin. The strength of operational processes—from production, distribution, sales, and services—will depend on the company's operational capabilities.

The operations can also affect productivity—in terms of inputs and outputs—because strong operational capabilities can convert inputs from the same number of resources into higher outputs compared to companies with similar products. Operations must be built so that everything can run flawlessly from preparation to execution. The focus of the operations should hinge on the ability to use the company's existing resources as efficiently as possible to produce products and supporting services of the highest quality while simultaneously preserving a degree of flexibility. The operations element is

[4]https://www.forbes.com/sites/ralphjennings/2021/01/11/taiwan-chipmaker-tsmc-revenues-hit-record-high-in-2020-stocks-follow/?sh=220c30343077

also an intermediary between marketing, which usually focuses on the top line, and finance, which prioritizes the bottom line in the income statement.

Rigidity Is Natural

We can find rigidity everywhere; it usually forms when a start-up becomes more established in running its business. At this point, a firm might settle into its routines and systems. It may find comfort in maintaining the status quo. Look again in Chapter 6. The following sections delineate several factors that frequently lead to rigidity.

Weak Entrepreneurial Mindset

An entrepreneurial spirit shines through flexibility in dealing with various obstacles and the decision-making process. When this doesn't occur, companies can grow stiff and fail.

For example, HMV, a CD and DVD seller, shut down in 2018. Prior to closing its doors, the company had the opportunity to address three trends that would become threats: discounting supermarkets, online retailers, and downloadable music. The company rejected these projections and did business as usual. The corporation began investing in internet activities in the late 1990s. However, by then it was too little, too late.[5]

Stagnation of Creativity and Innovation

Often, a company is initially very passionate, rich in ideas, and always ready to innovate in the early stages of its operations. After a while, routines set in and creativity fades. Team members shy away from words like *agile* and *adapting*. At this point, rigidity settles in.

Ignoring the Competition

A company can be blinded by its success, even though both existing competitors and newcomers continue to race to find the best market position. This complacent attitude will typically lead the firm to become stagnant. Unfortunately, this is sometimes noticed only when the company begins to experience a crisis and plunges into a death spiral trap.

---

[5]https://www.theguardian.com/commentisfree/2013/jan/15/why-did-hmv-fail

Not Taking Care of Customers

Companies that have gained many customers often forget that these individuals may not always be loyal. Or management may assume that it will be easy to find new customers when the current ones leave. This view and attitude are usually are a sign of impending rigidity.

Not Transforming the Business Model

The dynamic business environment will affect how the company conducts its business. After a long time running, an organization will usually need to check whether its business model is still feasible. Unfortunately, organizations often lock into outdated systems and are reluctant to transform.

Ignoring Macro-Environment Changes

Elements in the macroenvironment are fast-changing and often unpredictable. If a firm does not pay attention to these trends, it can miss new opportunities. It may also not see warning signs that it needs to pivot and change.

Weak Digitization Orientation

Some companies are slow to adopt digital models and tools. Others invest heavily but fail to account for the organization's overarching goals and strategy. Some firms implement digital tools and then don't look ahead to spot upcoming changes that might be needed. In these cases, the rigidity causes the firm to overlook key digital tools that could drive profits.

The Value Chain Is Not Dead

It is sometimes said that the value chain concept developed by Michael Porter in the mid-1980s is no longer applicable. The idea surfaced during an era when digitalization was not connecting the world as it is now. Thus, the value chain concept becomes invalid when everything is increasingly digitally connected.

However, the development of digital technology enables us to simplify, combine, or even eliminate several sub-elements that are unneeded so that they can be bypassed or outsourced to partners. Hence, the company can avoid carrying out some activities that are not adding significant value. This will speed up the ideation stage to commercialization, reduce costs, and increase the use of tangible and intangible assets.

For example, WhatsApp outsourced their engineers by contracting an IT team from Russia. The decision was made because their starting capital was very limited during their early years, and they couldn't afford engineers in the US. They decided to seek talented engineers elsewhere to get a more competitive talent rate.[6] This scheme successfully kept WhatsApp afloat until its acquisition by Facebook in 2014. This method simplified WhatsApp's operational management and supported its competitive advantage.

Continual Adjustment of Value Chain

From the previous explanation and examples, we can say that the value chain concept is not dead and remains relevant as long as the company continues to make adjustments to facets of its value chain. All primary and supporting elements must be fully integrated digitally but at the same time can still work modularly. Companies must also have the courage to determine which activities they will ultimately carry out on their own—they will be referred to as core activities—and which ones they should hand over to partners.

Both big and small companies sometimes need to outsource in the current business situation. A common reason to outsource is to reduce cost. Another reason is that an outsourcing system can be beneficial for small-scale companies. For start-ups, an outsourcing plan can help the business run as usual when the internal team reaches its maximum capacity.[7]

With a more concise value chain, companies can also increase the quality of their products by focusing on areas such as creativity and innovation while reducing unnecessary costs. By creating a more efficient value chain, companies can speed up delivery processes, even for some customized products. Supporting services can be the basis for creating differentiation in the value chain.

The Supply Chain Is Even More Relevant

The role of a robust supply chain, both upstream (supply side) and downstream (demand side), grows even more relevant in this digitalized era. With the increasingly connected supply chain elements, companies can share

---

[6]https://www.daxx.com/blog/development-trends/outsourcing-success-stories; https://biz30.timedoctor.com/outsourcing-examples/
[7]https://www.forbes.com/sites/forbestechcouncil/2021/06/09/why-poland-should-be-the-next-go-to-it-outsourcing-for-us-startups/?sh=40d0dc1a74d9

information with the supply side to support their flexibility. Good coordination from upstream to downstream partners helps a company achieve a high level of efficiency in supply chain processes, which can meet changing customer demands—both B2B and B2C.[8] Strong supply chain integration triggers rigidity while allowing flexibility for companies to respond to market dynamics. It also provides space for suppliers to adapt quickly to meet the demand.

Integration and Strategic Flexibility

Integrating a company with the supply chain enables the company to have strategic flexibility. Companies can become better at sensing external changes and formulate what they must do by using resources and operational activities. However, the firm does not need to own all its resources. It can outsource some of its operations.

Companies can concentrate on their core competencies while outsourcing the rest. They can also focus on activities related to these core competencies and even create a distinctive competence. This condition is in line with the sharing economy concept, which is increasingly popular in the digital era. It enables different parties to connect in a specific business domain.

Some US-based companies, such as Microsoft, American Express, Dell, and General Electric, serve millions, if not billions, of global customers. These companies outsource their help desk services to third-party companies in India. The country is an essential destination to outsource customer support activities because of low labor cost, IT talent, English fluency, and a 12-hour time zone difference that can help companies provide 24/7 call center service for their customers.[9]

Integration, Bargaining Position, and QCD

If we relate these topics to Masaaki Imai's quality, cost, and delivery (QCD) concept, we see that nonideal conditions will cause QCD not to be optimized. The strength of an integration and bargaining position between suppliers and buyers will determine the level of vulnerability of the QCD (see Figure 17.2).

---

[8]https://jorgdesign.springeropen.com/articles/10.1186/s41469-018-0035-4
[9]https://www.magellan-solutions.com/blog/companies-that-outsource-to-india/; https://www.outsource2india.com/india/outsourcing-customer-support-india.asp

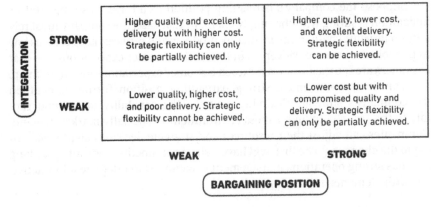

FIGURE 17.2   The impact of integration and bargaining position on QCD

No matter how good the value chain is in a company, it will be challenging to provide high-quality products and services if access to production factors is limited. In the case of B2B, for example, if the company's bargaining position as a buyer is weak and the integration is weak, then all elements of the QCD will be very vulnerable. The company will also find it challenging to reduce multiple costs because the supplier determines the prices of production factors. If the supply of production factors to the company is also not smooth, it might disrupt the delivery.

If the company's bargaining position as a buyer is strong enough, but the integration is weak, the company can focus only on the cost element, while quality and delivery remain vulnerable. However, if the company's bidding position as a buyer is weak but the integration is strong, the company has a better chance of providing quality products and services and excellent delivery to customers. However, the vulnerability remains high for the cost element. These two conditions lead to less flexibility for the company and more space to form its competitive advantage.

For example, Apple—a strong buyer for TSMC (mentioned at the beginning of the chapter)—has a vast ecosystem and demands a top-quality chip for all their gadgets. As one of the leading brands in innovative consumer electronic goods, Apple requested a specific chip from TSMC. This particular demand of three-nanometer production helped TSMC improve its operational experience. Given this, only TSMC could complete the chip's manufacturing process. This form of business relationship establishes a healthy interdependence between Apple and TSMC.[10]

---

[10]Shih, Chien, Shih, and Chang (2009); https://appleinsider.com/articles/21/11/02/apple-gets-preferential-treatment-in-close-tsmc-partnership

Suppose the company's bargaining position as a buyer is strong, and its integration is strong with the supply chain. In that case, the company must rely only on its value chain to ensure quality products and services, keep costs as low as possible, and ensure delivery is in line with customer expectations—so that customers are satisfied—or even exceed customer expectations to delight them.

This integration and a strong bargaining position further strengthen the company's strategic flexibility, namely, the capability to respond rapidly to the fast-changing business environment—especially market demand. Companies can adjust their resources and strategic decisions swiftly according to the changes.[11] The firm will have a strong competitive advantage as long as it has strong operations management capabilities to integrate all its activities with elements in the supply chain.[12]

Insufficiency of Linear Relationship

Even if the value chain is firmly integrated with the upstream supply chain—that is, the suppliers (S1 to S5), and downstream supply chain, that is, the distributors (D1 to D3)—it is still not necessarily the ideal condition (see Figure 17.3). This is the case if the firm is not yet an integrated part of a business ecosystem. Moreover, if the relationship is still linear, then the dynamics may not necessarily match the speed of change in the overall business environment, especially from the customer side.

To pursue a dynamic and often chaotic situation, a linear supply chain approach is no longer suitable, especially one that is independent or not integrated. Due to this insufficiency, there is an urgency for the value chain to evolve into a very dynamic ecosystem. This ecosystem will function as a value web that optimizes all elements involved.[13]

If companies rely on a single aspect in supply chains, such as supplies, production, sales, or distribution, it could accidentally harm a business. They might be held hostage for payments they haven't made or a price hike. For example, if an organization can't receive raw material, a machine fails, a website crashes, or it cannot find inventory in a warehouse, the entire operations may have to shut down to avoid bottlenecks.[14]

---

[11]Katsuhiko Shimizu and Michael A. Hitt, "Strategic Flexibility: Organizational Preparedness to Reverse Ineffective Strategic Decisions," *The Academy of Management Executive (1993–2005)* 18, no. 4 (November 2004): 44–59.

[12]https://keydifferences.com/difference-between-supply-chain-and-value-chain.html

[13]Referring to Eamonn Kelly and Kelly Marchese in https://www2.deloitte.com/content/dam/insights/us/articles/platform-strategy-new-level-business-trends/DUP_1048-Business-ecosystems-come-of-age_MASTER_FINAL.pdf

[14]https://smallbusiness.chron.com/strengths-weaknesses-supply-chain-75987.html

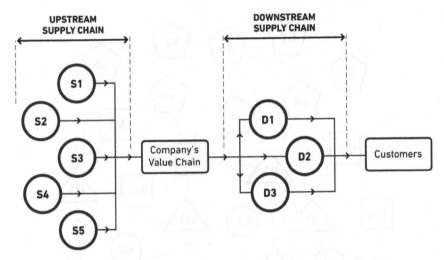

FIGURE 17.3   The linear relationship between a company's value chain and supply chain

The Business Ecosystem Is the Ultimate Domain

According to BCG, a business ecosystem should solve a business challenge and be organized to achieve a specific value proposition. Access to a wide range of capabilities, the ability to scale quickly, and flexibility and resilience are all advantages of business ecosystems. For instance, Steve Jobs opened the iPhone to third-party app developers, allowing for a flood of new and inventive apps.[15]

In the end, a company must become an active part of a business ecosystem, both conventional and digital. By connecting all elements in an ecosystem, all parties, consisting of suppliers (S), manufacturers (M), distributors (D), and customers (C), will have vast access and flexibility to collaborate and co-create, which will provide superior performance for all parties involved.[16] As part of a strong business ecosystem, there is a significant chance that a company can improve its dynamic capabilities, which are an essential foundation for building a competitive advantage (see Figure 17.4).

A company and its partners will enjoy benefits from the ecosystem, which will provide some advantages. The higher the interdependence in an ecosystem, the higher the rigidity. However, it also provides flexibility for all

[15]https://www.bcg.com/publications/2019/do-you-need-business-ecosystem
[16]https://www2.deloitte.com/us/en/insights/focus/business-trends/2015/supply-chains-to-value-webs-business-trends.html

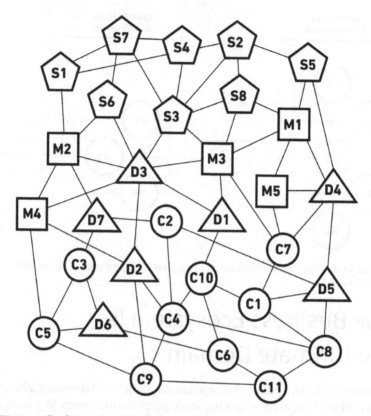

FIGURE 17.4 Business ecosystem[17]

parties involved in the business ecosystem in dealing with swift environmental changes. This condition is in line with the principle of strategic flexibility.

Advantages of a Business Ecosystem

Business ecosystems can provide several advantages to the parties who are part of them:

Provide a substantial entry barrier. The business ecosystem can function as a strong barrier for new entrants. It is not enough for new competitors to rely merely on their value chain's strength to win the competition.

[17]https://www2.deloitte.com/us/en/insights/focus/business-trends/2015/supply-chains-to-value-webs-business-trends.html

Newcomers now have to face the ecosystem as a whole, which, of course, has the collective power of all parties in it.

Enable solutions for more extensive problems. An optimized ecosystem facilitates a company to innovate and provide solutions. This can occur both to solve individual company's problems and to collectively address social and environmental issues on a global scale.[18] A dynamic ecosystem consisting of shared resources, capabilities, and competencies with increasingly blurred boundaries allows for discovering new values. It will be instrumental for companies to help them face this fierce world independently.[19]

Provide versatile platforms. The business ecosystem is a platform for accelerating the learning process, developing ideas, sharing knowledge, and producing techniques and technologies for collective use. It is a catalyst for innovations, enabling multiple parties to collaborate and co-create in a cross-sector network to support commercialization processes. This platform can increase efficiency and effectiveness both per company and collectively due to the possibility of spreading operating and investment costs to many parties in the ecosystem.[20]

Operations at the Center Stage

As companies become more integrated into a business ecosystem, the role of operations becomes more central, as seen in the omnihouse model. On the one hand, the marketing function within a company is primarily to understand the market and provide solutions through its various products and services. On the other hand, the financial function aims to determine whether multiple marketing innovations will provide good margins and make productive use of the company's capital. The role of the operations function is to enable the execution of value creation that can fulfill the objectives of those two functions.

Various technologies support operational functions, especially those in line with this increasingly digitalized world. This technology also allows a company to be part of a business ecosystem to share roles and burdens and

[18]https://www.investopedia.com/terms/b/business-ecosystem.asp
[19]https://smallbizclub.com/run-and-grow/innovation/how-is-a-business-ecosystem-a-key-driver-to-success/; https://www2.deloitte.com/content/dam/insights/us/articles/platform-strategy-new-level-business-trends/DUP_1048-Business-ecosystems-come-of-age_MASTER_FINAL.pdf
[20]https://www.timreview.ca/article/227 and https://smallbizclub.com/run-and-grow/innovation/how-is-a-business-ecosystem-a-key-driver-to-success/; https://www.tallyfox.com/insight/what-value-business-ecosystem

support operational activities within the company. Companies can take advantage of the multiple advantages in an ecosystem to provide the best to customers, shareholders, and the community. The operations function is also an essential part of realizing the idea of technology for humanity.

New Character of Operational Excellence

In line with the increasing importance of a company's involvement in a business ecosystem, operational excellence cannot rely solely on the capabilities of the company's internal management, internal disciplines, or company values. Indeed, companies still need to pay serious attention to their internal processes. At the same time, they should find ways to align internal processes with interactions involving other parties in a business ecosystem.

In addition to maintaining existing operational excellence in the company, it is crucial to understand what conditions can improve the company's operational excellence after it has become part of a business ecosystem. The goal is to achieve optimum flexibility regardless of the rigid interdependency between companies in that business ecosystem. Here are some of the characteristics of a company's new operational excellence:

Seamless interdependency. How much does a company cooperate with parties in the same business ecosystem? What is the extent of the interdependence between a company and other parties, and is the relationship seamless? The more parties that cooperate with a company and the higher the interdependence, and the more seamless a relationship or connection is, the higher the level of needed integration.

Flawless compatibility. We have to see how compatible the technology used in the operational activities of a company is with other organizations in an ecosystem. It means that we have to see whether those organizations employ a similar process and methodology, whether the company uses the same protocol as other parties, whether they all refer to universal governance within an ecosystem, or whether the people's culture is consistent with other organizations. These must be completely compatible and flawless in interacting with an ecosystem. The more perfect the compatibility of an organization in a business ecosystem, the more the company shows the character of new operational excellence.

Immediate responsiveness. Being part of a business ecosystem allows a company to maintain its relevance in an ever-changing business environment. Companies can take advantage of the business ecosystem to quickly respond to changes even if they show discontinuous trajectories.

The faster the operational responsiveness of the company supported by its ecosystem, the stronger the indication that the company performs new operational excellence.

This new operational excellence capability is what we call post-operational excellence. Combining those three aspects of post-operational excellence will determine a high degree of flexibility because a company can run operational processes modularly and easily adjust whenever necessary. The maximum point of the three aspects will form the flexibility frontier (see Figure 17.5).

Suppose the business environment shows dynamics that exceed the imaginary flexibility frontier. In that case, all parties in the ecosystem must work hard to jointly take advantage of their interdependence as a collective strength, improve their compatibility, and increase their ability to respond. These three efforts can push the flexibility frontier outward beyond the dynamics of the business environment so that all parties in the business ecosystem can remain relevant. However, given that the flexibility frontier is already ahead of the business dynamics, it depends on each company's efforts as part of the ecosystem to maximize the available opportunities and possibilities.

With this flexibility, management can accelerate scaling up the company. The market is becoming wide open. As long as the available logistics system can reach them, the company can certainly serve that market. Further, a company can also streamline the product development process and supporting services. The possibilities for diversification are also getting more significant. Finally, the company must answer the fundamental question again regarding its core competency and the extent to which its core competence will remain relevant, and even give it a distinctive competence.

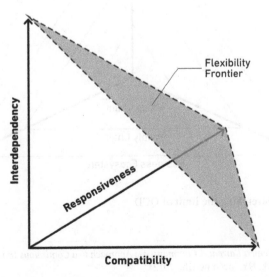

FIGURE 17.5   The flexibility frontier

Stretching the QCD

Companies can improve their achievements in the three elements of QCD that rely not only on internal company processes that refer to cross-functional collaboration but also on processes that multiple partners in a business ecosystem can handle. Organizations can reduce costs by relying on efficiency from the designing phase to selling a product and depending on the collective efficiency of a business ecosystem. Firms can also deliver those products and services according to customer requests faster.[21]

Initially, QCD depended only on the company's limited value chain flexibility or, at a higher level, the relationships with upstream and downstream value chains that were linear in nature. But now, companies can have much greater flexibility if they rearrange all their operational processes to become more congruent with the ecosystem where they participate, mainly if they can position themselves closer to the flexibility frontier. In short, companies can stretch their limit of QCD (see Figure 17.6).

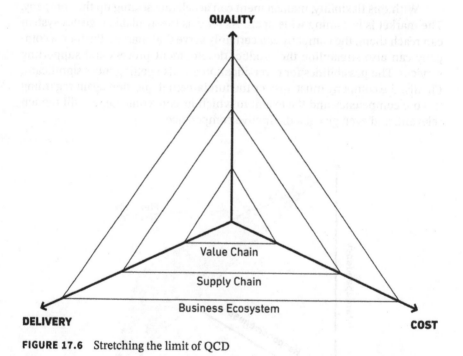

FIGURE 17.6 Stretching the limit of QCD

[21]Masaaki Imai, *Gemba Kaizen: A Commonsense Approach to a Continuous Improvement Strategy* (New York, NY: McGraw-Hill, 2012).

Managing Rigidity and Flexibility

We have indeed entered a completely different era with a new business landscape. It is full of discontinuities in trajectories in many industries. All of these affect the way a company operates. Post-operational excellence is needed based on a more advanced business ecosystem by managing three aspects, namely, interdependency, compatibility, and responsiveness.

Although important, departmental integration is not sufficient to deal with the dynamics of the business environment now and in the future. The renowned value chain concept developed by Michael Porter will be even better if we don't see it as a one-way process but one that also allows an iterative process and flexibility at each point of the value chain. This iterative process and flexibility will enable the company to deliver faster and continuous customer value while adapting to external changes.

The company can use its internal resources, capabilities, and competencies within the division or intra-division to create competitiveness. However, on top of that, it should use external networks from critical partners to ensure a flexible value-creating process. Networking with strategic partners is why integration with the value chain plays a vital role in increasing the company's competitive advantage. This integration will also affect the company's operational management in a value-creation process.

Technology that enables connectivity with a business ecosystem enables companies to leverage the ecosystem advantages.[22] Companies must transform and embrace post-operational excellence as a new value or characteristic in their company. Organizational structures with large inertia no longer have a place. We must immediately remove the corporate culture that is not open-minded and is resistant to new things. Connectivity with ecosystems—especially those supported by digital technology—enables companies to discover and realize new values that were previously impossible if only relying on traditional value chains.[23]

In the end, a company must have the capability to manage rigidity and flexibility simultaneously. This capability—including coordination—will open up more significant opportunities to achieve economies of scope.[24] In short, today's companies must be able to build strategic flexibility to successfully head toward 2030, which is an important stepping stone to the following decades.[25]

---

[22]https://www.jbs.cam.ac.uk/wp-content/uploads/2020/08/wp1006.pdf

[23]https://www.linkedin.com/pulse/death-value-chain-new-world-order-requires-ecosystem-analysis-shwet

[24]For further discussion regarding the coordination mechanism, please see https://www.bptrends.com/bpt/wp-content/uploads/05–02–2017-COL-Harmon-on-BPM-Value-Chains.pdf

[25]Michael A. Hitt, Barbara W. Keats, and Samuel M. DeMarie, "Navigating in the New Competitive Landscape: Building Strategic Flexibility and Competitive Advantage in the 21st Century," *Academy of Management Perspectives* 12, no. 4 (November 1998). https://doi.org/10.5465/ame.1998.1333922

Key Takeaways

- Rigidity in a company can be caused by a weak entrepreneurial mindset, stagnation of creativity and innovation, ignoring the competition, not taking care of customers, not transforming the business model, ignoring macro-environment changes, and weak digitalization orientation.

- Strong supply chain integration creates rigidity while allowing flexibility for companies to respond to market dynamics.

- Business ecosystems can provide a barrier to entry, solutions to extensive problems, and versatile platforms.

Epilogue

Visioning the Next Curve

The core section of the omnihouse model—CI-EL and PI-PM, which are also inspired by mythological stories rooted in Javanese culture (see Appendix)—are necessary for companies to secure their journey to the future. However, on top of understanding the current conditions, we must also be able to observe what we will likely face in the future. The implementation of entrepreneurial marketing will not be optimal and will not significantly have an impact if we are not prepared to anticipate what will happen in the future.

What Are We Facing Now?

Learning from various developments in recent years, we are currently faced with the following conditions.

Collaboration Is a Must

Not all companies individually have access to advantages to help them face future challenges. Those whose sources of advantage are very limited or insufficient to overcome the challenges need to immediately redefine competition and think about how to collaborate with various other parties, even with their competitors. *Collaboration* is the critical word in bringing our company to the future.

Highly Sophisticated Customers

In an increasingly connected world, customers are also changing. Since the early 2010s, our customers seem to have metamorphosed into a new type of customer because they can easily find and absorb an extraordinary amount of information. They have become very sophisticated with increasingly strong bargaining power. Acquiring new customers is getting even more complicated, let alone satisfying them, so, we need to find new ways to handle them.

The Need to Converge Dichotomies

Companies must be able to adapt to significant changes in the business environment by relying on flexibility or agility. Companies must continually renew themselves to exist in the long term. For this reason, it is necessary to converge various dichotomies, for example, the generational dichotomy, technology dichotomy, and merging entrepreneurial mindset with professionalism. Carrying out the essential convergence process is a challenge for companies in general.

Sound Strategy and Tactics Are a Must

The increasingly dynamic and complex business environment requires us to sharply analyze the impact of all changes on the companies we manage. We should then identify various options, which is sometimes not easy to do, and at the same time, take into account the multiple competencies we have. Finally, we should develop a strong strategy and consistent tactics.

The Importance of Talented People

To ensure success, we need talented people with various capabilities. We cannot expect that one person can have all the necessary qualifications. Therefore, companies must find, attract, develop, and retain the best people. Companies must provide conditions that enable these talents to unleash their potential, fully engage with the company, and actualize themselves. Companies must have omni capabilities to remain relevant and continue to exist long term.

Integrating Inside and Outside

We should banish all silos within the company. If we cannot have an interdepartmental collaboration in a company due to these silos, then do not expect that we can collaborate well with various external parties and do something relevant and significant for the goodness of society. We have to ensure the integration of all divisions in the company first before we move on to aim for something bigger. We must dare to revise or update our value chain, become part of the business ecosystem (both conventional and digital), and use the ecosystem advantage to remain sustainable.

The Era of Tech-Driven Marketing

Tech-driven marketing has changed how we implement customer, product, and brand management now and in the future. Technology broadly also must be aimed at all humanity. Internally, we must provide various technologies to support our people so that they can maximize their value creation. We must provide technology to our customers, so our solutions are accessible. We also have to use various technologies to ensure that society and the environment are always taken care of in the best way possible.

Operational Flexibility Is Crucial

The operational aspect, of course, will also be affected. Companies must balance various rigid operating processes with very flexible market demands. At the same time, both B2C and B2B companies must improve the quality of their products and various supporting services with more efficient costs and delivery according to customer expectations (even delighting them). All touchpoints must be able to provide an outstanding customer experience.

What Lies Ahead Does Matter

Regardless of how severe the impact of the COVID-19 pandemic has been, it is time for us to bounce back. Despite the looming global uncertainty, there are several interesting phenomena that we need to anticipate in the next few years.

The Pending Golden Era of Gen Z

Referring to the World Economic Forum, compared to previous generations and based on data in 2020, we can see that the Gen Z unemployment rate has almost doubled in almost all OECD countries. This high unemployment is because Gen Z is looking for a job (most of them have just graduated from college or high school) and, coincidentally, are overrepresented in service industries such as travel and restaurants, which have recently been hit hard by the recent pandemic. Gen Z will lose their opportunity to accumulate work experience and training, which are essential for their capability building, affecting their career paths in the future.[1] Gen Z's golden era seems to have been delayed a bit.

---

[1]https://www.weforum.org/agenda/2021/03/gen-z-unemployment-chart-global-comparisons/
#:~:text=There%20are%20more%20than%202,about%2027%25%20of%20the%20workforce

The Beginning of Metaverse

The evolution of web communities is still ongoing; from Web 1.0, it has transformed into Web 2.0, and now we embark on the Web 3.0 era, the metaverse era. As widely discussed in various forums that the metaverse, which is still in its embryonic stage, will revolutionize everything from e-commerce, media, and entertainment to real estate. The metaverse can potentially transform how we interact socially, do business, and even make a giant leap forward in the internet economy.

Higher Relevance of ESG Criteria

ESG has become a critical nonfinancial criterion in investor analysis, which is the basis for understanding a company's real risks and growth potential. These metrics are now an integral part of the investment selection process.[2] The application of ESG metrics demonstrates the widespread adoption of the stakeholder approach in various companies. In addition, using ESG measurement simultaneously shows that different nonfinancial metrics are becoming increasingly significant in determining a company's value and seeing the extent to which it realizes its various values. ESG has become a standard that is now increasingly being adopted.[3]

SDGs' Deadline Is Approaching

The United Nations (UN) initiated the Sustainable Development Goals (SDGs) in 2015 to eradicate poverty, protect our planet, and ensure that by 2030 everyone can enjoy a life full of peace and prosperity. The SDGs have relevance to companies, although each company may have a different emphasis on each SDG goal. The SDGs are an essential guide so that companies can align their various strategies with the interests of today's society. Interestingly, the SDGs are also in line with the new genre of entrepreneurial marketing because they emphasize innovation and opportunities for opening new markets.[4]

The Wicked 7

Similar to the SDGs, what we find in Wicked 7 can enrich our insight related to various urgent problems hitting the world, including the death of nature,

[2]https://www.cfainstitute.org/en/research/esg-investing#:~:text=ESG%20stands%20 for%20Environmental%2C%20Social,material%20risks%20and%20growth%20 opportunities.&text=This%20guide%20takes%20fiduciary%20duty,important%20ESG%20 issues%20into%20account

[3]https://cglytics.com/what-is-esg/

[4]https://www.17goalsmagazin.de/en/the-relevance-of-the-sustainable-development-goals-sdgs-for-companies/

inequality, hate and conflict, power and corruption, work and technology, health and livelihood, and population and migration. Those seven problems are also part of the five sub-elements of change.[5]

The Era of Sharing and the Circular Economy

We are increasingly familiar with the term *sharing economy* in line with the increasing number of parties who adopt it. The sharing economy's development is inseparable from the ease with which everyone is connected through multiple digital networks and platforms.[6] In addition to the sharing economy, we are also increasingly familiar with the *circular economy*, which relies on three principles: eliminating waste and pollution, circulating products and materials at their highest value, and regenerating nature.[7] We should consider all the consequences of supporting reuse, reduce, and recycle initiatives.

The Next Curve

The next curve is our journey from 2022 to 2030. The journey to 2023, as predicted by the IMF, is seen as full of uncertainty. Beyond 2023 there is still not much to say right now, let alone the journey to 2030.

Referring to the economic growth published by the MF, we can see in Table E.1 that the world economy will continue to grow, even though after 2021, the projection shows that there will be slower growth until 2023.

TABLE E.1 **Global Economic Growth (%)**[8]

	2019	2020	2021	2022*	2023*
Global economy	2.9	−3.1	6.1	3.2	2.9
Advanced economies	1.7	−4.5	5.2	2.5	1.4
Emerging markets and developing economies	3.7	−2.0	6.8	3.6	3.9

*Projections

[5]Please refer to Christian Sarkar and Philip Kotler, *Brand Activism: From Purpose to Action* (Idea Bite Press, 2021).
[6]https://english.ckgsb.edu.cn/knowledges/what-happened-sharing-economy-in-china/
[7]https://ellenmacarthurfoundation.org/topics/circular-economy-introduction/overview
[8]https://www.imf.org/en/Publications/WEO/Issues/2020/06/24/WEOUpdateJune2020; https://www.imf.org/en/Publications/WEO/Issues/2022/07/26/world-economic-outlook-update-july-2022

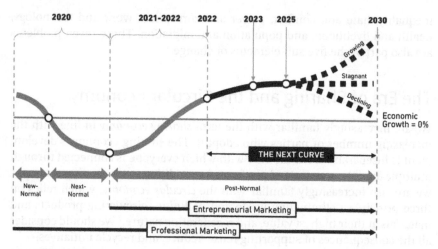

FIGURE E.1 The next curve 2022–2030

Consistently, the growth of emerging and developing economies looks higher than that of advanced economies. Despite slowing down after 2021, there is still positive economic growth. In addition, we can see that the projected global economic growth in 2022 is better than in 2019, and economic growth in 2023 is estimated to be the same as in 2019.

The IMF stated that the world economic outlook tends to be gloomy and uncertain. They believe there are several causes, including the declining performance of large countries considered economic powerhouses, namely, China, Russia, and the US. The war in Ukraine also contributed to the deteriorating condition of the global economy, especially in Europe, due to the cessation of gas supplies from Russia. Geopolitical fragmentation also continues to overshadow and can hinder global cooperation and trade. The world inflation rate is also expected to increase.[9]

The global economy may improve, stagnate, or even worsen after 2023. Our current attitude in dealing with various possibilities between now and 2025 is very decisive. Whatever happens in the next curve in this post-normal era, we can't just stand still. This uncertain condition also suggests that a holistic approach to entrepreneurial marketing is becoming increasingly relevant in dealing with a world that will be very challenging (see Figure E.1).

During the worst moment of the COVID-19 pandemic, although many companies then experienced a decline in performance, it turned out that there were many companies that could survive even without significant growth

[9]https://www.imf.org/en/Publications/WEO/Issues/2022/07/26/world-economic-outlook-update-july-2022

(being stagnant). Other companies could grow, not only because of the influence of the windfall but also because they had successfully converged their professional approach with an entrepreneurial mindset.

Policies on Resources, Capabilities, and Competencies

Companies that can still grow should optimize their resources, align different capabilities to suit their purpose-driven strategic direction, and identify their distinctive competencies in a growing condition. In a growing state, companies can even consider diversifying.

Companies with stagnant performance can emphasize their efforts to increase efficiency, effectiveness, and overall productivity. They can carry out several marketing strategies or tactics adjustments. This adjustment may require additional resources, upgrading the existing capabilities, calibrating them with the revitalization of strategic direction, and refocusing on core competencies.

In a declining situation, companies must conduct a renewal process by taking advantage of any business opportunities available. Companies might require additional resources on top of various existing resources and even look for new ones. Companies must also upgrade their current capabilities and establish new and unique capabilities. In the end, companies can revise their existing competencies or start forming new ones (see Table E.2).

TABLE E.2   Company's Performance and Options for the Next Steps

Company's Performance	Resources	Capabilities	Competencies
Growing	Optimize available resources	Align capabilities with purpose-driven strategic direction	Search for distinctive competency
Stagnant	Add more resources	Upgrade existing capabilities and calibrate with strategic revitalization direction	Refocus on core competency
Declining	Add more resources and/or acquire new resources	Upgrade existing capabilities and/or build new (unique) capabilities for renewal	Revive existing competencies or develop new competency

As the IMF has said, the journey ahead is full of uncertainty. Uncertainty is something that many people fear. A study revealed that unpredictability significantly increases people's discomfort, which according to Ema Tanovic can further intensify how we perceive threatening situations.[10] However, we should remain optimistic but also realistic when facing various challenges in the future.

On the one hand, the longer we delay or procrastinate change, the greater the potential for complications that arise over time, worsening the company's condition and eventually collapsing it. On the other hand, David Teece revealed that we could not avoid and deal with uncertainties even if we immediately executed the renewal process.

So, don't hesitate to collaborate. Use an entrepreneurial mindset together with professionalism. Converge various dichotomies, and develop and implement sound strategies and tactics. Make sure our talented people are not trapped in silos within the company and are ready to become part of the business ecosystem.

We should stay alert and anticipate several things in the future that will have a significant impact, for example, the arrival of the Gen Zer and the rise of the metaverse. Be flexible with changes, and don't be allergic to technology if it is a necessity.

There is nothing wrong with keeping our strong profit motive, but that does not mean we can forget various responsibility agendas related to social and environmental aspects of life. For those who haven't, this is the time to immediately incorporate the sustainability aspect into your company's business model.

The challenges on the next curve are not easy, but that doesn't mean we can't overcome them. It is proven that humans have survived uncountable catastrophes and challenges for thousands of years. If humans continually strengthen their minds, use their conscience, and use them as a marketing beacon, then the future is in hand. So, giving up is not an option.

Welcome to the next curve!

---

[10]https://www.bbc.com/worklife/article/20211022-why-were-so-terrified-of-the-unknown

Appendix: Punokawan and Pandava

The Indonesian Mythic Symbols of CI-EL and PI-PM in the Omnihouse Model

The concept of entrepreneurial marketing is intended to answer future challenges. The existence of digitalization and the COVID-19 pandemic does require leaders to be agile, flexible, and resilient in dealing with change. CI-EL is the answer so that business people, government officials, social activists, and leaders in various organizations do not stutter in responding to the dynamic environment.

The birth of this concept is also based on local Indonesian philosophy, especially from the *wayang* story, one of the cultural heritage stories in Indonesia. According to Javanese tradition, *wayang* stories are based on Indigenous mythologies and Indian epics.[1] *Wayang* flourished in the royal courts of Java—Indonesia's main islands—and Bali for ten centuries. It has also spread to neighboring islands—Lombok, Madura, Sumatra, and Kalimantan—where it has evolved into various local performance styles and musical accompaniments.

The story that is popularly performed in the *wayang* shows is the Mahabharata. It is one of ancient India's two primary epics in addition to the Ramayana.[2] The main protagonists in the story of the Mahabharata are the Pandava, five brothers called Yudhishthira, Bhima, Arjuna, Nakula, and Sadewa. They are nobles as well as knights with different supernatural powers.

In the Javanese tradition, there are also four local figures known as the Javanese version of clowns, called the Punokawan. They are the servants of the Pandava. The Punokawan comprise four characters: Semar, Gareng,

---

[1] https://ich.unesco.org/en/RL/wayang-puppet-theatre-00063
[2] Amaresh Datta, *The Encyclopaedia of Indian Literature* (Vol 2: Devraj to Jyoti). (New Delhi: Sahitya Akademi, 1988).

Petruk, and Bagong. Even though they are described as funny characters, the Punokawan have great abilities and wisdom. They are often helpers and advisors to the Pandava.

This collaboration between the Punokawan and Pandava inspired the CI-EL (creativity, innovation, entrepreneurship, and leadership) and PI-PM (productivity, improvement, professionalism, and management) concepts as one of the primary dichotomies in the omnihouse model. Punokawan, with all their uniqueness and funny behavior—often providing unexpected solutions—are symbols of CI-EL. Meanwhile, with their "elite" characters, the Pandava are the manifestation of PI-PM.

Punokawan as the Symbol of CI-EL

The youngest character of the Punokawan is Bagong. Bagong is short and chubby, but his eyes and mouth are wide.[3] He is a funny character, likes to entertain, and is intelligent. Although his movements are not as agile as his other brothers, Bagong is known to have many ideas. That's why we chose it as an icon of creativity.

The second figure of the Punokawan is Petruk. This character has a large sense of humor but is also an agile fighter. Petruk has a distinctive face, a tall body posture, and a long nose. Other body parts—hands, neck, and legs—have similar characteristics. Petruk has many magical abilities and is willing to test his abilities in various situations.[4] This character is similar to an innovator who likes experimenting with new ideas. So, Petruk is a symbol of innovation.

Gareng is the next Punokawan character. Unlike the other Punokawan, Gareng is described as a human figure with a body with some atypical features. He has crossed eyes, imperfect hands, and limp feet.[5] But actually, Gareng's physical imperfection implies his unique ability. Crossed eyes are not a weakness; it symbolizes accuracy and thoroughness in seeing the surrounding environment. With this accuracy, Gareng can see opportunities that others have missed. This ability to see opportunities is one of the main characteristics of entrepreneurship.

Among the other Punokawan, Semar is the most senior figure. He is the father figure to other Punokawan. Semar's character is described as fat and having a short posture, an ample backside, and a snub nose.[6] In Javanese

[3]https://www.indonesia.travel/gb/en/trip-ideas/wayang-s-own-four-musketeers-punokawan
[4]https://indonesiar.com/getting-to-know-the-punakawan-characters-petruk-in-javanese-puppetry/
[5]https://soedonowonodjoio.family/the-story-of-our-ancestors/dive-into-the-philosophical-meaning-of-gareng,-javanese-puppet-characters.html
[6]Claire Holt, *Art in Indonesia: Continuities and Change* (Ithaca, NY: Cornell University Press, 1967).

BAGONG   **PETRUK**   **GARENG**   **SEMAR**

FIGURE A.1 The Punokawan

wayang stories, he is the leader of other Punokawan and plays a central role as an advisor to the Pandava. Therefore, it is very appropriate that Semar represents leadership.

Pandava as the Symbol of PI-PM

The youngest of the five Pandava brothers are the twins Nakula and Sadewa. Nakula has a deep understanding of horse-keeping. He is also said to be a brilliant swordsman.[7] Sadewa, the younger brother, is the most junior of the Pandava, but he has high intelligence, especially in astrology. He also has the same swordsmanship abilities as his brother.[8] With their various skills and knowledge, the twins can provide multiple needs for their siblings. That is why they are suitable to represent productivity.

The next character is Arjuna. In the Mahabharata epic, he is the third among the Pandava. Arjuna was a great student in his boyhood, and his adored teacher, Drona, also favored him. As a grown-up, Arjuna develops into a skilled archer.[9] Arjuna always tries to improve his supernatural powers by meditating and practicing. Because of his persistence to keep improving, we chose Arjuna as a symbol of improvement.

[7]Kanjiv Lochan, *Medicines of Early India* (with appendix on a rare ancient text) (Varanasi: Chaukhambha Sanskrit Bhawan, 2003).
[8]https://dbpedia.org/describe/?uri=http%3A%2F%2Fdbpedia.org%2Fresource%2FSahadeva
[9]https://www.britannica.com/topic/Arjuna

NAKULA   SADEWA   ARJUNA   BHIMA   YUDHISTHIRA

FIGURE A.2   The Pandava

Bhima is a Pandava character with unique combat abilities. His tremendous stature and power set him apart from his brothers.[10] Because of his physical ability, it is not uncommon for Bhima to get a mission to lead the battle. He can complete heavy tasks with excellence. Therefore Bhima is the correct figure to represent professionalism.

Yudhishthira is the older brother of the four other Pandava figures. Honesty, justice, tolerance, and discernment are all qualities he possesses. He is also known to be very strict with the rules.[11] This characteristic sometimes causes him to be too rigid in directing the other Pandava. As the eldest of the Pandava, Yudhisthira is the most suitable figure to represent the management concept.

[10]https://detechter.com/bhima-who-slayed-all-kauravas-including-duryodhana/
[11]https://www.mahabharataonline.com/stories/mahabharata_character.php?id=59

About the Authors

PHILIP KOTLER is professor emeritus of marketing at the Kellogg School of Management, Northwestern University, where he held the S.C. Johnson & Son Distinguished Professor of International Marketing. He is one of the world's leading authorities on marketing, widely regarded as the "father of modern marketing," recipient of numerous awards and honorary degrees from schools around the world, and voted as the Number 1 Guru in Management in the list of Top 30 Gurus of Management (2022). The *Wall Street Journal* ranks him among the top six most influential business thinkers. He holds an MA from the University of Chicago and a PhD from MIT, both in economics. Philip has an incredible international presence—his books have been translated into more than 25 languages, and he regularly speaks on the international circuit.

HERMAWAN KARTAJAYA is the founder and chairman of MarkPlus, Inc. and was named by the United Kingdom's Chartered Institute of Marketing on the list of 50 Gurus Who Have Shaped the Future of Marketing. He received the Distinguished Global Leadership Award from the Pan-Pacific Business Association at the University of Nebraska-Lincoln. He is also the chairman of the Asia Council for Small Business and a cofounder of the Asia Marketing Federation.

HOOI DEN HUAN is an associate professor and former head of the Marketing and International Business Division and vice-dean at the Nanyang Business School, Nanyang Technological University (NTU), Singapore. He obtained his bachelor's degree from the University of Bradford and his PhD from the University of Manchester. He was chairman of the bachelor of business degree curriculum committee, which started the business degree programs at NTU. He was also the director of the university's Nanyang Technopreneurship Center.

JAYSON MUSSRY is the deputy chairman and chief executive officer at MarkPlus, Inc., where he helps many companies design corporate and marketing strategies and their training programs. He is also lecturing at several prominent universities in Indonesia, in addition to being active as a writer and speaker. He obtained his master's degree in marketing management and a doctorate in strategic management from the Faculty of Economics and Business, University of Indonesia.

Index